Gre

AMERICAN FLYER®
POCKET PRICE GUIDE

Edited by Roger Carp

KALMBACH BOOKS

Kalmbach Books
21027 Crossroads Circle
Waukesha, Wisconsin 53186
www.kalmbach.com/books

Published in 2014
Twenty-ninth Edition

Manufactured in the United States of America

ISBN: 978-1-62700-125-0
EISBN: 978-1-62700-131-1

Front cover photo: American Flyer no. 21234 Chesapeake & Ohio
GP7 Diesel

Back cover photo: American Flyer no. 23796 Sawmill

We constantly strive to improve Greenberg's Pocket Price Guides. If
you find missing items or detect misinformation, please contact us.
Send your comments, new information, or corrections via e-mail
to books@kalmbach.com or by mail to Lionel Pocket Price Guide
Editor at the address above.

CONTENTS

INTRODUCTION

The latest and greatest guide

Welcome to the latest edition of what hobbyists regard as the most authoritative and trusted price guide to the trains and accessories produced by the leading S gauge firms of the past 69 years. Whether you're a longtime S gauge enthusiast or a newcomer to the toy train hobby, in this guide, you'll find the information you need to identify and evaluate the thousands of items made by various S gauge manufacturers between 1946 and 2015. Most of all, you will have at your fingertips the most up-to-date prices for locomotives, freight cars, passenger cars, stations, tunnels, signals, track sections, transformers, and catalogs.

Over the years, hundreds of enthusiasts have contributed extensive research to each edition of the *American Flyer Pocket Price Guide*. This 2015 edition represents the culmination of tremendous effort by many contributors. As a result, this 29th edition contains information on just about every toy train product marketed by the A.C. Gilbert Co. for its American Flyer line between 1946 and 1966. Also collected between the two covers of this guide are complete listings of all the S gauge trains put out by Lionel (using Gilbert tooling as well as its own), American Models, S-Helper Service, and MTH.

What is listed and what isn't

When the first editions of this pocket price guide were published, the only S gauge products included were the classic trains and accessories developed by the A.C. Gilbert Co. for its American Flyer line. You'll still find those terrific models listed in **Section 1**, which includes locomotives, freight cars, and passenger cars cataloged between 1946 and 1966. Also included are American Flyer accessories, track sections, and transformers.

Gilbert released its final, abbreviated line of American Flyer trains in 1966 and declared bankruptcy a year later. In one of those "who'd-a-thunk-it?" scenarios, Lionel, which dominated the toy train industry in the postwar era, acquired the tools and dies that Gilbert had used to mass-produce American Flyer trains and related items.

Finally, in 1979, Lionel brought out a selection of Flyer trains and accessories. Ever since, thanks to old and new tooling, Lionel has been cataloging train sets, locomotives, cars, and accessories for its revamped American Flyer line.

Section 2 covers items that Lionel has produced or sponsored for that line since 1979. The vast majority of these items represent postwar models that Lionel has updated with different paint and lettering schemes and improved motors. Popular operating accessories have been revived, much to the delight of S gauge hobbyists as well as O gauge operators, who agree that particular freight loaders, light towers, and other accessories work equally well on their layouts. Other Lionel-produced models appear as uncataloged items offered by toy train collecting associations, museums, and other organizations for promotional purposes.

Section 3 covers every set, locomotive, and car made and marketed by American Models since the company entered the toy train field in 1981. Over the past 34 years, this firm has offered S gauge collectors and operators a wide range of popular electric-profile and diesel locomotives and, more recently, steam locomotives and tenders. The types of freight and passenger cars American Models has developed are impressive in terms of their variety and decoration. Also part of the company's S gauge line are sections of track and remote control switches.

Section 4 features the S gauge trains of MTH Electric Trains. MTH purchased the tooling of S-Helper Service's Showcase Line. MTH used this tooling to reintroduce and add to the freight cars and locomotives of S-Helper Service. Its locomotives include Proto-Sound, MTH's sound and control system.

Section 5 covers locomotives and cars made by S-Helper Service from 1994, when production began, through 2012, when its owners retired. The number of items this manufacturer put out is breathtaking—more than 1,500 train sets, diesel and steam locomotives, freight and passenger cars, switches, trucks, and couplers. Its locomotives and rolling stock feature an incredible array of railroad names.

Section 6 features a listing of the catalogs and other paperwork that A.C. Gilbert put out for consumers and dealers.

About the only notable American Flyer items not included in Section 1 are the boxed train sets that Gilbert cataloged. These S gauge sets are omitted from this guide because, to be considered complete, they must have all the items, including ancillary ones, that Gilbert packed with them. In addition, they should be in their original boxes. The level of completeness demanded for American Flyer sets puts them beyond the scope of this guide.

Also left out of the *American Flyer Pocket Price Guide* are rare items that have surfaced. These unique pieces include mock-ups of products that were assembled by members of Gilbert's Engineering Department. They also include models created for company executives to evaluate different paint and lettering schemes. These items, some of which are one of a kind, are so scarce that values cannot be assigned to them.

The guide's focus on S gauge trains of the post-World War II years explains other omissions. You won't find mention of the O gauge trains that Gilbert cataloged between 1939 and 1942 or the HO scale trains that it offered after the war. For the same reason, information on the Wide and O gauge trains produced by American Flyer Manufacturing is also absent.

How values are determined

Every user of the *American Flyer Pocket Price Guide* wants to know how the values are ascertained. There's nothing mysterious or arbitrary about the process. Over the years, we at Kalmbach Publishing Co. have gained the cooperation of many dealers and hobbyists, some of whom serve on our national review panel. These knowledgeable individuals share information about the trains and accessories they have bought and sold. They report on transactions conducted at meets across the United States, in retail outlets, and at live and online auctions. The editors of this guide study the information and supplement it with data from the publications of hobby groups that relates to buying and selling S gauge trains.

The values presented here are an averaged reflection of prices for items bought and sold across the country over the year prior to the publication of this edition. These values are offered as guidelines and should be viewed as starting points that buyers and sellers can use to begin informed and reasonable negotiations.

Values for individual items may differ from what is listed in this price guide due to a few key factors. Where collectible trains are scarce and demand outruns supply, actual values may exceed what is shown. Values may also rise where certain items are especially popular, often because of their road names. And as with all collectibles, national and local economic conditions will impact values, which tend to drop when times are tough and demand falls.

Another factor influencing what a toy train is worth relates to the venue in which it is being sold. Antiques dealers generally ask more for an item than do folks putting it out at a garage sale. Mail-order and retail outlets tend to charge more for trains than do individuals at shows because they need to be compensated for the additional costs generated by operating a store, compiling and distributing price lists, and packing and shipping trains. Of course, the cost of any item can balloon far beyond its listed value when two or more people compete for it at a live or online auction.

HOW TO READ THIS GUIDE

Number	Description	Condition——Good	Exc
24067	Keystone Line Boxcar, *60* * *u*	1350 2425	___
24076	Union Pacific Stock Car, *57–60*		
	(A) Knuckle couplers	30 85	___
	(B) Pike Master couplers	28 71	___

Reading an entry

Each section is arranged in numerical order by catalog numbers. Every item is listed by the product's catalog number or other number assigned by its manufacturer. A catalog number often appears on the product as its road number.

A basic description of the model follows the number. It gives the type of product, lists the name of any railroad identified with it, and includes identifying characteristics, such as color or lettering. If the item has a road number that differs from its catalog number, that number is shown in quotation marks. Abbreviations used in the descriptions, including those of railroad names, are found at the back of the price guide.

Next, you'll find the year or years during which that item was cataloged. The years are shown in italics. If one is followed by a *u*, then this item was uncataloged, most likely a promotional item and not part of the manufacturer's cataloged line.

In the American Models section, items are continually manufactured, so no years are listed. MTH and S-Helper Service products are also undated. Some entries show an asterisk (*) after the year. This mark indicates that a reproduction of the item has been made.

Some entries feature variations, each indicated by a separate letter (A, B, and so forth). Variations amount to slight yet noteworthy differences in appearance that distinguish models that otherwise seem identical. These differences can relate to color, lettering, and details that were added or deleted. For items having many variations, an entry may not include every variation.

An entry concludes with an indication of the item's value for several common conditions.

Condition

American Flyer and S gauge enthusiasts should be familiar with the condition and grading standards established by the Train Collectors Association, which are used as the basis for evaluating the condition of toy trains and accessories:

C-10 **Mint:** brand new—all original, unused, and unblemished.

C-9 **Factory New:** same condition as Mint but with evidence of factory rubs or slight signs of handling, shipping, and being test run at the factory.

C-8 **Like New:** complete and all original with no rust or no missing parts; may show effects of being displayed or signs of age and may have been run.

C-7 **Excellent:** all original and may have minute scratches and paint nicks; no rust, no missing parts, and no distortion of component parts.

C-6 **Very Good:** has minor scratches, paint nicks, or minor spots of surface rust; is free of dents and may have minor parts replaced.

C-5 **Good:** shows evidence of heavy use and signs of play wear—small dents, scratches, minor paint loss, and minor surface rust.

C-4 **Fair:** shows evidence of heavy use—scratches and dents, moderate paint loss, missing parts, and surface rust.

C-3 **Poor:** requires major body repair and is a candidate for restoration; major rust, missing parts, and heavily scratched.

C-2 **Restoration:** needs to be restored.

C-1 **Junk:** parts value only.

In this guide, Gilbert American Flyer trains are evaluated in Good (C-5) and Excellent (C-7) conditions. Lionel-produced trains are assessed in Mint (C-10) condition. American Models, MTH, and S-Helper items are listed with their last suggested retail price.

You may also see NRS listed as a value in the guide. NRS (No Reported Sales) refers to an item for which no adequate pricing data is available. Typically, these items are so scarce that only a handful have been reported.

Gilbert catalogs and paper items are evaluated in Good (P-5) and Excellent (P-7) conditions according to the following paper grading standards established by the Train Collectors Association:

P-10 **Mint:** Brand new, complete, all original as manufactured, and unused. Free of all flaws. Original folds are crisp with no signs of damage, and individual pages appear to have never been opened. No rusty staples, creases, tears, fading, or wear marks.

P-9 **Store New:** Complete, all original, and unused. Item may have merchant additions such as store stamps and price tags. May have been handled since leaving the original factory, but original folds are crisp without signs of wear.

P-8 **Like New:** Complete and all original. There is evidence of light use and aging. Item may have notations (discrete) added since leaving the manufacturer.

P-7 **Excellent:** Complete and all original. Item can show signs of moderate use, but it is completely intact. Original paper folds can show minute signs of damage including evidence of bending and folding. Item may have rusty staples that have not affected the paper.

P-6 **Very Good:** Complete and all original. Item shows signs of usage such as minor abrasions and creases. It is completely intact, but original paper folds show signs of damage. All printing is legible; however, there may be weathering, slight fading, pencil or ink marks, and soiling from rust, grease, or oil. Pages may have tears.

P-5 **Good:** Item shows substantial wear which can include moderate abrasions, creases, and folds. All existing printing is legible; however, the item is severely worn. Colors may be extensively faded, and original folds and edges may be damaged, Rusty staples may have stained pages. (Any paper having been repaired cannot be graded above P-5.)

P-4 **Fair:** Shows heavy damage but printing is generally legible. Paper may be brittle or have been repaired. Could have grease, oil, or water damage.

S GAUGE MARKETPLACE

When to consult this guide

Many readers of the *American Flyer Pocket Price Guide* use it after the fact. They already have some trains and accessories and now want to identify and evaluate those items. The *American Flyer Pocket Price Guide* can also help you think about what to acquire in the future. That's really when the fun begins! Once you have a general idea of how to enjoy this hobby, you can make informed decisions about which trains you want.

Postwar trains and accessories

This is an interesting time to be concentrating on postwar American Flyer. On the one hand, serious collectors are paying record prices for Like New and Mint items, boxes are escalating in value, and demand for original and complete sets, top-of-the-line locomotives, and scarce variations continues to rise.

On the other hand, the need that operators once felt to acquire postwar pieces to run on their S gauge layouts has all but vanished. The selection of realistic steam and diesel locomotives and colorful freight and passenger cars becomes greater each year.

As a result, folks who want to run trains can choose from models that promise superior performance and outstanding detail. Few S gauge enthusiasts can say that the postwar line from Gilbert surpassed what is available today, which is why operators are devouring new catalogs and paying less attention to what was offered 50 years ago.

Anyone who wants Good and even Excellent trains to display or operate will find that all but the most deluxe and exotic models are available in abundant supply and at affordable prices. Collectors with deep pockets and high standards may turn up their noses at common pieces as well as notable ones because those items are graded below Like New or do not come with all their original packaging.

So collectors willing to forgo a box and accept a scratch or paint chip may find items available that they once thought were beyond their aspirations. They may also benefit from the shift of operators away from postwar trains to contemporary ones. Operating cars, especially those models and road names that are considered fairly common, deserve more attention. In contrast, passenger cars continue to dazzle serious collectors, and so their prices have stayed at the same level or even climbed.

Demand for certain items in the higher grades seems stronger, which means that those same trains in Good or possibly Excellent condition may be overlooked. For example, the big steam locomotives, sleek PA diesels, realistic boxcars, and impressive tank cars that Gilbert cataloged in the 1950s continue to gain strength on the collector market. The same can be said of different freight loaders, figures, and stations. Originals draw more attention, probably because reproductions have flooded the market.

Consumer catalogs from the entire postwar period are available at low prices. As bound volumes of catalog reproductions go out of print, demand for originals should rise, which logically means that Gilbert's wish books in Excellent and better condition will go up in value. If you love the postwar era and don't have a complete set of catalogs, this is the time to buy the missing ones.

Now may be a great time to be collecting or operating postwar American Flyer trains, provided you're willing to make a few compromises in the appearance, performance, and packaging of the locomotives, cars, and accessories you buy.

Modern trains and accessories

Flip through Sections 2 through 5 and you'll come across S gauge models of many of the best-known diesel locomotives and any kind of freight or passenger car imaginable. Railroads, large and small, prominent and forgotten, are represented.

Increasing numbers of S gauge enthusiasts are jumping on the contemporary bandwagon and buying trains of recent vintage to operate. They have found dozens of locomotives to run, including the EMD diesels and GG1 electrics that Gilbert never made as well as a variety of steamers.

When it comes to cars for any of these powerful, detailed locomotives, hobbyists have a selection of rolling stock that overshadows what was available in the 1950s and 1960s. Lionel and other current manufacturers have brought out superb models of vintage and contemporary boxcars, tankers, refrigerator cars, and covered hoppers. The array of loads carried on flatcars is amazing, and the range of caboose styles and road names continues to grow.

			Good	Exc
____	1	Transformer, 25 watts, *49–52*	2	4
____	1	Transformer, 35 watts, *56*	4	9
____	1A	Transformer, 40 watts, *57 u*	3	10
____	1B	Transformer, 50 watts, *56*	1	5
____	1½	Transformer, 45 watts, *53*	1	5
____	1½	Transformer, 50 watts, *54–55*	1	5
____	1½ B	Transformer, 50 watts, *56*	1	5
____	2	Transformer, 75 watts, *47–53*	3	13
____	2B	Transformer, 75 watts, *47–48*	3	29
____	3	Transformer, 50 watts, *46 u*	1	6
____	4B	Transformer, 100 watts, *49–56*	10	28
	4B-EX	Transformer, 100 watts, made for export, *49–56*		
____			20	95
____	5	Transformer, 50 watts, *46*	1	6
____	5A	Transformer, 50 watts, *46*	1	6
____	5B	Transformer, 50 watts, *46*	3	6
____	6	Transformer, 75 watts, *46*	1	8
____	6A	Transformer, 75 watts, *46*	1	7
____	7	Transformer, 75 watts, *46 u*	2	9
____	7B	Transformer, 75 watts, *46*	2	9
____	8B	Transformer, 100 watts, *46–52*	11	40
	8B-EX	Transformer, 100 watts, made for export, *46–52*		
____			20	95
____	9B	Transformer, 150 watts, *46*	18	33
____	10	DC Inverter, *46*	6	17
____	11	Circuit Breaker, *46*	3	21
____	12B	Transformer, 250 watts, *46–52*	35	95
____	13	Circuit Breaker, *52–55*	4	10
____	14	Rectiformer, *47, 49*	9	94
____	15	Rectifier, *48–52*	5	39
____	15B	Transformer, 110 watts, *53*	13	66
____	16	Rectiformer, *50*	10	41
____	16B	Transformer, 175 watts, *54–56*	23	82
____	16B	Transformer, 190 watts, *53*	30	80
____	16C	Transformer, 35 watts, *58*	6	17
____	17B	Transformer, 190 watts, *52*	33	63
____	18	Filter, *50 u*		NRS
____	18B	Transformer, 175 watts, *54–56*	27	115
____	18B	Transformer, 190 watts, *53*	33	120
	18B-EX	Transformer, 175 watts, made for export, *54–56*		
____			35	140
____	19B	Transformer, 300 watts, *52–55*	60	149
____	21	Imitation Grass, *49–50*	15	30
____	21A	Imitation Grass, *51–56*	15	29
____	22	Scenery Gravel, *49–56*	13	31
____	23	Artificial Coal, *49–56*	14	30
____	24	Rainbow Wire, *49–56*	3	11
____	25	Smoke Cartridge, *47–56*	5	19

		Good	Exc	
26	Service Kit, *52–56*	8	32	___
27	Track Cleaning Fluid, *52–56*	2	9	___
28	Track Ballast, *50*	5	11	___
28A	Track Ballast, *51–53*	5	24	___
29	Imitation Snow, *50*	45	247	___
29A	Imitation Snow, *51–53*	50	294	___
30	Highway Signs, *49–52*	81	157	___
30B	Transformer, 300 watts, *53–56*	85	170	___
31	Railroad Signs, *49–50*	100	280	___
31A	Railroad Signs, *51–52*	75	190	___
32	City Street Equipment, *49–50*	55	206	___
32A	Park Set, *51*	55	200	___
33	Passenger and Train Figure Set, *51–52*	75	207	___
34	Railway Figure Set, *53*	105	765	___
35	Brakeman with lantern, *50–52*	95	196	___
40	Smoke Set, *53–56*	2	4	___
50	District School, *53–54*	90	171	___
91½ B	Transformer, 50 watts, made for export, *56*	20	95	___
160	Station Platform, *53*	263	590	___
161	Bungalow, *53*	115	240	___
162	Factory, *53*	80	175	___
163	Flyerville Station, *53*	130	311	___
164	Red Barn, *53*	105	513	___
165	Grain Elevator, *53*	105	182	___
166	Church, *53*	95	427	___
167	Town Hall, *53*	108	284	___
168	Hotel, *53*	120	276	___
247	Tunnel, *46–48*	20	42	___
248	Tunnel, *46–48*	20	45	___
249	Tunnel, *47–56*	14	43	___
270	News and Frank Stand, light or dark blue, *52–53*	55	124	___
271	Whistle Stop Set, 3 pieces, *52–53*	65	227	___
271-1	Waiting Station, brown, *52–53*	21	60	___
271-2	Refreshment Booth, white, *52–53*	21	60	___
271-3	Newsstand, green, *52–53*	21	60	___
272	Glendale Station and Newsstand, *52–53*	64	202	___
273	Suburban Railroad Station, *52–53*	65	262	___
274	Harbor Junction Freight Station, *52–53*	55	250	___
275	Eureka Diner, *52–53*	49	296	___
282	C&NW 4-6-2 Pacific Locomotive, *52–53*			
	(A) AF tender, plastic or metal, *52*	34	71	___
	(B) AF or AFL tender with coal pusher, *53*	44	78	___
283	C&NW 4-6-2 Pacific Locomotive, *54–57*	32	70	___
285	C&NW 4-6-2 Pacific Locomotive, *52*	42	121	___
287	C&NW 4-6-2 Pacific Locomotive, *54*	21	88	___
289	C&NW 4-6-2 Pacific Locomotive, *56 u*	332	404	___
290	American Flyer 4-6-2 Pacific Locomotive, *49–51*	38	77	___
293	NYNH&H 4-6-2 Pacific Locomotive, *53–58*			
	(A) Reverse in tender, *53–57*	74	123	___
	(B) Reverse in cab, *58 u*	150	390	___

			Good	Exc
____	295	American Flyer 4-6-2 Pacific Locomotive, *51*	95	180
____	296	NYNH&H 4-6-2 Pacific Locomotive, *55 u*	90	417
____	299	Reading 4-4-2 Atlantic Locomotive, *54 u*	72	186
	300	Reading 4-4-2 Atlantic Locomotive, *46–47, 52*		
____		(A) Reading, *46–47*	19	47
____		(B) Other variations, *47, 52*	15	35
	300AC	Reading 4-4-2 Atlantic Locomotive, *48–51*		
____		(A) 4-piece boiler, *48*	20	63
____		(B) Other variations, *49–51*	15	34
	301	Reading 4-4-2 Atlantic Locomotive		
____		(A) Metal tender, *46*	15	46
____		(B) Plastic tender, *53*	15	34
	302	Reading 4-4-2 Atlantic Locomotive, *48, 51–53*		
____		(A) Smoke in boiler	18	46
____		(B) Plastic boiler	17	35
	302AC	Reading 4-4-2 Atlantic Locomotive, *48, 50–52*		
____		(A) 4-piece boiler	17	48
____		(B) Other variations	18	39
____	303	Reading 4-4-2 Atlantic Locomotive, *54–56*	17	39
____	307	Reading 4-4-2 Atlantic Locomotive, *54–57*	18	66
____	308	Reading 4-4-2 Atlantic Locomotive, *56*	24	78
	310	PRR 4-6-2 Pacific Locomotive		
____		(A) Pennsylvania, *46 u*	39	105
____		(B) PRR-AFL, *47 u*	40	84
	312	PRR 4-6-2 Pacific Locomotive, *46–48, 51–52*		
____		(A) Pennsylvania, s-i-t, *46*	55	115
____		(B) Other variations	65	101
____	312AC	PRR 4-6-2 Pacific Locomotive, *49–51*	55	93
	313	PRR 4-6-2 Pacific Locomotive, *55–57*		
____		(A) Small motor, *55*	75	188
____		(B) Large motor, *56–57*	95	229
	314AW	PRR 4-6-2 Pacific Locomotive, *49–50*		
____		(A) Die-cast trailing truck, *49*		292
____		(B) One-piece trailing truck and drawbar assembly, *50*		223
____	315	PRR 4-6-2 Pacific Locomotive, *52*	75	240
____	316	PRR 4-6-2 Pacific Locomotive, *53–54*	70	213
	320	NYC 4-6-4 Hudson Locomotive, *46–47*		
____		(A) New York Central, *46*	50	170
____		(B) NYC-AFL, *47*	45	137
	321	NYC 4-6-4 Hudson Locomotive		
____		(A) New York Central, s-i-t, *46*	75	269
____		(B) NYC-AFL, *47*	50	185
	322	NYC 4-6-4 Hudson Locomotive, *46–49*		
____		(A) New York Central, s-i-t, *46*	47	119
____		(B) American Flyer Lines, s-i-t or s-i-b, *47–49*	38	102
____	322AC	NYC 4-6-4 Hudson Locomotive, *49–51*	44	142
____	324AC	NYC 4-6-4 Hudson Locomotive, *50*	70	160
____	325AC	NYC 4-6-4 Hudson Locomotive, *51*	60	159
	K325	NYC 4-6-4 Hudson Locomotive, *52*		
____		(A) Early coupler riveted to truck	155	400
____		(B) Other variations	55	194

		Good	Exc
326	NYC 4-6-4 Hudson Locomotive, *53–57*		
	(A) Small motor, *53–54*	60	158 ____
	(B) Large motor, *54–57*	115	284 ____
332	UP 4-8-4 Northern Locomotive, *46–49*		
	(A) AC, Union Pacific, s-i-t, *46*		NRS ____
	(B) AC, American Flyer Lines, s-i-t, *47*	1050	2800 ____
	(C) AC, American Flyer Lines, *47–48*	170	382 ____
	(D) DC, American Flyer Lines, *48–49*	170	542 ____
332AC	UP 4-8-4 Northern Locomotive, *51*	170	533 ____
332DC	UP 4-8-4 Northern Locomotive, *49*	155	416 ____
334DC	UP 4-8-4 Northern Locomotive, *50*	170	370 ____
K335	UP 4-8-4 Northern Locomotive, *52*	210	429 ____
336	UP 4-8-4 Northern Locomotive, *53–56*		
	(A) Small motor, *53*	170	467 ____
	(B) Large motor	190	555 ____
342	NKP 0-8-0 Switcher, *46–48, 52*		
	(A) Nickel Plate Road, s-i-t, *46*	500	1750 ____
	(B) American Flyer Lines, s-i-t, *47*	115	477 ____
	(C) Same as (B), but DC	110	428 ____
	(D) American Flyer Lines, *48*	95	253 ____
	(E) American Flyer, *52*	105	238 ____
342AC	NKP 0-8-0 Switcher, *49–51*	100	288 ____
342DC	NKP 0-8-0 Switcher, *48–50*	100	292 ____
343	NKP 0-8-0 Switcher, *53–58*		
	(A) Reverse in tender, *53–54*	115	289 ____
	(B) Reverse on motor, *55–57*	135	315 ____
346	NKP 0-8-0 Switcher, *55*	205	442 ____
350	Royal Blue 4-6-2 Pacific Locomotive, *48, 50*		
	(A) Wire handrails, *48*	50	131 ____
	(B) Cast handrails, *50*	43	90 ____
353	AF Circus 4-6-2 Pacific Locomotive, *50–51*		
	(A) Wire handrails, *50*	125	513 ____
	(B) Cast handrails, *51*	150	480 ____
354	Silver Bullet 4-6-2 Pacific Locomotive, *54*	100	249 ____
355	C&NW Baldwin Locomotive, *56–57*		
	(A) Unpainted green plastic	68	115 ____
	(B) Green-painted plastic	115	196 ____
356	Silver Bullet 4-6-2 Pacific Locomotive, *53*		
	(A) Chrome finish	65	134 ____
	(B) Satin silver-painted	80	160 ____
360/61	Santa Fe PA/PB Diesel Set, *50–51*		
	(A) Chrome finish, *50*	85	258 ____
	(B) Chrome finish with handrails, *50*	120	585 ____
	(C) Chrome finish with warbonnet, *50*	110	600 ____
	(D) Silver-painted with warbonnet, *51*	75	233 ____
360/64	Santa Fe PA/PB Diesel Set, *50–51*		
	(A) Silver-painted, Santa Fe, *50*	75	217 ____
	(B) Other variations		NRS ____
370	AF GM GP7 Diesel, *50–53*		
	(A) Link coupler bars, *50–52*	60	122 ____
	(B) Knuckle couplers, *53*	65	142 ____
371	AF GM GP7 Diesel, *54*	105	147 ____

			Good	Exc
	372	Union Pacific GP7 Diesel, *55–57*		
___		(A) Built by Gilbert	115	227
___		(B) Made by American Flyer	135	231
	374/75	Texas & Pacific GP7 Diesel, *54–55*		
___		(A) Sheet metal frame, *54*	175	444
___		(B) Die-cast frame, *55*	160	357
___	**375**	AF GM GP7 Diesel, *53*	490	595
___	**377/78**	Texas & Pacific GP7 Diesel, *56–57*	175	394
	405	Silver Streak PA Diesel, red stripe, *52*		
___		(A) Chrome finish	95	250
___		(B) Marblized chrome finish	110	290
___	**440**	Lamp	1	5
___	**441**	Lamp	1	5
___	**442**	Lamp	1	5
___	**443**	Lamp	1	10
___	**444**	Lamp	1	5
___	**451**	Lamp	1	5
___	**452**	Lamp	1	5
	453	Lamp, *46–48*		
___		(A) Single bulb	1	5
___		(B) 3 bulbs	1	6
___	**455**	Bulbs, 3 pieces	2	5
___	**460**	Bulbs, *51, 53–54*	34	225
___	**461**	Lamp	2	7
	466	AFL Comet PA Diesel, *53–55*		
___		(A) Chrome finish, *53*	103	164
___		(B) Silver-painted, decal, *54–55*	75	131
___		(C) Silver-painted, heat-stamped letters	90	235
___		(D) Silver-painted over Santa Fe lettering	85	203
___		(E) Silver-painted over Rocket lettering	90	250
___	**467**	AFL Comet PB Diesel, *55**		NRS
	470/71/73	SF PA/PB/PA Diesel Set, *53–58*		
___		(A) Chrome finish, metal steps, *53*	135	448
___		(B) Silver-painted, metal steps, *54–57*	120	427
___		(C) Silver-painted, cast plastic steps	245	705
___	**472**	Santa Fe PA Diesel, *56*	110	203
	474/75	Rocket PA/PA Diesel Set, *53–55*		
___		(A) Chrome finish, *53*	140	435
___		(B) Silver-painted, *54–55*	120	375
___	**476**	Rocket PB Diesel, *55**		NRS
	477/78	Silver Flash PA/PB Diesel Set, *53–54*		
___		(A) Chrome finish, *53*	175	470
___		(B) Silver-painted, *54*	170	510
___	**479**	Silver Flash PA Diesel, *55*	80	257
___	**480**	Silver Flash PB Diesel, *55**	600	2867
___	**481**	Silver Flash PA Diesel, *56*	136	374
___	**484/85/86**	Santa Fe PA/PB/PA Diesel Set, *56–57*	215	584
___	**490/91/93**	Northern Pacific PA/PB/PA Diesel Set, *56**	340	765
___	**490/92**	Northern Pacific PA/PA Diesel Set, *57*	200	497
___	**494/95**	New Haven PA/PA Diesel Set, *56*	195	550
___	**497**	New Haven PA Diesel, *57*	105	288
___	**499**	New Haven GE Electric, *56–57*	120	288

		Good	Exc
500	AFL Combination Car, *52 u*		
	(A) Satin silver-painted	140	425 ____
	(B) Chrome finish	125	287 ____
501	AFL Coach, *52 u*		
	(A) Satin silver-painted	150	396 ____
	(B) Chrome finish	110	299 ____
502	AFL Vista Dome Car, *52 u*		
	(A) Satin silver-painted	145	428 ____
	(B) Chrome finish	110	303 ____
503	AFL Observation Car, satin silver-painted, *52 u*	155	515 ____
520	Knuckle Coupler Kit, *54–56*	1	7 ____
521	Knuckle Coupler Kit		26 ____
525	Knuckle Coupler Trucks		45 ____
526	Knuckle Coupler Trucks		45 ____
529	Knuckle Coupler Trucks		48 ____
530	Knuckle Coupler Trucks		45 ____
531	Knuckle Coupler Trucks		45 ____
532	Knuckle Coupler Trucks		45 ____
541	Fuses, *46*		NRS ____
561	Billboard Horn, *55–56*		
	(A) Santa Fe Freight Train in Desert	50	60 ____
	(B) Santa Fe Alco with Steam Engine on Bridge	51	63 ____
	(C) Santa Fe Alco with Steam Engine on Bridge, green base	51	65 ____
	(D) Santa Fe Freight Train in Desert, green base	55	65 ____
566	Whistling Billboard, *51–55*	16	42 ____
568	Whistling Billboard, *56*	18	38 ____
571	Truss Bridge, *55–56*	11	35 ____
573	American Flyer Talking Station Record		NRS ____
577	Whistling Billboard, *46–50*		
	(A) Circus, *46–47*	21	69 ____
	(B) Fox Mart, *47*	500	2650 ____
	(C) Trains, *50*	24	40 ____
578	Station Figure Set, *46–52*	55	244 ____
579	Single Street Lamp, green or silver, *46–49*	10	30 ____
580	Double Street Lamp, green or silver, *46–49*	12	45 ____
581	Girder Bridge, *46–56*	11	33 ____
582	Blinker Signal, *46–48*	55	157 ____
583	Electromatic Crane, *46–49*	65	107 ____
583A	Electromatic Crane, *50–53*	65	145 ____
584	Bell Danger Signal, *46–47*	250	860 ____
585	Tool Shed, *46–52*	23	118 ____
586F	Wayside Station, *46–56*	29	97 ____
587	Block Signal, *46–47*	70	253 ____
588	Semaphore Block Signal, *46–48*	650	3725 ____
589	Passenger and Freight Station, *46–56*		
	(A) Green-painted roof	17	36 ____
	(B) Black-painted roof	15	61 ____
590	Control Tower, *55–56*	26	100 ____
591	Crossing Gate, *46–48*	25	58 ____
592	Crossing Gate, *49–50*	24	39 ____

			Good	Exc
___	**592A**	Crossing Gate, *51–53*	27	66
___	**593**	Signal Tower, *46–54*	41	67
___	**594**	Animated Track Gang, *46–47**	662	1300
___	**596**	Operating Water Tank, *46–56*	35	69
___	**598**	Talking Station Record, *46–56*	10	18
___	**599**	Talking Station Record, *56*	11	42
___	**600**	Crossing Gate with bell, *54–56*	30	67
___	**605**	American Flyer Lines Flatcar, silver or gray, *53*	11	24
___	**606**	American Flyer Lines Crane, *53*	25	47
___	**607**	AFL Work and Boom Car, gray base, *53*	9	35
___	**609**	American Flyer Lines Flatcar, *53*	10	25
___	**612**	Passenger and Freight Station with crane, *46–51, 53–54*	55	108
___	**613**	Great Northern Boxcar, *53*	21	62
___	**620**	Southern Gondola, *53*	22	60
___	**622**	General American Boxcar, *53**	16	40
___	**623**	Illinois Central Reefer, *53**	11	26
___	**625**	Shell Tank Car, *46–50*		
___		(A) Orange tank, plastic or painted	370	739
___		(B) Black tank	10	21
___		(C) Silver tank	6	22
___	**625**	Gulf Tank Car, *51–53*	8	20
___	**625G**	Gulf Tank Car, *51–53 u*	9	20
___	**627**	AFL Flatcar, die-cast base, *50*	14	24
___	**627**	C&NW Flatcar, plastic base, *46–50*	10	26
___	**628**	C&NW Flatcar, *46–53*		
___		(A) Metal or plastic	8	31
___		(B) Pressed wood	13	40
___	**629**	Missouri Pacific Stock Car, *46–53*	15	20
___	**630**	Reading Caboose, *46–52*	6	33
___	**630**	American Flyer Caboose, *52*	12	36
___	**630**	American Flyer Lines Caboose, *53*	8	23
___	**631**	Texas & Pacific Gondola, *46–53*		
___		(A) Unpainted green plastic	8	12
___		(B) Unpainted dark gray, *48 u*	85	295
___		(C) Red-painted, *52 u*	31	179
___		(D) Green-painted, *46–52*	4	19
___	**632**	Virginian Hopper, gray or blue-gray, die-cast, *46*	30	116
	632	Lehigh New England Hopper, *46–53*		
___		(A) Gray-painted, die-cast, *46*	30	105
___		(B) Black plastic, *46*	8	22
___		(C) Gray plastic, *47–49*	4	13
___		(D) White plastic, *50*	33	99
___		(E) Gray-painted plastic, *53*	9	24
___		(F) Black plastic, red filled circle in logo		250
___	**633**	Baltimore & Ohio Boxcar, *46–52*	10	25
	633	Baltimore & Ohio Reefer, *46–52*		
___		(A) Red, *52 u*	32	159
___		(B) Tuscan, *52 u*	45	260
___	**633F**	G. Fox & Co. Boxcar, *47* u*	990	1825

		Good	Exc
634	C&NW Floodlight "42597," *46–49, 53*		
	(A) Plastic base, *46*	20	71 ____
	(B) Die-cast base, *47–49*	11	27 ____
635	C&NW Crane, plastic base, *46*	15	56 ____
635	C&NW Crane, metal base, *47–49*		
	(A) Yellow cab	11	34 ____
	(B) Red cab	123	363 ____
	(C) Black roof		580 ____
636	Erie Flatcar, *48–53*		
	(A) AF, die-cast frame	13	28 ____
	(B) AFL, die-cast frame	50	235 ____
	(C) Pressed-wood frame, *53*	65	290 ____
637	MKT Boxcar, yellow-painted or yellow plastic, *49–53**	8	24 ____
638	American Flyer Caboose, *49–52*	6	10 ____
638	American Flyer Lines Caboose, *53*	5	10 ____
639	American Flyer Boxcar, *49–52*		
	(A) Unpainted yellow plastic	7	12 ____
	(B) Tuscan-painted	16	83 ____
	(C) Red-painted		555 ____
	(D) Yellow-painted	10	26 ____
639	American Flyer Reefer, *51–52*		
	(A) Yellow-painted or unpainted yellow plastic	6	10 ____
	(B) Unpainted cream plastic	64	219 ____
639	American Flyer Reefer, yellow-painted, *50–51*	10	19 ____
640	Wabash Hopper, *53*	10	23 ____
640	American Flyer Hopper, *49–53*		
	(A) Gray plastic body, white lettering	4	11 ____
	(B) Gray plastic body, black lettering	4	10 ____
	(C) White plastic body, black lettering	14	47 ____
641	American Flyer Gondola, *49–52*		
	(A) Red-painted or unpainted red plastic	10	15 ____
	(B) Unpainted gray plastic, *51 u*	65	283 ____
641	Frisco Gondola, *53*	11	20 ____
642	American Flyer Boxcar, *51–52*	10	16 ____
642	American Flyer Reefer, *52 u*		
	(A) Unpainted red plastic	7	15 ____
	(B) Red-painted	21	28 ____
	(C) Tuscan-painted	25	27 ____
642	Seaboard Boxcar, *53*	11	27 ____
643	American Flyer Circus Flatcar, *50–53**		
	(A) Yellow, metal, with door guides for load, *50*	100	525 ____
	(B) Yellow, metal	75	225 ____
	(C) Yellow, pressed wood	90	187 ____
	(D) Red, metal	120	517 ____
	(E) Metal car, no load	29	35 ____
644	American Flyer Crane Car, *50–53*		
	(A) Red cab, black boom, *50*	35	102 ____
	(B) Red cab, green boom, *50*	22	66 ____
	(C) Tuscan-painted cab, green boom, *50–51*	27	77 ____
	(D) Black cab, black boom	20	39 ____
645	AF Work and Boom Car, *50*	16	52 ____

			Good	Exc
____	**645A**	AF or AFL Work and Boom Car, *51–53*	16	29
	646	Erie Floodlight, *50–53*		
____		(A) Green-painted, die-cast generator, *50*	47	194
____		(B) Red or green plastic generator	15	32
____		(C) Red or green painted generator	15	33
____	**647**	Northern Pacific Reefer, *52–53*	13	43
____	**648**	American Flyer Flatcar, red or tuscan, *52–54*	11	21
	649	AF Circus Coach, *50–52*		
____		(A) Unpainted yellow plastic	23	38
____		(B) Yellow-painted	55	152
	650	New Haven Pullman Car, *46–53*		
____		(A) Red or green, plastic frame	21	74
____		(B) Red or green, die-cast frame	22	43
____		(C) Red or green, sheet metal frame	15	25
	651	New Haven Baggage Car, *46–53*		
____		(A) Red or green, plastic frame	12	56
____		(B) Red or green, die-cast frame	12	41
____		(C) Red or green, sheet metal frame	11	31
	652	Pullman Car, *46–53*		
____		(A) Red or green, long trucks	65	300
____		(B) Red, tuscan, or green, short trucks	41	130
____		(C) Red, maroon, or green, Pikes Peak	48	143
	653	Pullman Car, *46–53*		
____		(A) Red or green, long trucks	65	208
____		(B) Red or green, short trucks	40	100
	654	Pullman Observation Car, *46–53*		
____		(A) Red or green, long trucks	60	234
____		(B) Red or green, short trucks	41	94
	655	AFL Coach, *53*		
____		(A) Red-painted	22	66
____		(B) Green-painted	22	62
	655	Silver Bullet Coach, *53*		
____		(A) Chrome finish	25	89
____		(B) Satin silver-painted	20	139
	660	AFL Combination Car, *50–52*		
____		(A) Aluminum body	18	49
____		(B) Chrome finish, plastic body	27	118
	661	AFL Coach, *50–52*		
____		(A) Aluminum body	52	71
____		(B) Chrome finish, plastic body	44	78
____		(C) Satin silver-painted, plastic body	50	263
	662	AFL Vista Dome Car, *50–52*		
____		(A) Aluminum body	22	69
____		(B) Chrome finish, plastic body	30	88
____	**663**	AFL Observation Car, aluminum, *50–52*	22	79
____	**668**	Manual Switch, left hand, *53–55*	5	9
____	**669**	Manual Switch, right hand, *53–55*	5	9
____	**670**	Track Trip, *55–56*	2	13
____	**678**	Remote Control Switch, left hand, *53–56*	7	19
____	**679**	Remote Control Switch, right hand, *53–56*	6	16
____	**690**	Track Terminal, *46–56*		6
____	**691**	Steel Pins, *46–48*		1

GILBERT PRODUCTION 1946-1966

		Good	Exc
692	Fiber Pins, *46–48*		1 ____
693	Track Locks, dozen, *48–56*		5 ____
694	Couplers, Trucks, Wheels, and Axles, *46–53*	2	10 ____
695	Reverse Loop Relay, *55–56*	26	118 ____
695	Track Trip, *46*	6	12 ____
696	Track Trip, *55–57*		
	(A) Plastic shoe	10	13 ____
	(B) Die-cast shoe	10	22 ____
697	Track Trip, *50–54*	4	15 ____
698	Reverse Loop Kit, *49–50, 52–54*	17	85 ____
700	Straight Track, *46–56*		2 ____
701	Straight Track, half section, *46–56*		2 ____
702	Curved Track, *46–56*		2 ____
703	Curved Track, half section, *46–56*		2 ____
704	Manual Uncoupler, *52–56*		1 ____
705	Remote Control Uncoupler, *46–47*	1	5 ____
706	Remote Control Uncoupler, *48–56*	1	3 ____
707	Track Terminal, *46–59*		1 ____
708	Air Chime Whistle Control, *51–56*	3	11 ____
709	Lockout Eliminator, *50–55*	2	14 ____
710	Automatic Track Section, *46–47*	1	9 ____
710	Steam Whistle Control, *55–56*	10	78 ____
711	Mail Pickup, *46–47*	9	22 ____
712	Special Rail Section, *47–56*		1 ____
713	Special Rail Section with mail bag hook, *47–56*	8	30 ____
714	Log Unloading Car, *51–54*	16	45 ____
715	American Flyer Lines Flatcar, *46–54*		
	(A) Tootsietoy armored car	37	132 ____
	(B) Manoil coupe	25	46 ____
	(C) Tootsietoy racer		49 ____
716	American Flyer Lines Hopper, *46–51*		
	(A) Between-rail pickup, *46*	6	40 ____
	(B) Outside rail pickup, *47–51*	6	23 ____
717	American Flyer Lines Flatcar, *46–52*	15	25 ____
718	AFL Mail Pickup Car, *49–54*		300 ____
718	New Haven Mail Pickup Car, *46–54*		
	(A) Red body, red pickup arm	155	468 ____
	(B) Red or green body	31	127 ____
	(C) Maroon body		NRS ____
719	CB&Q Hopper Dump Car, *50–54*		
	(A) Tuscan-painted	25	57 ____
	(B) Red plastic	34	82 ____
720	Remote Control Switches, *46–49*	19	42 ____
720A	Remote Control Switches, *50–56*	23	40 ____
722	Manual Switches, *46–51*	10	24 ____
722A	Manual Switches, *52–56*	9	18 ____
725	90-degree Crossing, *46–56*	3	13 ____
726	Straight Rubber Roadbed, *50–56*	1	4 ____
727	Curved Rubber Roadbed, *50–56*	1	3 ____
728	Re-railer, *56*	3	33 ____

			Good	Exc
	730	Bumper, *46–56*		
____		(A) Green plastic	11	27
____		(B) Red, *51*	35	95
____		(C) Green-painted	23	90
____	**731**	Pike Planning Kit, *52–56*	11	24
	732	AF Operating Baggage Car, *51–54*		
____		(A) Unpainted red or green	29	77
____		(B) Green-painted	34	100
	734	American Flyer Operating Boxcar, *50–54*		
____		(A) Red plastic	20	48
____		(B) Red painted	25	80
____		(C) Tuscan painted	20	48
____		(D) Tuscan painted, AFL	30	92
____	**735**	NH Animated Station Coach, *52–54*	32	78
____	**736**	Missouri Pacific Stock Car, *50–54*	10	32
	740	AFL Motorized Handcar, *52–54*		
____		(A) No decals, no vent holes, black lettering, *52*	33	123
____		(B) Shield decal with stripes, *52*	20	47
____		(C) Shield decal with vent holes, no stripes	17	69
____	**741**	AFL Handcar and Shed, motorized, *53–54*	75	123
____	**742**	AFL Reversing Handcar, *55–56*	41	103
____	**743**	Track Maintenance Car		2750
____	**747**	Cardboard Trestle Set, u	7	22
____	**748**	Girder, Trestle, and Tower Bridge, *58 u*	22	50
	748	Overhead Foot Bridge, *51–52*		
____		(A) Gray/aluminum	17	32
____		(B) Bluish silver	28	51
____	**749**	Street Lamp Set, *50–52*	6	26
	750	Trestle Bridge, *46–56*		
____		(A) Black-painted	16	68
____		(B) Silver-painted	16	90
____		(C) Bluish gray-painted	25	110
____	**751**	Log Loader, *46–50*	69	184
____	**751A**	Log Loader, *52–53*	47	97
____	**752**	Seaboard Coaler, *46–50*	100	135
____	**752A**	Seaboard Coaler, *51–52*	115	165
____	**753**	Mountain Tunnel and Pass Set, *60 u*	17	51
____	**753**	Single Trestle Bridge, *52*	16	54
____	**754**	Double Trestle Bridge, *50–52*	50	98
	755	Talking Station, *48–50*		
____		(A) Green roof	50	66
____		(B) Blue roof	60	82
____	**758**	Sam the Semaphore Man, *49*	29	55
____	**758A**	Sam the Semaphore Man, *50–56*	36	90
____	**759**	Bell Danger Signal, *53–56*	22	52
____	**760**	Highway Flasher, *49–56*	9	29
____	**761**	Semaphore, *49–56*	22	75
____	**762**	Two-in-One Whistle, *49–50*	35	94
____	**763**	Mountain Set, *49–50*	46	120
____	**764**	Express Office, *50–51*	47	228
____	**766**	Animated Station, *52–54*	68	134

		Good	Exc	
K766	Animated Station, *53–55*	55	134	____
767	Roadside Diner, *50–54*			
	(A) Yellow plastic	40	89	____
	(B) Yellow-painted	50	146	____
768	Oil Supply Depot, *50–53*			
	(A) Shell	40	119	____
	(B) Gulf	60	136	____
769	Aircraft Beacon, *50*	16	42	____
769A	Aircraft Beacon, *51–56*	19	55	____
770	Girder Trestle Set, *60 u*	4	18	____
770	Loading Platform, *50–52*	31	85	____
771	Operating Stockyard, *50–54*	46	59	____
K771	Stockyard and Car, *53–56*	50	76	____
772	Water Tower, *50–56*			
	(A) Small tank	30	59	____
	(B) Small tank, with workman, *50*	207	510	____
	(C) Large checkerboard tank, metal shack	49	122	____
773	Oil Derrick, *50–52*			
	(A) American Flyer, *50*	48	78	____
	(B) Gulf logo		775	____
774	Floodlight Tower, *51–56*			
	(A) Red base, gray tower and platform	18	63	____
	(B) Red base, gray tower and platform, with workman	80	260	____
775	Baggage Platform with boxcar, link couplers, *53–55*	24	78	____
K775	Baggage Platform with boxcar, knuckle couplers, *53–55*	35	131	____
778	Street Lamp Set, *53–56*	11	25	____
779	Oil Drum Loader, *55–56*			
	(A) Tan plastic base	55	120	____
	(B) Gray-painted base	75	211	____
780	Trestle Set, *53–56*			
	(A) Black, *53*	15	26	____
	(B) Orange	10	24	____
781	Abutment Set, *53*	22	105	____
782	Abutment Set, *53*	17	121	____
783	Hi-Trestle Sections, *53–56*	6	42	____
784	Hump Set, *55*	75	354	____
785	Coal Loader, *55–56*	141	206	____
787	Log Loader, *55–56*	73	142	____
788	Suburban Station, *56*	11	56	____
789	Station and Baggage Smasher, *56–57*	93	168	____
790	Trainorama, *53 u*	48	169	____
792	Terminal, *54–56*	65	137	____
793	Union Station, *55–56*	16	83	____
794	Union Station, *54*	32	129	____
795	Union Station and Terminal, *54*	110	374	____
799	Talking Station, *54–56*	35	174	____
801	Baltimore & Ohio Hopper, *56–57*	11	14	____
802	Illinois Central Reefer, *56–57**			
	(A) Orange plastic	15	21	____
	(B) Orange-painted	100	280	____

			Good	Exc
____	803	Santa Fe Boxcar, tuscan, unpainted, *56–57*	17	24
____	804	Norfolk & Western Gondola, *56–57*	6	14
____	805	Pennsylvania Gondola, tuscan, *56–57*	7	13
____	806	American Flyer Lines Caboose, *56–57*	7	10
	807	Rio Grande Boxcar, *57*		
____		(A) Unpainted, nonopening door	19	28
____		(B) Opening door		NRS
____		(C) White-painted, nonopening door		415
____	900	NP Combination Car, *56–57**	100	238
____	901	NP Coach, *56–57**	100	242
____	902	NP Vista Dome Car, *56–57**	100	242
____	903	NP Observation Car, *56–57**	100	235
____	904	AFL Caboose, *56*	11	18
____	905	AFL Flatcar, gray or blue-gray, *54*	11	34
____	906	AFL Crane, gray or blue-gray, *54*	16	45
____	907	AFL Work and Boom Car, *54*	13	38
____	909	AFL Flatcar, gray or blue-gray, *54*	11	30
____	910	Gilbert Chemical Tank Car, *54**	70	219
	911	C&O Gondola, *55–57*		
____		(A) Silver pipes, black-painted or black body	10	31
____		(B) Brown pipes, black-painted body, *55*	39	195
	912	Koppers Tank Car, *55–57*		
____		(A) Die-cast frame	38	51
____		(B) Plastic frame	25	59
	913	Great Northern Boxcar, *53–58*		
____		(A) Decal goat logo	14	44
____		(B) Painted goat logo	14	43
____	914	American Flyer Lines Flatcar, *53–57*	17	59
	915	American Flyer Lines Flatcar, *53–57*		
____		(A) Black and red, yellow ramp, with TootsieToy racer	12	70
____		(B) gray, brown ramp, with Renwal gas truck	12	81
____	916	Delaware & Hudson Gondola, *55–56*	9	28
	918	American Flyer Lines Mail Car, *53–58*		
____		(A) American Flyer Lines	29	79
____		(B) New Haven	35	162
____	919	CB&Q Dump Car, *53–56*	41	60
____	920	Southern Gondola, *53–56*	14	31
____	921	CB&Q Hopper, *53–56*	8	27
	922	General American Boxcar, *53–57**		
____		(A) Decal	15	33
____		(B) Stamped	15	59
____	923	Illinois Central Reefer, *54–55**	13	18
____	924	Jersey Central Hopper, *53–56*	9	23
	925	Gulf Tank Car, *52–57*		
____		(A) Early knuckle coupler, *52*	28	176
____		(B) Die-cast frame	15	29
____		(C) Plastic frame	10	22
	926	Gulf Tank Car, *55–57*		
____		(A) Die-cast frame	10	45
____		(B) Plastic frame	10	43

		Good	Exc
928	C&NW Flatcar, *52–54*		
	(A) Pressed-wood base, *52*	24	98 ___
	(B) Die-cast base, *53–54*	9	23 ___
928	New Haven Log Car, *56 u*	17	28 ___
928	New Haven Lumber Car, *56–57*	11	32 ___
929	Missouri Pacific Stock Car, *52–57*		
	(A) Closed slats, tuscan or red	10	31 ___
	(B) Open slats, tuscan, *57*	100	900 ___
930	American Flyer Caboose, *52*		
	(A) Early knuckle coupler	28	112 ___
	(B) Red	15	37 ___
	(C) Tuscan	9	28 ___
930	American Flyer Lines Caboose, *53–57*		
	(A) Type I or II body	28	46 ___
	(B) Type III body	28	119 ___
931	T&P Gondola, green, *52–55*	5	20 ___
933	B&O Boxcar, *53–54*	19	43 ___
934	American Flyer Lines Caboose, *54 u*	16	39 ___
934	C&NW Floodlight "42597," gray or blue-gray, *53–54*	10	26 ___
934	Southern Pacific Floodlight, *54 u*	14	32 ___
935	AFL Bay Window Caboose, *57*	21	58 ___
936	Erie Flatcar, *53–54*	12	43 ___
936	Pennsylvania Flatcar, *55–57*	40	124 ___
937	MKT Boxcar, *53–58*		
	(A) All yellow	10	40 ___
	(B) Yellow and tuscan	10	34 ___
938	American Flyer Lines Caboose, *54–55*	5	16 ___
940	Wabash Hopper, *53–56*	7	21 ___
941	Frisco Lines Gondola, *53–56*	7	21 ___
942	Seaboard Boxcar, *54*	9	21 ___
944	American Flyer Crane, *52–57*		
	(A) Gray die-cast body, black cab	22	53 ___
	(B) Blue-gray die-cast body, black cab	30	63 ___
945	AF or AFL Work and Boom Car, *52–57*		
	(A) Die-cast base, *52–56*	10	41 ___
	(B) Plastic base, *57*	15	39 ___
946	Erie Floodlight Car, *53–56*		
	(A) Red or green painted generator	13	41 ___
	(B) Red, green, or yellow plastic generator	13	41 ___
947	Northern Pacific Reefer, *53–58*	12	43 ___
948	AFL Flatcar, *53–57*	11	30 ___
951	AFL Baggage Car, *53–57*		
	(A) Red or maroon	15	62 ___
	(B) Green	18	58 ___
952	AFL Pullman Car, *53–58*		
	(A) No silhouettes, maroon or green	36	164 ___
	(B) Silhouettes, maroon	50	176 ___
953	AFL Combination Car, *53–58*		
	(A) No silhouettes, maroon or green	43	115 ___
	(B) Silhouettes, maroon	55	160 ___

			Good	Exc
	954	AFL Observation Car, *53–56*		
___		(A) No silhouettes, maroon or green	36	119
___		(B) Silhouettes, maroon	105	160
	955	AF or AFL Coach, *54–55*		
___		(A) Satin silver-painted	30	81
___		(B) Green-painted	31	73
___		(C) Maroon-painted, silhouettes, "955"	21	80
___		(D) Maroon-painted, silhouettes, white-outlined windows	29	90
___	**956**	Monon Flatcar, *56*	21	57
___	**957**	Erie Operating Boxcar, *57 u*	47	113
	958	Mobilgas Tank Car, plastic or metal frame, *57 u*		
___			23	90
	960	AFL Columbus Combination Car, *53–56*		
___		(A) Satin silver	30	92
___		(B) Blue, green, or red band	56	114
___		(C) Chestnut band	75	182
___		(D) Orange band	50	131
___		(E) Chrome finish	50	114
	961	AFL Jefferson Pullman Car, *53–58*		
___		(A) Satin silver	40	272
___		(B) Green or red band	45	115
___		(C) Chestnut band	108	271
___		(D) Orange band	65	159
___		(E) Chrome finish	50	108
	962	AFL Hamilton Vista Dome Car, *53–58*		
___		(A) Satin silver	40	114
___		(B) Blue, green, or red band	41	110
___		(C) Chestnut band	90	238
___		(D) Orange band	65	164
___		(E) Chrome finish	50	113
	963	AFL Washington Observation Car, *53–58*		
___		(A) Satin silver	40	107
___		(B) Blue, green, or red band	36	123
___		(C) Chestnut band	85	223
___		(D) Orange band	65	157
___		(E) Chrome finish	50	110
	969	Rocket Launcher Flatcar, *57 u*		
___		(A) Black plastic	20	63
___		(B) Black-painted	80	285
___	**970**	Seaboard Operating Boxcar, *56–57*	48	90
	971	Southern Pacific Lumber Unloading Car, *56–57*		
___		(A) Tuscan plastic	39	80
___		(B) Tuscan-painted plastic	50	620
___	**973**	Gilbert's Operating Milk Car, *56–57*	65	135
___	**974**	AFL Operating Boxcar, *53–54*	27	78
___	**974**	Erie Operating Boxcar, *55*	48	151
___	**975**	AFL Operating Coach, *54–55*	29	75
___	**976**	MP Operating Cattle Car, *53–62*	25	46
___	**977**	AFL Caboose, metal or rubber man, *55–57*	26	43
___	**978**	AFL Grand Canyon Observation Car, *56–58*	130	448
___	**979**	AFL Bay Window Caboose, *57*	62	104
___	**980**	Baltimore & Ohio Boxcar, *56–57*	35	102

		Good	Exc	
981	Central of Georgia Boxcar, *56–57*			
	(A) Shiny black paint	44	122	___
	(B) Dull black paint	70	201	___
982	BAR Boxcar, *56–57*	48	91	___
983	MP Boxcar, *56–57*	48	94	___
984	New Haven Boxcar, *56–57*	30	64	___
985	B&M Boxcar, *57*	55	91	___
988	ART Reefer, *56–57*	49	93	___
989	Northwestern Reefer, *56–58*	60	170	___
994	Union Pacific Stock Car, *57*	55	162	___
C1001	White's Discount Centers Boxcar, *61* u*	345	1267	___
1023A	Trestle Set		220	___
1-1024A	Trestle Set, *52 u*	10	44	___
C2001	Post Boxcar, *62 u*	13	22	___
L2001	Game Train 4-4-0 Locomotive, *63*	15	39	___
L2002	Burlington Route 4-4-0 Locomotive, *63 u*	50	295	___
L2004	Rio Grande F9 Diesel, *62*	80	190	___
C2009	Texas & Pacific Gondola, *62–64*			
	(A) Unpainted dark green or dark green-painted		2000	___
	(B) Unpainted light green	7	18	___
21004	PRR 0-6-0 Switcher, *57 u*	115	358	___
21005	PRR 0-6-0 Switcher, *57–58*	125	381	___
21084	C&NW 4-6-2 Pacific Locomotive, *57 u*	41	154	___
21085	C&NW or CMStP&P 4-6-2 Pacific Locomotive, *58–65*			
	(A) Plastic drivers	32	58	___
	(B) Metal drivers	32	68	___
21088	FY&P Franklin 4-4-0 Locomotive, red, black, or green, *59–60*	49	85	___
21089	FY&PRR Washington 4-4-0 Locomotive, *60–61*	65	249	___
21095	NYNH&H 4-6-2 Pacific Locomotive, *57*		NRS	___
21099	NYNH&H 4-6-2 Pacific Locomotive, *58*	128	482	___
21100	Reading 4-4-2 Atlantic Locomotive, *57 u*	14	31	___
21105	Reading 4-4-2 Atlantic Locomotive, *57–60*			
	(A) Aluminum drive wheels	100	200	___
	(B) Die-cast wheels with white tires	40	67	___
	(C) Black plastic drive wheels	20	41	___
21106	Reading 4-4-2 Atlantic Locomotive, *59 u*	105	253	___
21107	PRR or BN 4-4-2 Atlantic Locomotive, *64–66 u*	10	20	___
21115	PRR 4-6-2 Pacific Locomotive, *58*	215	1061	___
21129	NYC 4-6-4 Hudson Locomotive, *58*	318	1354	___
21130	NYC 4-6-4 Hudson Locomotive, *59–60*	140	320	___
21139	UP 4-8-4 Northern Locomotive, *58–59*	265	1428	___
21140	UP 4-8-4 Northern Locomotive, *60*	525	2014	___
21145	NKP 0-8-0 Switcher, *58*	165	1060	___
21155	0-6-0 Switcher, *58*	90	285	___
21156	0-6-0 Switcher, *59*	75	200	___
21158	0-6-0 Switcher, *60 u*	41	99	___
21160	Reading 4-4-2 Atlantic Locomotive, *58–60 u*	15	26	___
21161	Reading 4-4-2 Atlantic Locomotive, *60 u*			
	(A) American Flyer Lines	11	22	___
	(B) Prestone Car Care Express	83	414	___

			Good	Exc
___	**21165**	Erie 4-4-0 Locomotive, *61–62, 65–66 u*	10	26
	21166	Burlington Route 4-4-0 Locomotive, *63–65*		
___		(A) White letters in black box	10	32
___		(B) Black letters in white box	85	204
	21168	Southern 4-4-0 Locomotive, *61–63*		
___		(A) Knuckle coupler, *61*	25	64
___		(B) Pike Master couplers, *62–63*	10	44
___	**21205/-1**	B&M Twin F9 Diesels, *61–62 u*		
___		(A) Twin A units	110	252
___		(B) Single unit	75	197
___	**21206/-1**	SF Twin F9 Diesels, *61–62 u*	105	352
___	**21207/-1**	GN Twin F9 Diesels, *63–64*	100	333
___	**21210**	Burlington F9 Diesel, *61*	65	262
___	**21215/-1**	UP F9 Diesel, *61–62*	95	298
___	**21215/16**	UP Twin F9 Diesels, *61*		2100
	21234	Chesapeake & Ohio GP7 Diesel, *59–61*		
___		(A) Long steps	145	411
___		(B) Short steps	165	694
	21551	Northern Pacific PA Diesel, *58*		
___		(A) Plastic steps, portholes filled in	135	298
___		(B) Sheet-metal steps, portholes open	135	373
	21561	New Haven PA Diesel, *57–58*		
___		(A) Plastic steps	125	307
___		(B) 1-rivet metal steps	125	328
	21573	New Haven GE Electric, *58–59*		
___		(A) Shiny black, *58*	145	355
___		(B) Dull black, *59*	200	450
___	**21720**	Santa Fe PB Diesel, *58 u*	275	1135
	21801	C&NW Baldwin Locomotive, *57–58*		
___		(A) Unpainted	42	107
___		(B) Painted	70	320
	21801-1	C&NW Baldwin Locomotive, *58 u*		
___		(A) Unpainted	70	172
___		(B) Painted	85	290
___	**21808**	C&NW Baldwin Locomotive, *58 u*	50	97
___	**21812**	Texas & Pacific Baldwin Locomotive, *59–60*	75	127
___	**21813**	M&StL Baldwin Locomotive, *58 u, 60 u*	190	646
	21831	Texas & Pacific GP7 Diesel, *58*		
___		(A) American Flyer Lines	150	323
___		(B) Texas & Pacific	185	541
___	**21910/-1/-2**	SF PA/PB/PA Diesel Set, *57–58*	370	811
___	**21918/-1**	Seaboard Baldwin Locomotive, *58*	320	484
___	**21920**	Missouri Pacific PA Diesel, *63–64*	185	527
___	**21920/-1**	Missouri Pacific PA/PA Diesel Set, *58**	340	1032
___	**21922/-1**	Missouri Pacific PA/PA Diesel Set, *59–60*	275	852
___	**21925/-1**	Union Pacific PA/PA Diesel Set, *59–60**	235	889
___	**21927**	Santa Fe PA Diesel, *60–62*	110	206
___	**22004**	Transformer, 40 watts, *59–64*	2	10
___	**22006**	Transformer, 25 watts, *63*	2	9
___	**22020**	Transformer, 50 watts, *57–64*	2	8
___	**22030**	Transformer, 100 watts, *57–64*	4	21
___	**22033**	Transformer, 25 watts, *65*	2	5

		Good	Exc	
22034	Transformer, 50 watts, *65*	4	12	____
22035	Transformer, 175 watts, *57–64*	16	78	____
22040	Transformer, 110 watts, *57–58*	5	18	____
22050	Transformer, 175 watts, *57–58*	12	42	____
22060	Transformer, 175 watts, *57–58*	12	39	____
22080	Transformer, 300 watts, *57–58*	34	195	____
22090	Transformer, 350 watts, *59–64*	63	173	____
23021	Imitation Grass, *57–59*	6	22	____
23022	Scenery Gravel, *57–59*	6	22	____
23023	Imitation Coal, *57–59*	5	17	____
23024	Rainbow Wire, *57–64*	4	10	____
23025	Smoke Cartridges, *57–59*	4	25	____
23026	Service Kit, *59–64*	6	27	____
23027	Track Cleaning Fluid, *57–59*	1	4	____
23028	Smoke Fluid Dispenser, *60–64*	2	17	____
23032	Equipment Kit, *60–61*	33	105	____
23036	Money Saver Kit, *60, 62, 64*	32	295	____
23040	Mountain Tunnel and Pass Set, *58*		140	____
23249	Tunnel, *57–64*	9	48	____
23561	Billboard Horn, *57–59*	10	43	____
23568	Whistling Billboard, *57–64*	11	73	____
23571	Truss Bridge, *57–64*	7	30	____
23581	Girder Bridge, *57–64*	8	35	____
23586	Wayside Station, *57–59*	25	113	____
23589	Passenger and Freight Station, *59 u*	15	55	____
23590	Control Tower, *57–59*	20	110	____
23596	Water Tank, *57–58*	25	103	____
23598	Talking Station Record, *57–59*	5	19	____
23599	Talking Station Record, *57*	9	36	____
23600	Crossing Gate with bell, *57–58*	13	105	____
23601	Crossing Gate, *59–62*	13	83	____
23602	Crossing Gate, *63–64*	13	69	____
23743	Track Maintenance Car, *60–64*	90	129	____
23750	Trestle Bridge, *57–61*	26	75	____
23758	Sam the Semaphore Man, *57*	29	85	____
23759	Bell Danger Signal, *56–60*	12	79	____
23760	Highway Flasher, *57–60*	9	42	____
23761	Semaphore, *57–60*	22	68	____
23763	Bell Danger Signal, *61–64*	11	70	____
23764	Flasher Signal, *61–64*	12	42	____
23769	Aircraft Beacon, *57–64*	13	75	____
23771	Stockyard and Car, *57–61*	29	113	____
23772	Water Tower, *57–64*	20	150	____
23774	Floodlight Tower, *57–64*	16	109	____
23778	Street Lamp Set, *57–64*	8	39	____
23779	Oil Drum Loader, *57–61*	55	198	____
23780	Gabe the Lamplighter, *58–59*			
	(A) Dark green base	305	563	____
	(B) Light green base	900	901	____
23785	Coal Loader, *57–60*	130	216	____
23786	Talking Station, *57–59*	60	104	____
23787	Log Loader, *57–60*	90	253	____

			Good	Exc
___	**23788**	Suburban Station, *57–64*	10	60
___	**23789**	Station and Baggage Smasher, *58–59*	55	217
	23791	Cow on Track, black/white or brown/white,		
___		*57–59*	26	100
___	**23796**	Sawmill, *57–64*	105	216
___	**23830**	Piggyback Unloader, *59–60*	39	88
	24003	Santa Fe Boxcar, *58*		
___		(A) Unpainted tuscan plastic	14	41
___		(B) Tuscan-painted		713
___	**24006**	Great Northern Boxcar, *57–58*		2500
___	**24016**	MKT Boxcar, *58*	260	1149
___	**24019**	Seaboard Boxcar, *58, 61 u*	18	39
___	**24023**	Baltimore & Ohio Boxcar, *58–59*	34	119
___	**24026**	Central of Georgia Boxcar, *58*	32	162
	24029	BAR Boxcar		
___		(A) Knuckle couplers, *57–60*	58	89
___		(B) Pike Master couplers, *61*	100	180
	24030	MKT Boxcar, *60 u*		
___		(A) Unpainted yellow plastic	10	17
___		(B) Yellow-painted plastic	50	945
___	**24033**	Missouri Pacific Boxcar, *58*	52	131
___	**24036**	New Haven Boxcar, *58–60*	24	88
	24039	Rio Grande Boxcar, *59*		
___		(A) Unpainted white plastic	10	66
___		(B) Unpainted ivory plastic	10	41
___		(C) White-painted		228
___	**24043**	Boston & Maine Boxcar, *58–60*	33	114
___	**24045**	MEC Boxcar		NRS
___	**24047**	Great Northern Boxcar, *59*	55	215
___	**24048**	M&StL Boxcar, *59–62*	47	121
	24052	UFGE Boxcar, *61*		
___		(A) Unpainted yellow plastic	11	19
___		(B) Yellow-painted	150	208
	24054	Santa Fe Boxcar, *62–64, 66*		
___		(A) Red-painted plastic, *62–64*	20	54
___		(B) Unpainted red plastic, *66*	9	34
	24055	Gold Belt Line Boxcar, *60–61*		
___		(A) Opening with door	14	52
___		(B) Opening without door	14	35
	24056	Boston & Maine Boxcar, *61*		
___		(A) Blue-painted black plastic	70	283
___		(B) Unpainted blue plastic	27	136
	24057	Mounds Boxcar, *62*		
___		(A) White	5	11
___		(B) Ivory	9	19
	24058	Post Boxcar, white or ivory, *63–64*		
___		(A) Cereal	8	14
___		(B) Cereals	11	20
___	**24059**	Boston & Maine Boxcar, *63*	48	189
___	**24060**	M&StL Boxcar, *63–64*	39	130

		Good	Exc	
24065	NYC Boxcar, *60–64*			
	(A) Knuckle couplers	41	98	___
	(B) Pike Master couplers	30	75	___
24066	L&N Boxcar, blue-painted, *60*	80	206	___
24067	Keystone Line Boxcar, *60* * u	1350	2425	___
24068	Planters Peanuts Boxcar, *61* * u		NRS	___
24076	Union Pacific Stock Car, *57–60*			
	(A) Knuckle couplers	30	85	___
	(B) Pike Master couplers	28	57	___
24077	Northern Pacific Stock Car, *59–62*			
	(A) Knuckle couplers	85	313	___
	(B) Pike Master couplers	60	152	___
24103	Norfolk & Western Gondola, black plastic, *58, 63–64*	7	20	___
24106	Pennsylvania Gondola, *60 u*			
	(A) Unpainted tuscan plastic	7	19	___
	(B) Tuscan-painted	36	160	___
24109	C&O Gondola with pipes, *57–60*			
	(A) Silver plastic or cardboard pipes	24	47	___
	(B) Orange cardboard pipes	45	125	___
24110	Pennsylvania Gondola, *59 u*	5	12	___
24113	Delaware & Hudson Gondola, *57–59*	14	28	___
24116	Southern Gondola, *57–60*	19	102	___
24120	Texas & Pacific Gondola, *60 u*			
	(A) Unpainted green plastic	14	58	___
	(B) Green-painted	100	300	___
24124	Boston & Maine Gondola, *63–64*			
	(A) Unpainted blue	5	16	___
	(B) Dark blue-painted	72	222	___
24125	Bethlehem Steel Gondola, *60–66*			
	(A) Gray-painted with rail load	24	124	___
	(B) Unpainted gray without load	9	21	___
24126	Frisco Gondola, tuscan, *61*	33	136	___
24127	Monon Gondola, *61–65*			
	(A) Knuckle couplers	5	14	___
	(B) Pike Master couplers	4	11	___
24130	Pennsylvania Gondola, *60 u*			
	(A) Pike Master couplers	9	18	___
	(B) Fixed or operating knuckle couplers	4	12	___
24203	Baltimore & Ohio Hopper, *58, 63–64*			
	(A) Unpainted black, *58*	20	30	___
	(B) Black-painted, *58*	150	275	___
	(C) Marbleized, *58*	150	275	___
	(D) PM trucks and couplers, *63–64*	17	52	___
24206	CB&Q Hopper, *58*	32	119	___
24209	Jersey Central Hopper, *57–60*	27	121	___
24213	Wabash Hopper, *58–60*	15	29	___
24216	Union Pacific Hopper, *58–60*	22	66	___
24219	Western Maryland Hopper, *58–59*	42	130	___
24221	C&EI Hopper, *59–60*	35	128	___
24222	Domino Sugar Hopper, *63–64**	138	383	___

			Good	Exc
	24225	Santa Fe Hopper, *60–65*		
___		(A) Red-painted, knuckle couplers	10	43
___		(B) Red-painted, PM couplers	10	37
___		(C) Unpainted red plastic, PM couplers	25	42
	24230	Peabody Hopper, *61–64*		
___		(A) Knuckle couplers	21	75
___		(B) Pike Master couplers	21	69
___	24309	Gulf Tank Car, *57–58*	4	19
___	24310	Gulf Tank Car, *58–60*	5	22
	24313	Gulf Tank Car, *57–60*		
___		(A) Full tank	21	49
___		(B) Open-bottom tank		1000
	24316	Mobilgas Tank Car, *57–61, 65–66*		
___		(A) Knuckle couplers, complete tank	20	53
___		(B) Knuckle couplers, open-bottom tank	70	240
___		(C) Pike Master couplers	5	28
___	24319	PRR Salt Tank Car, *58**	155	455
	24320	Deep Rock Tank Car, *60–61*		
___		(A) Complete tank, *60*	50	341
___		(B) Open-bottom tank, *61*	100	459
___	24321	Deep Rock Tank Car, *59*	20	82
	24322	Gulf Tank Car, *59*		
___		(A) Full tank	15	21
___		(B) Open-bottom tank	25	99
	24323	Baker's Chocolate Tank Car, *59–60**		
___		(A) Type II frame white, white ends	480	1476
___		(B) Type II frame white, gray-painted ends	118	392
___		(C) Type III frame white, open-bottom tank		2100
___	24324	Hooker Tank Car, *59–60*	31	141
	24325	Gulf Tank Car, *60*		
___		(A) Type II plastic frame	6	18
___		(B) Type III plastic frame, open-bottom tank	15	143
	24328	Shell Tank Car, *62–66*		
___		(A) Yellow plastic	7	22
___		(B) Yellow-painted	300	450
___	24329	Hooker Tank Car with platform, *61*	10	32
___	24329	Hooker Tank Car, no platform or number, *62–65 u*	9	27
___	24330	Baker's Chocolate Tank Car, *61–62*	27	172
	24403	Illinois Central Reefer		
___		(A) Unpainted orange plastic	13	23
___		(B) Orange-painted		300
___	24409	Northern Pacific Reefer, *58*	355	1322
___	24413	ART Reefer, *57–60*	38	141
___	24416	Northwestern Reefer, *58*	680	2027
___	24419	Canadian National Reefer, *58–59*	112	280
___	24420	Simmons Reefer, *58** *u*	660	1047
___	24422	Great Northern Boxcar, *63–65, 66 u*	50	148
	24422	Great Northern Reefer, *63–65, 66 u*		
___		(A) Unpainted green plastic, non-opening door	12	18
___		(B) Green-painted plastic, opening door	65	193
___		(C) Green-painted plastic, non-opening door	60	192

		Good	Exc	
24425	BAR Reefer, *60*			
	(A) Knuckle couplers	175	608	____
	(B) Pike Master couplers	200	473	____
24426	Rath Packing Reefer, *60–61*	200	389	____
24516	New Haven Flatcar, *57–59*	12	40	____
24519	Pennsylvania Flatcar, *58*	265	734	____
24529	Erie Floodlight, *57–58*	10	48	____
24533	American Flyer Lines Flatcar, *58–66*	10	31	____
24536	Monon Flatcar, *58*	385	1666	____
24537	New Haven Flatcar, *58 u*	10	33	____
24539	New Haven Flatcar, *58–59, 63–64*			
	(A) Silver plastic or cardboard pipes, *58–59*	12	31	____
	(B) Orange cardboard pipes, *63–64*	17	50	____
	(C) Orange pipes, no number, *63–64*	25	57	____
24540	New Haven Flatcar, *60 u*	47	305	____
24543	American Flyer Lines Crane, *58*	11	44	____
24546	AFL Work and Boom Car, *58–64*	10	59	____
24547	Erie Floodlight, *58*	265	692	____
24549	Erie Floodlight, *58–66*			
	(A) Yellow generator, knuckle couplers	15	47	____
	(B) Red generator, PM couplers	12	25	____
	(C) Yellow generator, PM couplers	8	21	____
24550	Monon Flatcar, *59–64*	23	90	____
24553	Rocket Transport Flatcar, *58–60*	22	85	____
24556	Rock Island Flatcar, *59*	22	52	____
24557	U.S. Navy Flatcar, *59–61*	29	107	____
24558	Canadian Pacific Flatcar with trees, *59–60*	102	473	____
24559	New Haven Flatcar, *59 u*	80	333	____
24561	American Flyer Lines Crane, *59–61*			
	(A) Gray-painted frame, knuckle couplers, *59*	10	40	____
	(B) Unpainted gray frame, PM couplers, *60–61*	8	26	____
24562	New York Central Flatcar, *60*	14	35	____
24564	New Haven Flatcar, *60 u*			
	(A) Silver-gray plastic pipes	9	38	____
	(B) Orange cardboard pipes	25	60	____
24565	FY&PRR Flatcar with cannon, *60–61**	38	156	____
24566	National Car Flatcar, *61–65*	26	86	____
24566	New Haven Flatcar, *61–64*			
	(A) Unpainted black body, blue or red tractor	27	184	____
	(B) Unpainted gray body, *61*	300	892	____
24569	AFL Crane, *62–66*	11	25	____
24572	U.S. Navy Flatcar with 2 jeeps, *61*			
	(A) Gray plastic or painted, knuckle couplers	38	156	____
	(B) Gray plastic, Pike Master couplers	75	189	____
24574	U.S. Air Force Flatcar with rocket fuel tanks, *60–61*			
	(A) Knuckle couplers	40	163	____
	(B) Pike Master couplers	39	130	____
24575	Borden's Milk Flatcar, unmarked, *66 u*	9	37	____
24575	National Car Co. Flatcar, *60–66*			
	(A) Knuckle couplers	17	68	____
	(B) Pike Master couplers	17	47	____

			Good	Exc
	24577	Illinois Central Flatcar, *60–61, 63–64*		
____		(A) Knuckle couplers	45	175
____		(B) Pike Master couplers	42	175
____	**24578**	New Haven Flatcar with Corvette, *62–63*	113	385
	24579	Illinois Central Flatcar, *60–61*		
____		(A) Silver pipes, knuckle couplers	45	213
____		(B) Orange pipes, PM couplers	50	210
	24603	AFL Caboose, *57–58*		
____		(A) Unpainted red plastic	5	15
____		(B) Painted red plastic		NRS
____	**24610**	AFL Caboose, *58–60 u*	5	18
____	**24619**	AFL Bay Window Caboose, *58*	20	144
____	**24626**	AFL Caboose, *58*	9	33
____	**24627**	AFL Caboose, *59–60*	4	17
____	**24630**	AFL Caboose, *59–61 u*	4	18
	24631	AFL Caboose, yellow-painted, *59–61, 63–65*		
____		(A) Knuckle couplers, stripe, *59–61*	8	34
____		(B) Pike Master couplers, stripe, *63–65*	6	29
____		(C) Pike Master couplers, no stripe, *65*	80	165
____	**24632**	American Flyer Lines Caboose, *59*	28	62
____	**24633**	AFL Bay Window Caboose, *59–62*	19	87
	24634	AFL Bay Window Caboose, *63–66*		
____		(A) Unpainted red plastic, illuminated	20	36
____		(B) Red-painted, illuminated	20	62
____		(C) Nonilluminated, plastic wheels	8	20
	24636	American Flyer Lines Caboose, *60–66*		
____		(A) Red plastic	6	16
____		(B) Yellow-painted	150	628
____		(C) Red-painted		500
____	**24638**	AFL Bay Window Caboose, *62*	27	93
	24720	FY&PRR Coach, *59–61*		
____		(A) Unpainted yellow	23	50
____		(B) Yellow-painted	29	56
	24730	FY&PRR Overland Express Baggage Car, *59–60*		
____		(A) Unpainted yellow	17	35
____		(B) Yellow-painted	29	56
____	**24733**	AFL Pikes Peak Coach, *57*	145	611
____	**24739**	AFL Niagara Falls Combination Car, *57*		NRS
____	**24740**	Baggage Express Combination Car, *60*	28	41
____	**24750**	FY&PRR Combination Car, *60–61*	50	145
____	**24773**	AFL Columbus Combination Car, *57–58, 60–62*	65	152
____	**24776**	AFL Columbus Combination Car, *59*	60	157
____	**24793**	AFL Jefferson Coach, *57–58, 60–62*	70	193
____	**24794**	AFL Jefferson Coach, *59*		1700
____	**24813**	AFL Hamilton Vista Dome Car, *57–58, 60–62*	60	140
____	**24816**	AFL Hamilton Vista Dome Car, *59*	60	160
____	**24833**	AFL Washington Observation Car, *57–58, 60–62*	60	127
____	**24836**	AFL Washington Observation Car, *59*	60	121
____	**24837**	Union Pacific Combination Car, *59–60**	85	245
____	**24838**	Union Pacific Coach, *59–60**	90	347
____	**24839**	Union Pacific Vista Dome Car, *59–60**	95	330

		Good	Exc	
24840	Union Pacific Observation Car, *59–60**	95	311	___
24843	Northern Pacific Combination Car, no lights, *58*	90	255	___
24846	Northern Pacific Coach, no lights, *58*	90	305	___
24849	Northern Pacific Vista Dome Car, no lights, *58*	90	301	___
24853	Northern Pacific Observation Car, no lights, *58*	90	240	___
24856	MP Eagle Hill Combination Car, *58, 63–64**	125	325	___
24859	MP Eagle Lake Coach, *58, 63–64**	130	435	___
24863	MP Eagle Creek Coach, *58, 63–64**	120	443	___
24866	MP Eagle Valley Observation Car, *58, 63–64**	120	385	___
24867	AFL Combination Car, no lights, *58 u, 60 u*	46	177	___
24868	AFL Observation Car, no lights, *58 u, 60 u*	50	213	___
24869	AFL Coach, no lights, *58 u, 60 u*	50	185	___
24963	Car Assortment, *58*		NRS	___
25003	American Flyer Log Car, *57–60*			
	(A) Number and lettering on bin	85	388	___
	(B) No number or lettering on bin	20	55	___
25005	Mail Car, *57*		NRS	___
25016	Southern Pacific Flatcar, *57–60*	44	125	___
25019	Operating Milk Car, *57–60*	65	255	___
25025	CB&Q Dump Car, *58–60*	75	271	___
25031	AFL Caboose, *58*		NRS	___
25042	Erie Operating Boxcar, *58*	70	215	___
25045	Rocket Launcher Flatcar, *57–60*	16	60	___
25046	Rocket Launcher Flatcar, *60*	14	94	___
25049	Rio Grande Boxcar, *58–60*	85	243	___
25052	AFL Bay Window Caboose, *58*	53	162	___
25056	USM Boxcar and Rocket Launcher Flatcar, *59*	125	426	___
25057	TNT Exploding Boxcar, *60*	70	309	___
25058	Southern Pacific Flatcar, *61–64*	48	152	___
25059	Rocket Launcher Flatcar, *60–64*	21	105	___
25060	CB&Q Dump Car, *61–64*	80	414	___
25061	TNT Exploding Boxcar, *61*	100	365	___
25062	Mine Carrier Exploding Boxcar, *62–64*			
	(A) Silver roof and ends	125	703	___
	(B) Tuscan roof and ends	125	539	___
25071	AF Tie-Jector Car, *61–64*	7	25	___
25081	NYC Operating Boxcar, *61–64*	15	30	___
25082	New Haven Operating Boxcar, *61–64*	11	35	___
25515	U.S. Air Force Flatcar, black, *60–63*			
	(A) Unpainted yellow sled	78	299	___
	(B) Yellow-painted sled	200	885	___
26101	Curved Track Panel, *65–66*	3	25	___
26121	Straight Track Panel, *65–66*	4	35	___
26122	Straight Panel with whistle, *65–66*	7	50	___
26141	Switch Panel, right hand, *65–66*	7	54	___
26142	Switch Panel, left hand, *65–66*	7	54	___
26151	Crossover Panel, *65–66*	7	24	___
26261	Curved Snow Panel		88	___
26262	Straight Snow Panel		88	___
26263	Snow Switch, right hand		138	___

			Good	Exc
___	26264	Snow Switch, left hand		138
___	26265	Crossover Snow Panel		94
___	26300	PM Straight Track, *61–64*		1
___	26301	PM Straight Track, *61–64*		1
___	26302	PM Straight Track with uncoupler, *61–64*		2
___	26310	PM Curved Track, *61–64*		1
___	26320	PM Remote Switch, right hand, *61–64*	6	13
___	26321	PM Remote Switch, left hand, *61–64*	7	12
___	26322	PM 90-degree Crossing, *61–64*	1	3
___	26323	PM Manual Switch, right hand, *61–64*	1	5
___	26324	PM Manual Switch, left hand, *61–64*	1	5
___	26340	PM Steel Track Pins, *61–64*		1
___	26341	PM Insulating Pins, *61–64*		1
___	26342	PM Adapter Pins, *61–64*		1
___	26343	PM Track Locks, *61–64*		1
___	26344	PM Track Terminal, *61–64*		1
___	26415	Track Assortment, *60, 62*		NRS
___	26419	Accessory Package	4	15
___	26421	Accessory Package, *60*		375
___	26425	Track Assortment Pack, *60*	6	11
___	26428	Accessory Pack with box, *58 u*		410
___	26520	Knuckle Coupler Kit, *57–64*	1	5
___	26521	Knuckle Coupler Kit, *57–58*		12
___	26601	Fiber Roadbed, *59–62*		1
___	26602	Fiber Roadbed, *59, 61–62*		1
___	26611	4-Level Trestle Display, *59—61*		600
___	26670	Track Trip, *57–58*	4	16
___	26671	Track Trip, *59*	3	11
___	26672	Track Trip, *60*	2	8
___	26673	Track Trip, *61–64*	2	7
___	26690	Track Terminal, with envelope, *57–59*	1	2
___	26691	Steel Pins, *57–60, 64*		1
___	26692	Fiber Pins, *57–60, 64*		1
___	26693	Track Locks, dozen, *57–60, 64*	2	6
___	26700	Straight Track, *57–64*		1
___	26704	Manual Uncoupler		1
___	26708	Horn Control, *57–58*	4	9
___	26710	Straight Track, half section, *57–64*		1
___	26718	Remote Control Switch, left hand, *57*	6	17
___	26719	Remote Control Switch, right hand, *57*	6	17
___	26720	Curved Track, *57–64*		1
___	26722	Curved Track, dozen	6	11
___	26726	Straight Rubber Roadbed, half section, *58*	1	2
___	26727	Rubber Roadbed, half section, *58*	1	2
___	26730	Curved Track, half section, *57–64*		1
___	26739	Whistle Control, *57–58*	13	40
___	26742	Remote Control Switches, pair, *57*	9	50
___	26744	Manual Switches, pair, *57–58*	4	16
___	26745	Railroad Crossing, *57–64*	1	21
___	26746	Rubber Roadbed, *57–64*		2
___	26747	Rubber Roadbed, *57–64*		2
___	26748	Re-railer, *57–64*	3	22

GILBERT PRODUCTION 1946-1966

		Good	Exc
26749	Bumper, *57–60*	2	16 _____
26751	Pike Planning Kit, *57–59*	8	24 _____
26752	Remote Control Uncoupler, *57–58, 60–61*	1	5 _____
26756	Bumper, *61–64*	5	17 _____
26760	Remote Control Switches, pair, *58–64*	11	41 _____
26761	Remote Control Switch, left hand, *58–64*	7	17 _____
26762	Remote Control Switch, right hand, *58–64*	7	17 _____
26770	Manual Switches, pair, *59–64*	4	15 _____
26781	Trestle Set, *57*	10	33 _____
26782	Trestle Set, *58–60*	4	24 _____
26783	Hi-Trestles, *57*	8	32 _____
26790	Trestle Set, *61–64*	13	30 _____
26810	Pow-R-Clips, *60–64*		1 _____
27441	Lamps, 3 bulbs, red	1	4 _____
27443	Lamps, 3 bulbs, green	1	3 _____
27458	Lamps, 3 bulbs, clear	1	4 _____
27460	Lamp Assortment, *59, 64*	10	24 _____

Unnumbered Items

	Good	Exc
Buffalo Hunt Gondola, *63–64*	4	14 _____
Freight Ahead Caboose, *63*	3	7 _____

Mint

			Mint
____	**0700**	Boxcar, NASG, *81 u*	113
____	**2300**	Oil Drum Loader, *83–87*	58
____	**2321**	Operating Sawmill, *84, 86–87*	95
____	**8150/52**	Southern Pacific Alco PA1 Diesel AA Set, *81*	363
____	**8151**	Southern Pacific Alco PA1 Diesel B Unit, *82*	185
____	**8153/55**	Baltimore & Ohio Alco PA1 Diesel AA Set, *81, 83*	275
____	**8154**	Baltimore & Ohio Alco PA1 Diesel B Unit, *81, 83*	100
____	**8251/53**	Erie Alco PA1 Diesel AA Set, *82*	250
____	**8252**	Erie Alco PA1 Diesel B Unit, *82*	102
____	**8350**	Boston & Maine GP7 Diesel, *83*	300
____	**8458**	Southern GP9 Diesel, *84*	208
____	**8459**	Chessie System GP20 Diesel, *84*	271
____	**8551**	Santa Fe GP20 Diesel, *86*	205
____	**8552**	New York Central GP9 Diesel, *86*	188
____	**9000**	B&O Flatcar with trailers, *81, 83*	44
____	**9002**	B&M Flatcar with logs, *83*	85
____	**9004**	Southern Flatcar with trailers, *84*	42
____	**9005**	NYC Flatcar with trailers, *86*	33
____	**9100**	Gulf 1-D Tank Car, *79*	57
____	**9101**	Union 76 1-D Tank Car, *80*	35
____	**9102**	B&O 1-D Tank Car, *81, 83*	27
____	**9104**	B&M 3-D Tank Car, *83*	92
____	**9105**	Southern 3-D Tank Car, *84*	28
____	**9106**	NYC 3-D Tank Car, *86*	26
____	**9200**	Chessie System Hopper with coal, *79*	38
____	**9201**	B&O Covered Hopper, *81, 83*	32
____	**9203**	Boston & Maine Hopper, *83*	78
____	**9204**	Southern Hopper, *84*	24
____	**9205**	Pennsylvania Covered Hopper, *84*	35
____	**9206**	New York Central Covered Hopper, *84*	29
____	**9207**	B&O Covered Hopper, *86*	30
____	**9208**	Santa Fe Covered Hopper, *86*	27
____	**9209**	New York Central Hopper, *86*	29
____	**9300**	Burlington Gondola, *80*	25
____	**9301**	B&O Gondola with canisters, *81, 83*	23
____	**9303**	Southern Gondola with canisters, *84*	27
____	**9304**	NYC Gondola with canisters, *86*	25
____	**9400**	Chessie System Bay Window Caboose, *80*	34
____	**9401**	B&O Bay Window Caboose, *81, 83*	31
____	**9402**	B&M Bay Window Caboose, *83*	68
____	**9403**	Southern Bay Window Caboose, *84*	35
____	**9404**	NYC Bay Window Caboose, *86*	34
____	**9405**	Santa Fe Bay Window Caboose, *86*	38
____	**9500**	Southern Pacific Combination Car, *81*	90
____	**9501**	Southern Pacific Coach, *81*	130
____	**9502**	Southern Pacific Vista Dome Car, *81*	123
____	**9503**	Southern Pacific Observation Car, *81*	90
____	**9504**	Erie Combination Car, *82*	55

		Mint
9505	Erie Coach, *82*	75 ____
9506	Erie Vista Dome Car, *82*	72 ____
9507	Erie Observation Car, *82*	55 ____
9700	Santa Fe Boxcar, *79*	
	(A) Door nibs	108 ____
	(B) No door nibs	64 ____
9701	Rock Island Boxcar, *80*	31 ____
9702	B&O Sentinel Boxcar, *81, 83*	52 ____
9703	Boston & Maine Boxcar, *83*	95 ____
9704	Southern Boxcar, *84*	38 ____
9705	Pennsylvania Boxcar, *84*	46 ____
9706	New York Central Pacemaker Boxcar, *84*	80 ____
9707	Railbox Boxcar, *84*	54 ____
9708	Conrail Boxcar, *84*	43 ____
9709	Baltimore & Ohio Boxcar, *86*	32 ____
9710	Santa Fe Boxcar, *86*	33 ____
9711	Southern Pacific Boxcar, *86*	31 ____
9712	Illinois Central Gulf Boxcar, *86*	34 ____
9713	New York Central Boxcar, *86*	35 ____
22678	B&M Baked Beans Boxcar (NETCA), *10*	45 ____
22997	Oil Drum Loader, *99*	113 ____
24213	Universal Lockon for S Gauge Track, *10*	4 ____
41003	Aluminum Ore Covered Hopper (TCA), *13*	70 ____
41942	Youngstown Steel "Spirit of '76" Baldwin Diesel Switcher, *14*	290 ____
42169	KCS SD70ACe Diesel Locomotive "4042," CC, *12*	480 ____
42173	KCS SD70ACe Diesel Locomotive "4022," gray, *12*	480 ____
42500	UP "Building America" SD70ACe Diesel "8348," CC, *12*	480 ____
42501	UP "Building America" SD70ACe Diesel, nonpowered, *12*	240 ____
42502	UP "Building America" SD70ACe Diesel "8461," CC, *12*	480 ____
42504	KCS SD70ACe Diesel "4042," CC, *12*	480 ____
42505	BNSF SD70ACe Diesel "9344," CC, *12*	480 ____
42506	CSX SD70ACe Diesel "4847," CC, *12*	480 ____
42507	KCS SD70ACe Diesel "4847," gray, *12*	480 ____
42508	SP UP Heritage SD70ACe Diesel "1865," CC, *12*	480 ____
42509	D&RGW UP Heritage SD70ACe Diesel "1870," CC, *12*	480 ____
42510	C&NW UP Heritage SD70ACe Diesel "1859," CC, *12*	480 ____
42511	MP UP Heritage SD70ACe Diesel "1851," CC, *12*	480 ____
42512	Santa Fe U33C Diesel "8525," CC, *12–13*	480 ____
42513	D&H U33C Diesel "761," CC, *12–13*	480 ____
42514	IC U33C Diesel "5057," CC, *12*	480 ____
42515	PC U33C Diesel "6560," CC, *12–13*	480 ____
42516	Milwaukee Road U33C Diesel "5705," CC, *12–13*	480 ____
42519	CNJ NS Heritage SD70ACe Diesel "1071," CC, *12*	480 ____
42520	CNJ NS Heritage SD70ACe Diesel "1834," nonpowered, *12*	240 ____
42521	DL&W NS Heritage SD70ACe Diesel "1074," CC, *12*	480 ____
42522	DL&W NS Heritage SD70ACe Diesel "1856," nonpowered, *12*	240 ____
42523	Erie NS Heritage SD70ACe Diesel "1068," CC, *12*	480 ____
42524	Erie NS Heritage SD70ACe Diesel "1835," nonpowered, *12*	240 ____

___	**42525** Illinois Terminal NS Heritage SD70ACe Diesel "1072," CC, *12*	480
___	**42526** Illinois Terminal NS Heritage SD70ACe Diesel "1899," nonpowered, *12*	240
___	**42527** NYC NS Heritage SD70ACe Diesel "1066," CC, *12*	480
___	**42528** NYC NS Heritage SD70ACe Diesel "1834," nonpowered, *12*	240
___	**42529** PC NS Heritage SD70ACe Diesel "1073," CC, *12*	480
___	**42530** PC NS Heritage SD70ACe Diesel "1971," nonpowered, *12*	240
___	**42531** Reading NS Heritage SD70ACe Diesel "1067," CC, *13*	480
___	**42532** Reading NS Heritage SD70ACe Diesel, nonpowered, *13*	240
___	**42533** Savannah & Atlanta NS Heritage SD70ACe Diesel "1065," CC, *13*	480
___	**42534** Savannah & Atlanta NS Heritage SD70ACe Diesel, nonpowered, *13*	240
___	**42535** Virginian NS Heritage SD70ACe Diesel "1069," CC, *13*	480
___	**42536** Virginian NS Heritage SD70ACe Diesel "1910," nonpowered, *13*	240
___	**42537** Wabash NS Heritage SD70ACe Diesel "1070," CC, *13*	480
___	**42538** Wabash NS Heritage SD70ACe Diesel "1880," nonpowered, *13*	240
___	**42542** Central of Georgia NS Heritage ES44AC Diesel "8101," CC, *13*	530
___	**42543** Central of Georgia NS Heritage ES44AC Diesel "1833," nonpowered, *13*	270
___	**42544** Conrail NS Heritage ES44AC Diesel "8098," CC, *13*	530
___	**42545** Conrail NS Heritage ES44AC Diesel "1976," nonpowered, *13*	270
___	**42546** Interstate NS Heritage ES44AC Diesel "8105," CC, *13*	530
___	**42547** Interstate NS Heritage ES44AC Diesel "1896," nonpowered, *13*	270
___	**42548** LV NS Heritage ES44AC Diesel "8104," CC, *13*	530
___	**42549** LV NS Heritage ES44AC Diesel "1847," nonpowered, *13*	270
___	**42550** Nickel Plate Road NS Heritage ES44AC Diesel "8100" CC, *13*	530
___	**42551** Nickel Plate Road NS Heritage ES44AC Diesel "1881," nonpowered, *13*	270
___	**42552** N&W NS Heritage ES44AC Diesel "8103," CC, *13*	530
___	**42553** N&W NS Heritage ES44AC Diesel "1838," nonpowered, *13*	270
___	**42554** PRR NS Heritage ES44AC Diesel "8102," CC, *13*	530
___	**42555** PRR NS Heritage ES44AC Diesel "1846," nonpowered, *13*	270
___	**42556** Southern NS Heritage ES44AC Diesel "8099," CC, *13*	530
___	**42557** Southern NS Heritage ES44AC Diesel "1894," nonpowered, *13*	270
___	**42558** Norfolk Southern NS Heritage ES44AC Diesel "8114," CC, *13*	530
___	**42559** Norfolk Southern NS Heritage ES44AC Diesel "1982," nonpowered, *13*	270
___	**42560** Monongahela NS Heritage ES44AC Diesel "8025," CC, *13*	530

42561	Monongahela NS Heritage ES44AC Diesel "1901," nonpowered, *13*	270 ____
42563	Bethlehem Steel 0-6-0 Dockside Steam Switcher "71," *13–14*	95 ____
42564	Reading 0-6-0 Dockside Steam Switcher "1242," *13–14*	95 ____
42565	C&O 0-6-0 Dockside Steam Switcher "65," *13*	95 ____
42566	AFL 0-6-0 Dockside Steam Switcher "269," *13–14*	95 ____
42567	Christmas 0-6-0 Dockside Steam Locomotive "2013," *13*	95 ____
42570	D&H Alco PA A-A Diesel Set "18-19," CC, *14*	650 ____
42573	SP Alco PA A-A Diesel Set "94-95," CC, *14*	650 ____
42580	BNSF ES44AC Diesel "6438," CC, *13*	530 ____
42581	BNSF ES44AC Diesel "6423," CC, *14*	530 ____
42582	CP ES44AC Diesel "8744," CC, *14*	530 ____
42583	CP ES44AC Diesel "8730," CC, *14*	530 ____
42584	CSX ES44AC Diesel "924," CC, *14*	530 ____
42585	CSX ES44AC Diesel "937," CC, *14*	530 ____
42586	KCS ES44AC Diesel "4692," CC, *14*	530 ____
42587	KCS ES44AC Diesel "4696," CC, *14*	530 ____
42588	UP ES44AC Diesel "7523," CC, *14*	530 ____
42589	UP ES44AC Diesel "7494," CC, *14*	530 ____
42597	CP Baldwin Diesel Switcher "7070," *14*	290 ____
42598	UP Baldwin Diesel Switcher "1206," *14*	290 ____
48000	Southern Pacific GP9 Diesel "8000," *87*	190 ____
48001	Illinois Central Gulf GP20 Diesel "8001," *87*	195 ____
48002	SP GP9 Diesel Dummy Unit "8002," *88*	135 ____
48003	Santa Fe GP20 Diesel Dummy Unit "8553," *88*	122 ____
48004	Chessie System GP20 Diesel Dummy Unit "8460," *88*	160 ____
48005	Pennsylvania GP9 Diesel "8005," *89*	167 ____
48007	Burlington Northern GP20 Diesel "8007," *90*	304 ____
48008	New Haven EP-5 Electric Locomotive "8008," *91*	200 ____
48009	American Flyer GM GP7 Diesel "8009," *91*	173 ____
48010	MILW EP-5 Electric Locomotive "8010," *92*	218 ____
48013	Conrail GP7 Diesel "5600," *95*	230 ____
48014	Northern Pacific GP9 Diesel "8014," *95*	190 ____
48016	"Merry Christmas" GP20 Diesel "1225," *95*	227 ____
48017	Nickel Plate Road GP9 Diesel Set, *97*	289 ____
48019	SP GP20 Diesel "4060," *98*	175 ____
48020	Milwaukee Road GP9 Diesel "304," *98*	220 ____
48023	Santa Fe Merger GP9 Diesel "2927," *99*	373 ____
48033	Rock Island GP9 Diesel "1272," *02*	250 ____
48034	Seaboard Baldwin Switcher "1413," *03*	198 ____
48035	Santa Fe Baldwin Switcher "2257," *03*	205 ____
48036	NYC 2-8-2 Light Mikado Locomotive "1849," *04*	593 ____
48038	GN EP-5 Electric Locomotive "5011," *04–05*	210 ____
48039	Baltimore & Ohio 0-6-0 Dockside Switcher, *05*	93 ____
48040	Santa Fe 0-6-0 Dockside Switcher, *05*	100 ____
48041	UP Light Mikado Locomotive "2549," RailSounds, *05*	510 ____
48042	Southern Light Mikado Locomotive "4501," RailSounds, *05*	448 ____
48043	NYC Baldwin Switcher "8100," *04*	180 ____

___	48044	Southern Baldwin Switcher, *04*	200
___	48047	UP 4-8-4 Northern Locomotive "800," RailSounds, *06*	395
___	48048	DM&IR SD9 Diesel, *05*	220
___	48049	Southern Pacific SD9 Diesel, *05*	220
___	48051	Burlington SD9 Diesel "373," *06*	202
___	48052	Erie 4-6-2 Pacific Locomotive "2934," TMCC, *06*	555
___	48053	Pennsylvania 2-8-2 Mikado "9628," CC, *06*	473
___	48054	UP 4-8-4 Northern Locomotive "809," *06*	475
___	48055	Bethlehem Steel 0-6-0 Dockside Switcher, *06*	100
___	48056	NYC 0-6-0 Dockside Switcher, *06*	96
___	48058	Chessie System SD9 Diesel, *06*	235
___	48059	North Pole Central Switcher "25," *06*	100
	48060	C&O 2-8-2 Mikado Locomotive "1068," RailSounds, *07–09*	
___			525
	48061	B&O 4-6-2 Pacific Locomotive "5213," RailSounds, *07–09*	
___			475
___	48062	PRR Dockside Switcher, *07–09*	103
___	48063	UP Dockside Switcher, *07–09*	110
	48064	MILW 4-8-4 Northern Locomotive "261," RailSounds, *07–09*	
___			382
___	48065	American Flyer SD9 Diesel "1956," *07*	275
___	48066	UP SD9 Diesel, *07*	275
___	48067	C&NW Baldwin Switcher "1044," *07*	265
___	48070	UP 4-8-8-4 Big Boy Locomotive "4014," CC, *08–09*	682
___	48071	CN GP9 Diesel "4232," *08*	275
___	48072	ACL 4-6-2 Pacific Locomotive "1523," CC, *08*	650
___	48075	NH EP-5 Electric Locomotive "378," *08–09*	234
___	48078	Commemorative Handcar and Shed, *09*	110
___	48081	WP 2-8-2 Mikado Locomotive "319," CC, *10*	700
___	48082	UP Challenger Steam Locomotive "3985," CC, *11*	1000
___	48084	UP Greyhound Challenger Locomotive "3977," CC, *11*	1000
___	48085	Denver & Rio Grande Western 4-6-6-4 Challenger, *10*	1000
___	48087	Commemorative Dockside Switcher "1958," *11–13*	110
___	48088	Christmas GP9 Diesel, *11–12*	300
	48089	Clinchfield Challenger Steam Locomotive "675," CC, *11*	
___			1000
___	48090	NP Challenger Steam Locomotive "5121," CC, *11*	1000
___	48091	WP Challenger Steam Locomotive "402," CC, *11*	1000
___	48092	GN Challenger Steam Locomotive "4000," CC, *11*	1000
___	48094	Spokane Portland & Seattle Steam Locomotive, *11*	1000
___	48096	AF Christmas Handcar with shed, *12*	120
___	48097	Clear 0-6-0 Dockside Steam Switcher "1967," *12*	110
___	48100/01	Wabash Alco PA1 AA Set, *88*	245
___	48102/03	C&O Alco PA1 AA Set, *89*	334
___	48106/07	UP Alco PA1 AA Set, *90*	477
___	48112/13	MP Alco PA1 AA Set, *91*	452
___	48114/15/16	NP Alco PA1 ABA Set, *92*	420
___	48117	NP Alco PA1 Diesel B Unit "8117," RailSounds, *92*	105
___	48118	MP Alco PA1 Diesel B Unit "8118," RailSounds, *92 u*	130
___	48119	UP Alco PA1 Diesel B Unit "8119," RailSounds, *92 u*	165
___	48120/21	WP Alco PA1 Diesel AA Set, *93*	225
___	48122	WP Alco PA1 Diesel B Unit, RailSounds, *93*	123
___	48123	SP Alco PA1 Diesel B Unit "8123," RailSounds, *93*	140

		Mint	
48126/27	Silver Flash Alco Diesel PA1 AB Set, *95*	522	___
48128	Silver Flash Alco PA1 Diesel B Unit "480," *95*	90	___
48129	Silver Flash Alco PA1 Diesel Dummy A Unit "479," *96*	105	___
48130	SF Alco PA1 and PB-1 Diesel Set, *97*	305	___
48135	NYC Alco PA Diesel B Unit "4302," *03*	145	___
48136	Santa Fe Alco PB Diesel B Unit, *04*	145	___
48139	Pennsylvania Alco PB Diesel B Unit, RailSounds, *05*	135	___
48141	WM Baldwin Switcher "132," *06*	230	___
48142	Erie-Lackawanna U33C Diesel "3320," CC, *09*	370	___
48144	PRR Baldwin Switcher "5618," *08*	245	___
48146	SP U33C Diesel "8773," CC, *09*	370	___
48147	ATSF Alco PA Diesel AA Set, *09*	370	___
48155	D&RGW Alco PA Diesel AA Set, *10*	370	___
48158	Burlington Northern U33C Diesel, *10*	440	___
48159	Great Northern U33C Diesel, *10*	440	___
48161	Northern Pacific U33C Diesel, *10*	440	___
48162	Texas Special Alco PA Diesel AA Set, *11, 13–14*	470	___
48165	M&StL Baldwin Diesel Switcher, *12–14*	290	___
48166	UP "Building America" SD70ACe Diesel "8348," *12–14*	480	___
48167	UP "Building America" SD70ACe Diesel, nonpowered, *12–13*	240	___
48169	KCS SD70ACe Diesel "4042," CC, *12–13*	480	___
48168	UP "Building America" SD70ACe Diesel "8461," CC, *12–13*	480	___
48170	NS SD70ACe Diesel "1011," CC, *12–13*	480	___
48171	BNSF SD70ACe Diesel "9344," CC, *12*	480	___
48172	CSX SD70ACe Diesel "4847," CC, *12–13*	480	___
48173	KCS SD70ACe Diesel "4022," gray, CC, *12*	480	___
48174	SP UP Heritage SD70ACe Diesel "1865," CC, *12–14*	480	___
48175	D&RGW UP Heritage SD70ACe Diesel "1870," CC, *12–14*	480	___
48176	C&NW UP Heritage SD70ACe Diesel "1859," CC, *12–13*	480	___
48177	MP UP Heritage SD70ACe Diesel "1851," CC, *12–13*	480	___
48178	AT&SF 2-8-8-2 Steam Locomotive "1795," CC, *12–13*	1000	___
48179	PRR 2-8-8-2 Steam Locomotive "374," CC, *12–13*	1000	___
48180	N&W 2-8-8-2 Steam Locomotive "2009," CC, *12–13*	1000	___
48181	UP 2-8-8-2 Steam Locomotive "3672," CC, *12–13*	1000	___
48182	Virginian 2-8-8-2 Steam Locomotive "741," CC, *12–13*	1000	___
48185	AT&SF U33C Diesel Locomotive "8522," CC, *12*	480	___
48186	AT&SF U33C Diesel Locomotive "8509," CC, *12*	480	___
48187	D&H U33C Diesel Locomotive "755," CC, *12*	480	___
48188	D&H U33C Diesel Locomotive "752," CC, *12*	480	___
48189	IC U33C Diesel Locomotive "5054," CC, *12*	480	___
48190	IC U33C Diesel Locomotive "5052," CC, *12*	480	___
48191	MILW U33C Diesel Locomotive "5702," CC, *12*	480	___
48192	MILW U33C Diesel Locomotive "8002," CC, *12*	480	___
48193	PC U33C Diesel Locomotive "6552," CC, *12*	480	___
48194	PC U33C Diesel Locomotive "6541," CC, *12*	480	___
48195	Christmas U33C Diesel "1225," CC, *12*	480	___

			Mint
_____	48197	Santa Fe 2-8-8-2 Steam Locomotive "1797," CC, _13_	1000
_____	48198	N&W 2-8-8-2 Steam Locomotive "2020," CC, _13_	1000
_____	48200	ATSF Boxcar (TCA), _97_	113
_____	48203	NYC Reefer (TTOS), _97_	60
_____	48204	D&RGW Boxcar (TCA), _97_	70
_____	48205	Pacific Fruit Express Reefer (NASG), _97_	52
_____	48208	New England Hopper (TCA), _98_	55
_____	48209	Cotton Belt Boxcar (TTOS), _98_	105
_____	48210	New England Hopper (TCA), _98_	83
_____	48211	Magnolia Tank Car (NASG), _98_	58
_____	48212	SP Tank Car (TTOS), _99_	70
_____	48213	L&N Boxcar (TCA), _99 u_	129
_____	48214	GN Caboose (NASG), _99 u_	55
_____	48215	Monsanto Hopper, _99 u_	91
_____	48217	SP Gondola (TTOS), _00_	110
_____	48218	SP Crane Car (TTOS), _00_	110
_____	48219	"Ship It on the Frisco" Boxcar (TCA), _01 u_	75
_____	48220	Deep Rock Tank Car (NASG), _00 u_	115
_____	48221	Norfolk Southern 2-bay Hopper (TCA), _01_	105
_____	48222	British Columbia Tank Car (TTOS), _00_	70
_____	48223	Toy Train Museum 1-D Tank Car (TCA), _01 u_	80
_____	48224	Gulf Tank Car (NASG), _01_	80
_____	48225	Salt Lake Route Boxcar (TTOS), _02 u_	102
_____	48226	Toy Train Museum Flatcar with wheel load (TCA), _02 u_	93
_____	48227	D&S Hopper (TTOS), _02 u_	60
_____	48228	Cook Paint Tank Car (NASG), _02 u_	117
_____	48229	D&RGW Tank Car (TTOS), _03_	78
_____	48230	Toy Train Museum Gondola with pipe load (TCA), _03 u_	60
_____	48231	Linde Boxcar (TTOS), _03_	110
_____	48232	NH Flatcar with N.E. Transport trailer (NETCA), _03_	110
_____	48233	UP 1-D Tanker (NASG), _03_	82
_____	48234	Toy Train Museum Boxcar (TCA), _04_	55
_____	48235	Forest Service/Smokey Bear Tank Car (TTOS), _04_	103
_____	48236	BNSF Icicle Reefer (TTOS), _04_	90
_____	48237	Poland Spring Boxcar (NETCA), _04_	110
_____	48238	GE Cable Reel Car (NASG), _04_	125
_____	48239	Gilbert's Milk Tank Car (TTOS), _05_	95
_____	48240	Toy Train Museum Combination Car (TCA), _05_	73
_____	48241	Las Vegas & Tonopah Boxcar (TTOS), _05_	70
_____	48242	Fisk Tire Boxcar (NETCA), _05_	110
_____	48243	GE Twin Searchlight Car (NASG), _05_	90
_____	48244	Ward Kimball Boxcar (TTOS Cal-Stewart), _05_	85
_____	48245	A.C. Gilbert Coach (TTOS), _06_	85
_____	48246	SP Flatcar with trailers (TTOS), _06_	84
_____	48247	Toy Train Museum Idler Caboose (TCA), _06_	68
_____	48248	Indian Motocycle Boxcar (NETCA), _06_	250
_____	48249	Yule Marble Flatcar (TCA), _07_	106
_____	48250	GE Crane Car (NASG), _06_	87
_____	48253	Coors Reefer (TCA), _07_	91
_____	48254	Toy Train Museum Crane Car, _07_	80
_____	48255	PRR 2-bay Hopper with coal load (TTOS), _07_	68
_____	48256	Forest Service/Smokey Bear Boxcar (TTOS), _08_	83

48257	Oilzum Tanker 2-car Set (NETCA), *08*	100 ____
48260	Sacramento Northern Reefer (SVAFC), *07*	112 ____
48261	UP Generator Car (St. Louis S Gaugers), *07*	99 ____
48261X	C&NW Safety and Generator Car (St. Louis S Gaugers), *11*	90 ____
48262	Union Tank Car (TTOS), *07*	87 ____
48263	Cape Cod Potato Chip Boxcar (NETCA), *07*	103 ____
48264	GE Boom Car (NASG), *07*	81 ____
48265	Life Savers Tank Car (TTOS Cal-Stewart), *07*	86 ____
48267	Rutland Boxcar (TCA), *08*	80 ____
48268	Rutland Boxcar (TCA), *08*	80 ____
48269	ATSF Grand Canyon Reefer (TCA), *09*	85 ____
48270	GE Baldwin Diesel Switcher, *08*	345 ____
48271	Hoover Dam Power Co. Flatcar (TCA), *09*	50 ____
48272	Forest Service/Smokey Bear Flatcar with airplane (TTOS), *08*	84 ____
48273	Northwestern Reefer (TTOS), *09*	60 ____
48274	Western Pacific Stock Car (TTOS), *09*	85 ____
48275	Life Savers Wild Cherry Tank Car (TTOS Cal-Stewart), *08*	93 ____
48276	Bay State Beer Reefer (NETCA), *09*	73 ____
48281	GN Boxcar (Southeastern Michigan S Gaugers), *10*	75 ____
48284	Elgin, Joliet & Eastern Gondola with coil covers (NASG), *09*	70 ____
48285	Karo Tank Car (Southern California S Gaugers), *10*	125 ____
48286	Carling Black Label Beer Reefer #1 (TCA), *10*	80 ____
48287	Carling Black Label Beer Reefer #2 (TCA), *10*	80 ____
48288	Life Savers Pep-O-Mint Tank Car (TTOS Cal-Stewart), *09*	60 ____
48290	Life Savers Butter Rum Tank Car (TTOS Cal-Stewart), *10*	75 ____
48291	Jenney 3-D Tank Car (NASG), *10*	85 ____
48292	Sacramento Canning Tank Car (TCA), *11*	90 ____
48293	Charleston & West Carolina Boxcar (TTOS), *11*	95 ____
48294	Dixie Honey 1-D Tank Car (NASG), *11*	80 ____
48295	Flatcar with Howard Johnson trailers (NETCA), *11*	75 ____
48296	Life Savers Wint O Green Tank Car (TTOS Cal-Stewart), *12*	90 ____
48298	Spreckels Sugar Hopper (TCA Rocky Mountain), *12*	65 ____
48300	Southern Pacific Overnight Boxcar, *87*	41 ____
48301	D&RGW Boxcar, *87*	37 ____
48302	Canadian Pacific Boxcar, *87*	42 ____
48303	Chessie System Boxcar, *87*	42 ____
48304	Burlington Northern Boxcar, *87*	44 ____
48305	Wabash Boxcar, *88*	31 ____
48306	Seaboard Coast Line Boxcar, *88*	36 ____
48307	Western Pacific Boxcar, *88*	37 ____
48308	Maine Central Boxcar "8308," *90*	74 ____
48309	Christmas Boxcar "8309," *90 u*	206 ____
48310	MKT Boxcar "8310," *91*	39 ____
48311	Christmas Boxcar "8311," *91 u*	53 ____
48312	Missouri Pacific Boxcar "8312," *92*	45 ____
48313	BAR State of Maine Boxcar "8313," *92*	52 ____

			Mint
____	**48314**	Christmas Boxcar "8314," *92 u*	68
____	**48316**	Bangor & Aroostook Reefer "29425," *93*	37
____	**48317**	Rath Packing Reefer "29426," *93*	36
____	**48318**	A.C. Gilbert Boxcar "8318," *93*	42
____	**48319**	Christmas Boxcar "8319," *93*	45
____	**48320**	NKP Boxcar, *94*	34
____	**48321**	Christmas Boxcar "8321," *94*	37
____	**48322**	New Haven Boxcar, *95*	47
____	**48323**	Christmas Boxcar, *95*	47
____	**48324**	AF 50th Anniversary Boxcar "1946-1996," *96*	53
____	**48325**	Holiday Boxcar, *96*	38
____	**48326**	B&O Boxcar (TCA), *96*	65
____	**48327**	AF Christmas Boxcar "900," *97*	44
____	**48328**	GN Boxcar "900-197," *97*	33
____	**48329**	ATSF Boxcar "900-297," map graphic, *97*	28
____	**48330**	PRR Boxcar "900-397," *97*	30
____	**48332**	MKT Boxcar "937," *98*	43
____	**48333**	Bangor & Aroostook Boxcar "982," *98*	39
____	**48334**	Seaboard Boxcar "942," *98*	25
____	**48335**	Christmas Gondola, *98*	50
____	**48340**	American Flyer Christmas Car, *00*	70
____	**48341**	American Flyer Christmas Car, *99*	93
____	**48342**	American Flyer Christmas Boxcar, *01*	49
____	**48343**	Great Northern Boxcar, *01*	50
____	**48346**	Christmas Boxcar, *02*	55
____	**48347**	C&O Boxcar "2701," *02*	48
____	**48348**	NP Boxcar "31226," *02*	57
____	**48349**	Goofy Boxcar, *03*	34
____	**48351**	Donald Duck Boxcar, *04–05*	28
____	**48352**	Pennsylvania Boxcar "47133," *03*	50
____	**48353**	American Flyer Christmas Boxcar, *03–04*	45
____	**48354**	Southern Pacific Boxcar, *04*	50
____	**48355**	American Flyer Christmas Boxcar, *05*	45
____	**48356**	Pluto Boxcar, *05*	32
____	**48357**	Winnie the Pooh Boxcar, *04–05*	26
____	**48358**	Santa Fe Boxcar "272197," *05*	43
____	**48359**	Holiday Boxcar, *05*	48
____	**48362**	Burlington Boxcar "63114," *06*	55
____	**48363**	Holiday Boxcar, *06*	55
____	**48364**	Gilbert AF 60th Anniversary Boxcar, *06*	62
____	**48365**	Western Maryland Boxcar, *06*	125
____	**48366**	Jersey Central Boxcar "20958," *07*	43
____	**48367**	CP Rail Stock Car "277315," *07*	55
____	**48368**	American Flyer Holiday Boxcar, *07*	48
____	**48370**	UPS Centennial Boxcar "1937," *07*	39
____	**48372**	CN Boxcar "36298," *08*	60
____	**48373**	UP Stock Car "48155D," *08*	60
____	**48374**	American Flyer Holiday Boxcar, *08*	60
____	**48375**	American Flyer Stock Car with reindeer, *08*	52
____	**48376**	American Flyer Holiday Boxcar, *09*	70
____	**48378**	IC Boxcar "400664," *09*	70
____	**48379**	GN Stock Car, *09*	70

		Mint
48380	American Flyer Circus Stock Car "3636," *09–10*	60 ____
48381	1953 Catalog Art Boxcar, *09*	50 ____
48383	U.S. Mail Post Office Boxcar "8383," *09–11*	70 ____
48384	American Flyer Holiday Boxcar, *10*	55 ____
48385	American Flyer 1959 Catalog Art Boxcar, *10*	55 ____
48386	NYC Pacemaker Stock Car "23243," *10*	70 ____
48387	Airco Boxcar "4838," *10*	70 ____
48388	WP Boxcar "1955," *10*	70 ____
48389	Angela Trotta Thomas "Flyer Fantasy" Boxcar, *10*	55 ____
48390	American Flyer 1955 Catalog Art Boxcar, *11*	70 ____
48391	Timken Boxcar, *11*	70 ____
48393	Keystone Camera Boxcar, *11*	70 ____
48394	Holiday Boxcar, *11*	70 ____
48395	NP "Pig Palace" Stock Car, *11–13*	70 ____
48396	Coca-Cola Christmas Boxcar, *11–13*	70 ____
48397	Halloween Boxcar, *11–13*	70 ____
48399	Ringling Bros. Boxcar, *11*	70 ____
48400	SP 3-D Tank Car, *87*	34 ____
48402	Penn Salt 1-D Tank Car "24319," *92*	66 ____
48403	British Columbia 1-D Tank Car "8403," *93*	87 ____
48404	U.S. Army 1-D Tank Car, *94*	44 ____
48405	Shell 1-D Tank Car "8681," *95*	54 ____
48406	Celanese Chemicals Tank Car, *96*	46 ____
48407	Gilbert Chemicals Tank Car, *96*	47 ____
48408	Sunoco 1-D Tank Car "625," *97*	38 ____
48410	Tank Train 1-D Tank Car "44587," *99*	75 ____
48411	Gilbert Chemicals Tank Car "48411," *02*	67 ____
48412	Alaska 3-D Tank Car, *02*	50 ____
48413	Diamond Chemicals Tank Car "19418," *03*	42 ____
48414	Nestle Nesquik 1-D Tank Car "48414," *04*	48 ____
48415	Hooker Chemicals 3-D Tank Car "48515," *04*	47 ____
48416	Campbell's Soup 1-D Tank Car, *04*	46 ____
48417	Pillsbury 1-D Tank Car, *05*	49 ____
48418	Protex 3-D Tank Car "PDAX 1054," *05*	45 ____
48419	Jack Frost 1-D Tank Car "107," *06*	55 ____
48420	Union Pacific 3-D Tank Car, *06*	49 ____
48421	Philadelphia Quartz 1-D Tank Car "806," *07*	55 ____
48422	Simonin's 3-D Tank Car "9565," *07*	43 ____
48424	American Flyer Candy Cane 1-D Tank Car, *08*	60 ____
48425	NYC 3-D Tank Car, *08*	60 ____
48426	American Flyer Commemorative Freight Car 3-pack, *08–09*	165 ____
48428	DM&IR 1-D Tank Car "817," *09*	70 ____
48430	Comet 1-D Tank Car, *09*	70 ____
48431	Sunoco 1-D Tank Car, *09–10*	65 ____
48433	Coca-Cola 1-D Tank Car, *10–11*	70 ____
48434	American Flyer Smoke Fluid 1-D Tank Car, *12–13*	70 ____
48435	Hershey's 1-D Tank Car, *11*	70 ____
48437	Gilbert Chemicals 3-D Tank Car, *11*	70 ____
48438	Cities Service 3-D Tank Car, *12–13*	70 ____
48440	Track Cleaning Fluid 3-D Tank Car, *13–14*	50 ____
48442	AFL Air Service 1-D Tank Car, *13–14*	50 ____

____	**48459** Chessie GP20 Diesel, *07*	258
____	**48470** Jersey Central Boxcar (NASG), *88 u*	165
____	**48471** MKT 1-D Tank Car "120089" (NASG), *89 u*	243
____	**48472** Pennzoil 3-D Tank Car "390" (NASG), *90 u*	160
____	**48473** Central of Georgia Boxcar (TCA), *90 u*	68
____	**48474** C&NW Reefer "70165" (TCA), *91 u*	197
____	**48475** American Flyer Lines Smoking Caboose, *11*	80
____	**48475** Boraxo Covered Hopper "591" (NASG), *91 u*	70
____	**48476** NYC Reefer "491" (NASG), *91 u*	70
____	**48477** Ralston Purina Boxcar "11492" (TCA), *92 u*	92
____	**48478** Burlington Boxcar "792" (NASG), *92 u*	93
____	**48479** NKP Flatcar "20602" with Ertl trailer (NASG), *92 u*	127
____	**48480** Susquehanna Boxcar "993" (NASG), *93 u*	91
____	**48481** REA Reefer "893" (NASG), *93 u*	67
____	**48482** Great Northern Boxcar "3993" (TCA), *93 u*	92
____	**48483** A.C. Gilbert Society "Boys Club" Boxcar, *93 u*	65
____	**48484** A.C. Gilbert Society "Boys at the Gate" Boxcar, *93 u*	80
____	**48485** Northern Pacific Boxcar "1094" (NASG), *94 u*	72
____	**48486** NYNH&H Boxcar "1194" (NASG), *94 u*	51
____	**48487** Yorkrail Boxcar "1994" (TCA), *94 u*	93
____	**48489** Pennsylvania Dutch Boxcar "91653" (TCA), *97 u*	286
____	**48490** Western Pacific Boxcar "101645" (TTOS), *95 u*	70
____	**48491** BN Flatcar "1995" with trailers (TCA), *95 u*	100
____	**48492** Northern Pacific Boxcar "1261" (TCA), *95 u*	74
____	**48493** SP TTUX Flatcar Set with trailers (NASG), *95 u*	75
____	**48494** LV Covered Grain Hopper "1295" (NASG), *95 u*	60
____	**48495** Monsanto 1-D Tank Car, white (St. Louis S Gaugers), *95 u*	148
____	**48496** Monsanto 1-D Tank Car, orange (St. Louis S Gaugers), *95 u*	1018
____	**48497** MKT 3-D Tank Car "117018" (TCA), *95 u*	105
____	**48498** Western Pacific Boxcar "31337" (TTOS), *96 u*	80
____	**48500** SP Gondola with canisters, *87*	25
____	**48501** Southern Pacific Flatcar with trailers, *87*	41
____	**48502** Wabash Flatcar with trailers, *88*	46
____	**48503** Wabash Gondola with canisters, *88*	22
____	**48505** IC Gulf Bulkhead Flatcar "8505," *90*	40
____	**48507/08** U.S. Army Flatcars with 2 tanks, *95*	61
____	**48509** AF Flatcar with 2 farm tractors, *95*	45
____	**48510** Nickel Plate Road Gondola with canisters, *95*	34
____	**48511** TTUX Triple Crown Flatcars with trailers, *96*	70
____	**48513** CSX Flatcar with generator, *96*	28
____	**48514** Intermodal TTUX Set with 2 cars and 2 trailers, *97*	53
____	**48515** New Haven Flatcar, *97*	50
____	**48516** SP Searchlight Car "627," *97*	47
____	**48524** Borden's Flatcar, *01*	50
____	**48525** Burlington Gondola, *01*	39
____	**48526** Reading Gondola "38708" with pipes, *02*	40
____	**48527** Santa Fe Flatcar "90019" with jet rocket, *02*	46
____	**48528** Conrail Flatcar with wheel loader, *02*	53
____	**48529** NYC Flatcar with wheel load, *02*	48
____	**48531** Chessie Depressed Center Flatcar with cable reel, *03*	59
____	**48532** SP Flatcar "513183" with trailers, *03*	48

		Mint	
48533	PFE Flatcar with trailers, *04–05*	42	___
48534	NYC Depressed Center Flatcar with cable reel, *04*	55	___
48535	GN Bulkhead Flatcar "48535," *04–05*	46	___
48536	Southern Flatcar with wheel load, *04*	65	___
48537	Nestle Nesquik Flatcar with milk containers, *04–05*	48	___
48538	Hood's Flatcar with milk containers, *04–05*	46	___
48539	REA Flatcar "TLCX2" with trailers, *05*	48	___
48540	B&O Flatcar "8652" with girder, *05*	49	___
48541	D&H Gondola "13903" with pipe load, *05*	45	___
48542	UPS Flatcar with trailer, *05*	45	___
48543	Supplee Flatcar with milk containers, *06*	55	___
48544	WM Flatcar "2632" with girder, *06*	55	___
48545	DM&IR Gondola "4290" with pipe load, *06*	55	___
48546	Alaska Depressed Center Flatcar with cable reel, *06*	59	___
48547	Chessie System Gondola, *06*	100	___
48548	PRR Flatcar "480078" with trailers, *07*	35	___
48549	UP Gondola with canisters, *07*	41	___
48550	GN Depressed Center Service Car, *07*	44	___
48553	AF Christmas Gondola with candy canes, *07*	55	___
48554	Bethlehem Steel Gondola with coil covers, *08*	50	___
48555	Reading Flatcar "9314" with wheel load, *08*	60	___
48559	Christmas Gondola with presents, *09*	36	___
48560	BNSF Flatcar with jet engine, *09–11*	53	___
48561	CNJ Flatcar with boat, *10*	70	___
48563	Reindeer Express Agency Flatcar with trailers, *10*	70	___
48565	Commemorative Flatcar with piggyback trailers, *11*	70	___
48566	Gondola with Christmas trees, *11*	70	___
48568	Ringling Bros. Flatcar with piggyback trailers, *11*	70	___
48569	Buttermilk Bay Creamery Flatcar with milk containers, *11*	70	___
48570	PRR Gondola with coil covers, *12–13*	70	___
48571	Flatcar with Santa's sleigh, *12–13*	70	___
48572	Naughty or Nice Gondola, coil covers, *13*	70	___
48576	AFL Gilbert Dairy Flatcar with milk containers, *13–14*	50	___
48577	Flatcar with Santa's sleigh, *13*	70	___
48579	AFL Depressed Center Flatcar with cable reel, *14*	50	___
48580	U.S. Navy Flatcar with Jeeps, *14*	70	___
48600	Southern Pacific Hopper, *87*	31	___
48601	Union Pacific Covered Hopper, *87*	30	___
48602	Erie Covered Hopper, *87*	29	___
48603	Wabash Hopper with coal load, *88*	26	___
48604	Milwaukee Road Covered Hopper, *88*	31	___
48605	Burlington Northern Covered Hopper, *88*	36	___
48609	D&H Covered Hopper "8609," *93*	37	___
48610	NKP Covered Hopper, *94*	31	___
48611	Cargill Covered Grain Hopper, *95*	37	___
48612	ADM 3-bay Covered Hopper, *97*	42	___
48613	B&LE Hopper 4-pack, *98*	218	___
48614	B&LE Hopper, *98*	77	___
48619	Union Pacific Hopper, *01*	42	___
48620	B&O Hopper "435350," *02*	50	___
48621	CN Covered Hopper, *02*	41	___

____	**48622**	Burlington Hopper "170616," *03*	32
____	**48623**	"Naughty & Nice" Hopper 2-pack, *04–05*	88
____	**48627**	Southern Hopper with ballast load, *04*	55
____	**48628**	DM&IR Hopper, *05*	51
____	**48629**	CP Hopper, *06*	55
____	**48630**	Milwaukee Road 3-bay Hopper, *07*	38
____	**48631**	NYC 2-bay Hopper, *07*	30
____	**48632**	Santa's Candy Shop 2-bay Hopper, *09–10*	70
____	**48633**	UP 2-bay Hopper "82173," *09–10*	60
____	**48635**	Hershey's Special Dark 2-Bay Hopper, *12*	70
____	**48636**	WP 3-Bay Hopper, *12*	70
____	**48637**	Santa Fe Midnight Chief 2-Bay Hopper, *13–14*	50
____	**48638**	North Pole Express Hopper, *12–14*	70
____	**48639**	CN Scale Cylindrical Hopper "370708," *12*	80
____	**48640**	BN Scale Cylindrical Hopper "458856," *12*	80
____	**48641**	MP UP Heritage Scale Cylindrical Hopper "27421," *12*	80
____	**48642**	Saskatchewan Scale Cylindrical Hopper "397015," *12*	80
____	**48643**	SP Scale Cylindrical Hopper "491020," *12*	80
____	**48644**	D&RGW UP Heritage Scale Cylindrical Hopper, *12*	80
____	**48645**	C&NW UP Heritage Scale Cylindrical Hopper, *12*	80
____	**48646**	UP "Building America" Scale Cylindrical Hopper, *12*	80
____	**48647**	AFL Artificial Coal 3-Bay Hopper, *13–14*	50
____	**48648**	Alberta Cylindrical Hopper "396161," *12*	80
____	**48649**	PRR Cylindrical Hopper "260411," *12*	80
____	**48650**	Govt. of Canada Cylindrical Hopper "607002," *12*	80
____	**48651**	NS Cylindrical Hopper "81022," *12*	80
____	**48652**	CNJ NS Heritage Cylindrical Hopper "68110," *12*	80
____	**48653**	DL&W NS Heritage Cylindrical Hopper "11254," *12*	80
____	**48654**	Erie NS Heritage Cylindrical Hopper "91068," *12*	80
____	**48655**	Illinois Terminal NS Heritage Cylindrical Hopper "107296," *12*	80
____	**48656**	NYC NS Heritage Cylindrical Hopper "18292," *12*	80
____	**48657**	PC NS Heritage Cylindrical Hopper "32428," *12*	80
____	**48658**	Reading NS Heritage Cylindrical Hopper, *13*	80
____	**48659**	Savannah & Atlanta NS Heritage Cylindrical Hopper "19065," *13*	80
____	**48660**	Virginian NS Heritage Cylindrical Hopper, *13*	80
____	**48661**	Wabash NS Heritage Cylindrical Hopper, *13*	80
____	**48662**	AFL Scenery Gravel 3-Bay Hopper, *13–14*	80
____	**48664**	Christmas Cylindrical Hopper, *13*	80
____	**48665**	Central of Georgia NS Heritage Cylindrical Hopper, *13*	80
____	**48666**	Conrail NS Heritage Cylindrical Hopper, *13*	80
____	**48667**	Interstate NS Heritage Cylindrical Hopper "13488," *13*	80
____	**48668**	LV NS Heritage Cylindrical Hopper, *13*	80
____	**48669**	Nickel Plate Road NS Heritage Cylindrical Hopper, *13*	80
____	**48670**	N&W NS Heritage Cylindrical Hopper, *13*	80
____	**48671**	PRR NS Heritage Cylindrical Hopper, *13*	80
____	**48672**	Southern NS Heritage Cylindrical Hopper, *13*	80
____	**48673**	Norfolk Southern NS Heritage Cylindrical Hopper, *13*	80
____	**48674**	Monongahela NS Heritage Cylindrical Hopper, *13*	80
____	**48700**	SP Bay Window Caboose, *87*	35
____	**48701**	Illinois Central Gulf Bay Window Caboose, *87*	40
____	**48702**	Wabash Square Window Caboose, *88*	42

Mint

		Mint	
48703	Union Pacific Square Window Caboose, *88*	36	____
48705	Pennsylvania Square Window Caboose, *89*	47	____
48706	BN Square Window Caboose "8706," *90*	46	____
48707	NH Square Window Caboose "8707," *91*	41	____
48710	Conrail Bay Window Caboose "21503," *95*	46	____
48711	Northern Pacific Bay Window Caboose "8711," *95*	43	____
48712	"Happy New Year" Bay Window Caboose "0101," *95*	48	____
48713	Nickel Plate Road Caboose, *97*	44	____
48714	SP Square Window Caboose "990," *97*	45	____
48715	Milwaukee Road Caboose, *97*	53	____
48718	C&NW Caboose, *98*	48	____
48721	Santa Fe Caboose "999628," *99*	70	____
48722	Rock Island Bay Window Caboose "17778," *02*	55	____
48723	Santa Fe Boom Car "206982," *03*	39	____
48724	Seaboard Square Window Caboose "49658," *03*	54	____
48725	NYC Caboose "17560," *03–04*	48	____
48726	NYC Boom Car "48726," *04–05*	42	____
48727	UP Bay Window Caboose "24554," *05*	71	____
48728	Southern Bay Window Caboose "X545," *05*	48	____
48729	Southern Boom Car, *04*	50	____
48730	DM&IR Extended Vision Caboose "C-227," *05*	55	____
48731	SP Bay Window Caboose "1338," *05*	55	____
48732	UP Boom Car, *05*	59	____
48733	Erie Caboose "C107," *06*	53	____
48734	PRR Caboose "477810," *08*	60	____
48735	Burlington Extended Vision Caboose "13853," *06*	55	____
48736	WM Caboose "1864," *06*	48	____
48738	Chessie System Caboose, *06*	45	____
48739	American Flyer Christmas Caboose, *06*	55	____
48740	M.O.W. Boom Car "916," *07*	55	____
48741	C&NW Extended Vision Caboose "13653," *07*	55	____
48742	American Flyer Caboose, *07*	55	____
48743	C&O Caboose "90877," *07*	55	____
48746	ACL Caboose "0400," *08*	60	____
48747	CN Extended Vision Caboose "79644," *08*	52	____
48750	Erie-Lack. Extended Vision Caboose, *09*	60	____
48751	Cotton Belt Bay Window Caboose, *09*	70	____
48752	BN Extended View Caboose, *11*	70	____
48754	WP Bay Window Caboose, *10–11*	70	____
48755	NP Extended View Caboose, *11*	70	____
48756	Conrail Extended View Caboose, *11*	70	____
48757	GN Extended View Caboose, *11*	70	____
48759	Clear Smoking Caboose "997," *12*	80	____
48800	Wabash Reefer, *88*	36	____
48801	Union Pacific Reefer, *88*	29	____
48802	Pennsylvania Reefer, *88*	37	____
48805	National Dairy Despatch Insulated Boxcar "8805," *90*	43	____
48806	REA Reefer "8806," *94*	32	____
48807	NKP Reefer "8807," *94*	32	____
48808	PFE Reefer "30000," *03*	49	____
48809	NP Reefer "139," *04*	36	____
48814	Fruit Growers Express Reefer "40703," *06*	52	____

____	**48815**	Needham Reefer "60500," *07–08*	55
____	**48823**	Hershey's Reefer, *10*	70
____	**48824**	Pacific Fruit Express Reefer "47760," *11*	70
____	**48825**	Holiday Boxcar, *12–13*	70
____	**48826**	American Flyer 1956 Catalog Art Boxcar, *12*	70
____	**48827**	M&StL Boxcar, *12–13*	70
____	**48828**	Mr. Goodbar Reefer, *12–14*	70
____	**48829**	Pabst Beer Reefer, *12*	70
____	**48830**	Schlitz Beer Reefer, *12*	70
____	**48831**	Angela Trotta Thomas "Circus Comes to Town" Boxcar, *12–13*	70
____	**48832**	American Flyer 1951 Catalog Art Boxcar, *13–14*	50
____	**48833**	Christmas Boxcar, *13*	50
____	**48835**	Boy Scouts of America Cub Scout Boxcar, *13–14*	55
____	**48836**	Boy Scouts of America Eagle Scout Boxcar, *13–14*	55
____	**48838**	Penguin Seafood Reefer, *13–14*	50
____	**48839**	Smoke Cartridge Transport Boxcar, *13–14*	50
____	**48844**	Christmas Mint Car, *13*	60
____	**48845**	Fort Knox Mint Car, *13*	60
____	**48846**	Gilbert Mines Mint Car, *13*	60
____	**48847**	New York Federal Reserve Mint Car, *13–14*	60
____	**48848**	San Francisco Federal Reserve Mint Car, *13–14*	60
____	**48851**	AFL Stockcar, *14*	50
____	**48852**	AT&SF Grand Canyon Line Boxcar, *14*	50
____	**48854**	Boston Federal Reserve Mint Car, *14*	60
____	**48856**	NH Waffle-sided Boxcar, *14*	50
____	**48857**	C&NW Waffle-sided Boxcar, *14*	50
____	**48858**	BNSF 57' Mechanical Reefer "798879," *14*	80
____	**48859**	UP 57' Mechanical Reefer "455995," *14*	80
____	**48860**	PFE 57' Mechanical Reefer "458455," *14*	80
____	**48861**	GN 57' Mechanical Reefer "8870," *14*	80
____	**48862**	Govt. of Canada Cylindrical Hopper "106010," *14*	80
____	**48863**	CN Cylindrical Hopper "369290," *14*	80
____	**48864**	Santa Fe Cylindrical Hopper "300022," *14*	80
____	**48865**	Frisco Cylindrical Hopper "81028," *14*	80
____	**48866**	GN Cylindrical Hopper "71600," *14*	80
____	**48868**	NP 57' Mechanical Reefer "794," *14*	80
____	**48870**	GN Boxcar, Steam RailSounds, *14*	170
____	**48871**	Erie Boxcar, Steam RailSounds, *14*	170
____	**48900**	C&O Combination Car, *89*	49
____	**48901**	C&O Coach, *89*	63
____	**48902**	C&O Vista Dome Car, *89*	58
____	**48903**	C&O Observation Car, *89*	49
____	**48904**	UP Combination Car "8904," *90*	54
____	**48905**	UP Coach "8905," *90*	90
____	**48906**	UP Vista Dome Car "8906," *90*	73
____	**48907**	UP Observation Car "8907," *90*	47
____	**48908**	UP Coach "8908," *90 u*	113
____	**48909**	UP Vista Dome Car "8909," *90 u*	111
____	**48910**	Missouri Pacific Combination Car "8910," *91*	50
____	**48911**	Missouri Pacific Vista Dome Car "8911," *91*	78
____	**48912**	Missouri Pacific Coach "8912," *91*	78

Mint

48913	Missouri Pacific Observation Car "8913," *91*	69	____
48914	Missouri Pacific Coach "8914," *91*	94	____
48915	Missouri Pacific Vista Dome Car "8915," *91*	75	____
48920	Northern Pacific Combination Car "8920," *92*	55	____
48921	Northern Pacific Coach "8921," *92*	67	____
48922	Northern Pacific Vista Dome Car "8922," *92*	67	____
48923	Northern Pacific Observation Car "8923," *92*	50	____
48924	Northern Pacific Vista Dome Car "8924," *92*	67	____
48925	Northern Pacific Coach "8925," *92*	72	____
48926	WP California Zephyr Combination Car "801," *93*	37	____
48927	WP California Zephyr Vista Dome Car "814," *93*	40	____
48928	WP California Zephyr Vista Dome Car "815," *93*	40	____
48929	WP California Zephyr Vista Dome Car "813," *93*	54	____
48930	WP California Zephyr Vista Dome Car "811," *93*	60	____
48931	WP California Zephyr Observation Car "882," *93*	37	____
48932	WP California Zephyr Dining Car "842," *93*	43	____
48933	Missouri Pacific Dining Car "8933," *94*	90	____
48934	Northern Pacific Dining Car "8934," *94*	90	____
48935	New Haven Combination Car, *95*	57	____
48936	New Haven Vista Dome Car, *95*	55	____
48937	New Haven Observation Car, *95*	57	____
48938	Silver Flash Combination Car "960," *95*	75	____
48939	Silver Flash Coach "961," *95*	67	____
48940	Silver Flash Observation Car "963," *95*	79	____
48941	Union Pacific Vista Dome Dining Car "8941," *95*	93	____
48942	Vista Dome Car "962," *96*	140	____
48943	New Haven Vista Dome Dining Car, *96*	65	____
48944	ATSF Super Chief Passenger Car 4-pack, *97*	260	____
48961	NYC Streamliner Passenger Car 2-pack, *02*	160	____
48964	NYC Baggage Car "9149," *03*	50	____
48965	B&O Passenger Car 2-pack, *03*	157	____
48968	Santa Fe Passenger Car 2-pack, *04–05*	85	____
48975	Pennsylvania Passenger Car 2-pack, *05*	130	____
48976	Pennsylvania Baggage Car, *05*	75	____
48977	Pennsylvania Dining Car, *05*	75	____
48978	UP Heavyweight Passenger Car 4-pack, *06*	334	____
48983	UP Heavyweight Passenger Car 2-pack, *06*	148	____
48990	NYC Heavyweight Passenger Car 4-pack, *07*	265	____
48991	NYC Heavyweight Passenger Car 2-pack, *07*	140	____
48992	PRR Heavyweight Passenger Car 4-pack, *07*	265	____
48993	Pennsylvania Heavyweight Passenger Car 2-Pack, *07*	140	____
48994	Blue Comet Heavyweight Passenger Car 2-pack, *07*	140	____
49001	NYC Searchlight Car "9001," *90*	48	____
49002	B&M Flatcar with logs, *83*	83	____
49003	Union Pacific Searchlight Car "9003," *91*	45	____
49006	MILW Animated Square Window Caboose, *92*	47	____
49009	AFL Flatcar with derrick, *96*	32	____
49010	"Stable of Champions" Horse Car, *96*	32	____
49011	UP Moe & Joe Animated Flatcar "15100," *03*	65	____
49012	Santa Fe Crane Car "199707," *03*	68	____
49013	PRR Depressed Center Searchlight Car, *04–05*	80	____
49014	NYC Crane Car "X-15," *04–05*	63	____

			Mint
____	**49015**	Westside Lumber Moe & Joe Animated Flatcar, *04–05*	63
____	**49016**	Santa Fe Walking Brakeman Boxcar, *04–05*	65
____	**49017**	GN Animated Caboose "X84," *04–05*	62
____	**49019**	Southern Crane Car, *04*	65
____	**49021**	UP Crane Car "JPX-251," *05*	70
____	**49022**	M.O.W. Searchlight Car, *05*	69
____	**49023**	NYC Walking Brakeman Car "174226," *05*	68
____	**49024**	Pennsylvania Coal Dump Car "494979," *05*	73
____	**49025**	American Flyer Dump Car with presents, *05*	75
____	**49026**	American Flyer Operating Tie Car, *06*	58
____	**49027**	Pennsylvania Log Dump Car, *06*	80
____	**49028**	American Flyer Candy Cane Dump Car, *06*	78
____	**49029**	Santa Fe Animated Caboose, *06*	70
____	**49031**	GN Walking Brakeman Car, *06*	60
____	**49032**	Bethlehem Steel Depressed Center Searchlight Car, *06*	65
____	**49033**	NYC Coal Dump Car, *06*	74
____	**49035**	Southern Operating Coal Dump Car, *06*	65
____	**49037**	M.O.W. Crane Car "900," *07*	85
____	**49038**	D&RGW Walking Brakeman Car "69676," *07*	85
____	**49039**	Santa Fe Log Dump Car, *07–08*	85
____	**49040**	Chessie System Animated Caboose "3507," *07*	85
____	**49041**	C&O Tie Car, *07*	50
____	**49042**	Erie Coal Dump Car "05473," *07*	85
____	**49045**	American Flyer 915 Unloading Car, *08*	63
____	**49046**	American Flyer Santa Animated Caboose, *08*	73
____	**49047**	CP Rail Coal Dump Car "5522," *09*	90
____	**49048**	NYC Operating Boxcar "75509," *09*	68
____	**49049**	AF Commemorative Unloading Car, *10*	85
____	**49050**	Ringling Bros. Flatcar with Moe and Joe clowns, *11*	80
____	**49054**	GN Operating Log Dump Car, *10*	80
____	**49055**	Wabash Coal Dump Car, *10*	90
____	**49056**	NP Coal Dump Car, *11*	90
____	**49057**	WP Log Dump Car, *11*	85
____	**49060**	Ringling Bros. Searchlight Car, *11*	80
____	**49061**	Christmas Music Reefer, *12–13*	80
____	**49062**	Route of the Reindeer Animated Caboose, *12–13*	85
____	**49063**	Zombie Walking Brakeman Car, *13*	80
____	**49064**	NH Boxcar, Diesel RailSounds, *13–14*	170
____	**49066**	UP Boxcar, Diesel RailSounds, *13–14*	170
____	**49078**	Polar Express Elf Handcar, *14*	100
____	**49081**	70-Ton Truck with rotating bearing caps, pair, *14*	25
____	**49082**	C&O Coal Dump Car, *14*	80
____	**49083**	Santa Fe Depressed Center Searchlight Car, *14*	80
____	**49084**	PRR Gas Unloading Car, *14*	80
____	**49085**	FasTrack Activator Rail, *14*	20
____	**49600**	Union Pacific Pony Express Set, *90*	589
____	**49601**	Missouri Pacific Eagle Set, *91*	636
____	**49602**	Northern Pacific North Coast Limited Set, *92*	699
____	**49604**	Western Pacific California Zephyr Set, *93*	448
____	**49605**	New Haven Passenger Car Set, *95*	193
____	**49606**	Silver Flash Passenger Car Set, *95*	658
____	**49608**	Domino Sugar Covered Hopper, *92*	64

LIONEL PRODUCTION 1979-2015

Mint

49611	NYC Alco PA Diesel Passenger Set, *02*	610	
49612	B&O Passenger Car 4-pack, *03*	770	
49613	Southern Baldwin Switcher Work Train Set, *04*	413	
49614	Pennsylvania Alco PA Diesel Passenger Set, *05*	575	
49615	Chessie System SD9 Diesel Freight Set, *06*	424	
49616	Alton Limited Passenger Set, CC, *06*	740	
49617	Blue Comet Steam Passenger Set, *07*	763	
49618	NYC Dockside Switcher Freight Set, *07*	275	
49621	American Flyer Christmas Steam Train, *09*	350	
49622	Freedom Train Passenger Set, *08*	548	
49624	American Flyer 959 Defender Freight Set, *10*	600	
49625	Bakelite Plastics Freight Car 2-pack, *10*	135	
49626	Ringling Bros. GP9 Diesel Circus Train Set, *11*	550	
49627	Southern Crescent Limited Passenger Train Set, *11*	900	
49632	Polar Express Berkshire Steam Passenger Set, *14*	400	
49634	SP Dockside Switcher Steam Freight Set, *13–14*	270	
49805	American Flyer 23780 Gabe the Lamplighter, *01*	102	
49806	American Flyer 23796 Sawmill, *01*	75	
49807	American Flyer 752 Seaboard Coaler, *01*	139	
49808	American Flyer 594 Animated Track Gang Set, *06*	96	
49809	American Flyer 772 Water Tower, *02*	53	
49810	American Flyer 787 Log Loader, *04–05*	110	
49811	American Flyer 773 Oil Derrick, *04–05*	53	
49812	American Flyer 755 Talking Station, *04–05*	88	
49813	American Flyer 789 Baggage Smasher, *04–05*	74	
49814	American Flyer 774 Floodlight Tower, *04–05*	58	
49815	American Flyer 741 Handcar and Shed, *04–05*	98	
49818	American Flyer 23830 Piggyback Unloader and Flatcar, *04–05*	62	
49819	American Flyer 583A Electromagnetic Crane, *04–05*	148	
49820	American Flyer 758 Sam the Semaphore Man, *07–09*	95	
49824	American Flyer 770 Loading Platform and Car, *05*	125	
49825	American Flyer 571 Truss Bridge, *07–09*	27	
49827	54" Curved Track, *07–11*	3	
49828	10" Straight Track, *07–11*	3	
49829	36" Straight Track, *07–11*	9	
49830	Fiber Insulator Pins, *07–14*	2	
49831	Steel Pins, *07–14*	2	
49832	American Flyer 582 Blinking Signal, *07–08*	55	
49833	American Flyer 587 Block Signal, *07–08*	55	
49835	American Flyer 588 Semaphore Block Signal, *07–09*	55	
49838	American Flyer 792 Railroad Terminal, *08*	79	
49839	American Flyer 793 Union Station, *08–10*	53	
49843	Suburban Station, *09–10*	70	
49844	Christmas Animated Billboard, *10–13*	45	
49845	Truss Bridge, *10–14*	27	
49846	American Flyer 773 Sunoco Oil Derrick, *10*	76	
49847	American Flyer 774 Floodlight Tower, *10–12*	103	
49848	American Flyer Lines Girder Bridge, *10*	21	
49849	Lackawanna Girder Bridge, *10*	18	
49850	D&RGW Girder Bridge, *10–11*	21	
49851	Gilbert Oil Storage Tank, *11*	80	

___	**49852**	FasTrack 10" Straight Track, *12–14*	5
	49853	FasTrack R20 Curved Track, *12–14*	
___	**49854**	FasTrack 10" Terminal Track, *12–14*	8
___	**49856**	FasTrack R20 Switch, right hand, *12–14*	100
___	**49857**	FasTrack R20 Switch, left hand, *12–14*	100
___	**49858**	FasTrack Transition Track, *12–14*	10
___	**49859**	FasTrack R27 Wide-Radius Curved Track, *13–14*	9
___	**49855**	Illuminated Station Platform, *10*	35
___	**49860**	Sunoco Oil Storage Tank with light, *12*	80
___	**49861**	Classic Billboard Set, *12*	13
___	**49862**	FasTrack 30" Straight Track, *13–14*	16
___	**49863**	FasTrack 45-Degree Crossover, *13–14*	26
___	**49864**	FasTrack 90-Degree Crossover, *13–14*	26
___	**49865**	FasTrack Grade Crossing with Gates & Flashers, *13–14*	160
___	**49866**	FasTrack Straight Track with Illuminated Bumper, *13–14*	33
___	**49867**	FasTrack 5" Half Straight Track, *13–14*	6
___	**49868**	FasTrack R20 Manual Switch, left hand, *13–14*	50
___	**49869**	FasTrack R20 Manual Switch, right hand, *13–14*	50
___	**49870**	FasTrack R20 Manual Switch, left hand, CC, *13–14*	120
___	**49871**	FasTrack R20 Manual Switch, right hand, CC, *13–14*	120
___	**49872**	Telephone Poles, *13–14*	40
___	**49875**	American Flyer Replacement Wheel and Axle Packs, *13*	20
___	**49876**	Water Tower with shed, *13–14*	90
___	**49877**	Elevated Gilbert Oil Tank, *13–14*	90
___	**49878**	FasTrack R20 Half Curve, *13–14*	6
___	**49882**	Polar Express Girder Bridge, *14*	22
___	**49889**	FasTrack Figure-8 Add-On Track Pack, *14*	85
___	**49890**	FasTrack Inner Passing Loop Add-On Track Pack, *14*	127
___	**49891**	FasTrack 10" Grade Crossing, *14*	20
___	**49892**	FasTrack R27 Half Curve, *14*	8
___	**49893**	FasTrack Earthen Bumper, 2 pieces, *14*	13
___	**49895**	FasTrack Uncoupling Section, *14*	43
___	**49922**	Freedom Train Heavyweight Passenger Car 2-pack, *08*	150
___	**49923**	Alton Limited Heavyweight Passenger Car 2-pack, *08*	150
___	**49927**	UP Streamlined Baggage Car "8944," *09*	75
___	**49928**	MP Streamlined Baggage Car "8933," *09*	75
___	**49929**	American Freedom Display Car "3510," *09*	73
___	**49930**	ATSF Streamliner Passenger Car 3-pack, *09*	200
___	**49934**	C&O Streamliner Baggage Car "48190," *10*	80
___	**49935**	NP Streamliner Baggage Car "8929," *10*	80
___	**49936**	D&RGW Streamliner Passenger Car 3-pack, *10*	250
___	**49940**	ATSF Streamliner Full Vista Dome Car, *10*	80
___	**49941**	UP Streamliner Full Vista Dome Car, *10*	76
___	**49942**	NYC Streamliner Full Vista Dome Car, *10*	80
___	**49943**	D&RGW Streamliner Full Vista Dome Car, *11–14*	80
___	**49944**	Erie Streamliner Baggage Car, *11–14*	80
___	**49945**	D&RGW Streamliner Baggage Car "754," *10*	80
___	**49946**	SP Daylight Streamliner Baggage Car, *11–13*	80
___	**49947**	SP Daylight Streamliner Full Vista Dome Car, *11–13*	80
___	**49948**	Erie Streamliner Full Vista Dome Car, *11–14*	80

49949	Texas Special Streamliner Passenger Car 3-Pack, *11–13*	250 ___
49950	Texas Special Streamlined Combination Car, *12–13*	80 ___
49951	Texas Special Streamlined Vista Dome Car, *12–13*	80 ___
49952	Texas Special Streamlined Observation Car, *12–13*	80 ___
49956	Texas Special Streamlined Full Vista Dome Car, *12–14*	80 ___
49957	Texas Special Streamlined Baggage Car, *12–14*	80 ___
49958	AT&SF Streamlined Full Vista Dome Car, *12–14*	80 ___
49959	PRR Streamlined Vista Dome Car, *12–14*	80 ___
49960	North Pole Express Streamliner 3-Pack, *12–13*	250 ___
49972	Polar Express Abandoned Toy Car, *14*	70 ___
49973	Polar Express Baggage Car, *14*	70 ___
49977	American Flyer Work Crew People Pack, *14*	27 ___
49979	Winter Station, *14*	80 ___
49990	FasTrack Outer Passing Loop Add-On Track Pack, *14*	155 ___
49991	FasTrack Siding Track Add-On Track Pack, *14*	100 ___
52009	WP Stock Car (SVAFC), *09*	120 ___
52094	Ann Arbor Covered Grain Hopper "1496" (NASG), *96 u*	55 ___
52095	Mobil 1-D Tank Car "1596" (NASG), *96 u*	85 ___

		Retail
____ **100**	40' Boxcar	40
____ **102**	B&O 40' Boxcar	40
____ **103**	Cotton Belt 40' Boxcar	40
____ **105**	D&RGW 40' Boxcar	40
____ **108**	GN 40' Boxcar	43
____ **112**	Soo Line 40' Boxcar	40
____ **113**	NYC 40' Boxcar	40
____ **114**	PRR 40' Boxcar	40
____ **115**	ATSF 40' Boxcar	40
____ **116**	Seaboard 40' Boxcar	40
____ **116C**	Seaboard "Silver Comet" 40' Boxcar	40
____ **116L**	Seaboard "Robert E. Lee" 40' Boxcar	40
____ **117**	SP 40' Boxcar	40
____ **118**	UP 40' Boxcar	40
____ **119**	C&O 40' Boxcar	40
____ **119B**	C&O 40' Boxcar	40
____ **121**	NYC Pacemaker 40' Boxcar	43
____ **122**	Rutland 40' Boxcar	43
____ **123**	PRR Merchandise Service 40' Boxcar	46
____ **125**	P&LE 40' Boxcar	41
____ **126**	NP 40' Boxcar	41
____ **128**	NH 40' Boxcar	40
____ **129**	GN 40' Boxcar	40
____ **130**	GM&O 40' Boxcar	40
____ **131**	N&W 40' Boxcar	40
____ **132**	CP 40' Boxcar	40
____ **133**	M&StL 40' Boxcar	40
____ **134**	Erie-Lackawanna 40' Boxcar	40
____ **135**	SP 40' Boxcar	41
____ **136**	Susquehanna 40' Boxcar	46
____ **137**	C&NW 40' Boxcar	40
____ **138**	Conrail 40' Boxcar	40
____ **139**	Southern 40' Boxcar	40
____ **140**	MP 40' Boxcar	40
____ **141**	NYC 40' Boxcar	41
____ **142**	Rock Island 40' Boxcar	40
____ **143**	Virginian 40' Boxcar	40
____ **144**	SP 40' Boxcar, silver	41
____ **145**	CNJ 40' Boxcar	40
____ **146**	Wabash 40' Boxcar	40
____ **147**	Central of Georgia 40' Boxcar	45
____ **148**	B&M 40' Boxcar	45

149	Soo Line 40' Boxcar	40	____
150	D&RGW 40' Boxcar	43	____
151	B&O Sentinel 40' Boxcar	40	____
152	MKT 40' Boxcar	40	____
175	Illinois Central Gulf 40' Boxcar	46	____
176	Reading 40' Boxcar	46	____
177	Akron, Canton & Youngstown 40' Boxcar	40	____
178	BN 40' Boxcar	40	____
179	Burlington 40' Boxcar	43	____
180G	NP 40' Boxcar, green	43	____
180R	NP 40' Boxcar, red	43	____
200	2-bay Rib-sided Hopper	30	____
201	C&O 2-bay Rib-sided Hopper	30	____
202	WM 2-bay Rib-sided Hopper	30	____
204	Erie 2-bay Rib-sided Hopper	30	____
205	N&W 2-bay Rib-sided Hopper	30	____
206	NYC 2-bay Rib-sided Hopper	30	____
207	PRR 2-bay Rib-sided Hopper	30	____
208	Peabody 2-bay Rib-sided Hopper	30	____
209	Southern 2-bay Rib-sided Hopper	30	____
210	UP 2-bay Rib-sided Hopper	30	____
211	SP 2-bay Rib-sided Hopper	30	____
212	D&RGW 2-bay Rib-sided Hopper	30	____
213	Virginian 2-bay Rib-sided Hopper	30	____
214	Reading 2-bay Rib-sided Hopper	30	____
215	CB&Q 2-bay Rib-sided Hopper	30	____
216	LV 2-bay Rib-sided Hopper	30	____
217	Interstate 2-bay Rib-sided Hopper	30	____
218	BN 2-bay Rib-sided Hopper	30	____
223	Burlington Express 40' Plug Door Boxcar	31	____
250	2-bay Offset-sided Hopper	30	____
251	ATSF 2-bay Offset-sided Hopper	30	____
252	CP 2-bay Offset-sided Hopper	30	____
253	GN 2-bay Offset-sided Hopper	30	____
254	NP 2-bay Offset-sided Hopper	30	____
255	IC 2-bay Offset-sided Hopper	30	____
256	NYC 2-bay Offset-sided Hopper	30	____
257	L&N 2-bay Offset-sided Hopper	30	____
258	MILW 2-bay Offset-sided Hopper	30	____
259	UP 2-bay Offset-sided Hopper	30	____
260	Frisco 2-bay Offset-sided Hopper	30	____
261	LNE 2-bay Offset-sided Hopper	30	____
262	D&H 2-bay Offset-sided Hopper	30	____
263	NKP 2-bay Offset-sided Hopper	30	____
264	MP 2-bay Offset-sided Hopper	30	____
265	Conrail 2-bay Offset-sided Hopper	30	____

____ 266	C&NW 2-bay Offset-sided Hopper	30
____ 267	Monon 2-bay Offset-sided Hopper	30
____ 268	B&O 2-bay Offset-sided Hopper	30
____ 352	CP 2-bay Offset-sided Hopper	30
____ 355	IC 2-bay Offset-sided Hopper	30
____ 359	UP 2-bay Offset-sided Hopper	30
____ 361	LNE 2-bay Offset-sided Hopper	30
____ 364	MP 2-bay Offset-sided Hopper	30
____ 366	C&NW 2-bay Offset-sided Hopper	30
____ 368	B&O 2-bay Offset-sided Hopper	30
____ 420	BN Gondola	30
____ 500	Tank Car	45
____ 501	Corn Products Tank Car	45
____ 502	GATX Tank Car	45
____ 503	Cargill Tank Car	45
____ 504	J.M. Huber Tank Car	45
____ 505	Englehard Tank Car	45
____ 506	Georgia Kao Tank Car	45
____ 507	New Jersey Zinc Tank Car	45
____ 508	BASF Wyandotte Tank Car	45
____ 509	American Maize Tank Car	45
____ 510	B.F. Goodrich Tank Car	45
____ 511	Elcor Chemical Tank Car	45
____ 512	Domino Sugar Tank Car	45
____ 513B	American Models Tank Car	45
____ 513G	American Models Tank Car, green	45
____ 514	Aeron Tank Car	45
____ 515	DuPont Tank Car	45
____ 517	Sinclair Diesel Tank Car	45
____ 518	Sinclair Gas Tank Car	45
____ 519	Texaco Tank Car	45
____ 520	Sunoco Tank Car	45
____ 521	Dow Tank Car	45
____ 772	Automatic Water Tower	80
____ 774	Floodlight Tower	80
____ 1100	40' Boxcar	31
____ 1100	WFE 40' Boxcar, Premium Series	32
____ 1102	B&O 40' Boxcar	31
____ 1103	Cotton Belt 40' Boxcar	31
____ 1105	BN/WFE 40' Boxcar	33
____ 1105	D&RGW 40' Boxcar	31
____ 1108	GN 40' Boxcar, Classic Series	35
____ 1112	Soo Line 40' Boxcar	25
____ 1113	NYC 40' Boxcar	31
____ 1114	PRR 40' Boxcar	31
____ 1115	ATSF 40' Boxcar	31

Retail

1116	Seaboard 40' Boxcar	31 ___
1117	SP 40' Boxcar	31 ___
1118	UP 40' Boxcar	31 ___
1119	C&O 40' Boxcar	31 ___
1121	NYC 40' Boxcar, Classic Series	35 ___
1122	Rutland 40' Boxcar, Classic Series	35 ___
1125	P&LE 40' Boxcar, Premium Series	32 ___
1126	NP 40' Boxcar, Premium Series	32 ___
1128	NH 40' Boxcar	31 ___
1129	GN 40' Boxcar	31 ___
1130	GM&O 40' Boxcar	31 ___
1131	N&W 40' Boxcar	31 ___
1132	CP 40' Boxcar	31 ___
1133	M&StL 40' Boxcar	31 ___
1133	NYC 40' Boxcar	31 ___
1134	Erie-Lackawanna 40' Boxcar	31 ___
1135	SP 40' Boxcar, Premium Series	32 ___
1136	Susquehanna 40' Boxcar, Classic Series	35 ___
1137	C&NW 40' Boxcar	31 ___
1138	Conrail 40' Boxcar	31 ___
1500	50' Rib-sided Boxcar	40 ___
1501	Railbox 50' Rib-sided Boxcar	40 ___
1502	Evergreen 50' Rib-sided Boxcar	40 ___
1503	MEC 50' Rib-sided Boxcar	40 ___
1504	C&NW 50' Rib-sided Boxcar	40 ___
1505	UP 50' Rib-sided Boxcar	42 ___
1506	Conrail 50' Rib-sided Boxcar	40 ___
1507	BN 50' Rib-sided Boxcar	40 ___
1508	Tropicana 50' Rib-sided Boxcar	40 ___
1509	D&RGW 50' Rib-sided Boxcar	40 ___
1510	Rail Link 50' Rib-sided Boxcar	40 ___
1511	CSX Link 50' Rib-sided Boxcar	41 ___
1512	Soo Line 50' Rib-sided Boxcar	40 ___
1513	Miller 50' Rib-sided Boxcar	40 ___
1514	PRR 50' Rib-sided Boxcar	40 ___
1515	NYC 50' Rib-sided Boxcar	40 ___
1516	Amtrak 50' Rib-sided Boxcar	42 ___
1516P3	Amtrak 50' Rib-sided Boxcar, Phase III	45 ___
1517	NS 50' Rib-sided Boxcar	41 ___
1518B	Rock Island 50' Rib-sided Boxcar, blue	40 ___
1518W	Rock Island 50' Rib-sided Boxcar, white	40 ___
2002	RI City of Chicago Observation (TCA)	55 ___
2003	RI City of Los Angeles Pullman Coach (TCA)	55 ___
2004	RI Redman/Fraley Pullman Combine (TCA)	55 ___
2200	40' Plug Door Boxcar	39 ___
2202	PFE 40' Boxcar, Premium Series	40 ___

____ **2203**	ART 40' Boxcar, Premium Series	40
____ **2204**	FGE 40' Boxcar, Premium Series	40
____ **2206**	Dubuque 40' Boxcar, Premium Series	40
____ **2207**	WP 40' Plug Door Boxcar	39
____ **2208**	CN 40' Plug Door Boxcar	39
____ **2209**	DT&I 40' Boxcar, Premium Series	40
____ **2210**	ATSF 40' Boxcar, Premium Series	40
____ **2211**	PRR 40' Plug Door Boxcar	39
____ **2212**	Soo Line 40' Plug Door Boxcar	39
____ **2213**	Milwaukee Road 40' Plug Door Boxcar	39
____ **2215**	NYC 40' Boxcar, Premium Series	40
____ **2216**	BN 40' Boxcar, Premium Series	40
____ **2217**	GN 40' Plug Door Boxcar	39
____ **2218**	CP 40' Plug Door Boxcar	39
____ **2219**	Pacific Great Eastern 40' Plug Door Boxcar	39
____ **2220**	B&A 40' Boxcar, Classic Series	42
____ **2221**	NP 40' Boxcar, Classic Series	42
____ **2222**	Miller 40' Plug Door Boxcar	39
____ **2223**	Burlington 40' Plug Door Boxcar, Classic Series	42
____ **2224**	CP 40' Plug Door Boxcar, Classic Series	42
____ **2225**	Frisco 40' Plug Door Boxcar, Classic Series	42
____ **2226**	ADM 40' Plug Door Boxcar	39
____ **2227**	State of Maine 40' Plug Door Boxcar	42
____ **2228**	Reading 40' Plug Door Boxcar	40
____ **2229**	Milwaukee Road 40' Plug Door Boxcar	40
____ **3200**	2-bay Rib-sided Hopper	37
____ **3201**	C&O 2-bay Rib-sided Hopper	37
____ **3202**	WM 2-bay Rib-sided Hopper	37
____ **3203**	B&O 2-bay Rib-sided Hopper	37
____ **3204**	Erie 2-bay Rib-sided Hopper	37
____ **3205**	N&W 2-bay Rib-sided Hopper	37
____ **3206**	NYC 2-bay Rib-sided Hopper	37
____ **3206R**	NYC 2-bay Rib-sided Hopper, red	37
____ **3207**	PRR 2-bay Rib-sided Hopper	37
____ **3208**	Peabody 2-bay Rib-sided Hopper	37
____ **3209**	Southern 2-bay Rib-sided Hopper	37
____ **3211**	SP 2-bay Rib-sided Hopper	37
____ **3213**	Virginia 2-bay Rib-sided Hopper	37
____ **3214**	Reading 2-bay Rib-sided Hopper	37
____ **3215**	CB&Q 2-bay Rib-sided Hopper	37
____ **3216**	LV 2-bay Rib-sided Hopper	37
____ **3217**	Interstate RR 2-bay Rib-sided Hopper	37
____ **3218**	Burlington 2-bay Rib-sided Hopper	37
____ **3218**	D&RGW 2-bay Rib-sided Hopper	37
____ **3219**	NH 2-bay Rib-sided Hopper	37
____ **3250**	2-bay Offset-sided Hopper	37

3251	ATSF 2-bay Offset-sided Hopper	37 _____
3252	CP 2-bay Offset-sided Hopper	37 _____
3253	GN 2-bay Offset-sided Hopper	37 _____
3254	NP 2-bay Offset-sided Hopper	37 _____
3255	IC 2-bay Offset-sided Hopper	37 _____
3256	NYC 2-bay Offset-sided Hopper	37 _____
3257	L&N 2-bay Offset-sided Hopper	37 _____
3258	MILW 2-bay Offset-sided Hopper	37 _____
3259	UP 2-bay Offset-sided Hopper	37 _____
3260	Frisco 2-bay Offset-sided Hopper	37 _____
3261	LNE 2-bay Offset-sided Hopper	37 _____
3262	D&H 2-bay Offset-sided Hopper	37 _____
3263	NKP 2-bay Offset-sided Hopper	37 _____
3264	MP 2-bay Offset-sided Hopper	37 _____
3265	Conrail 2-bay Offset-sided Hopper	37 _____
3266	C&NW 2-bay Offset-sided Hopper	37 _____
3267	Monon 2-bay Offset-sided Hopper	37 _____
3268	B&O 2-bay Offset-sided Hopper	37 _____
3269	ACL 2-bay Offset-sided Hopper	37 _____
3270	GM&O 2-bay Offset-sided Hopper	37 _____
3271	Reading 2-bay Offset-sided Hopper	37 _____
3272	Southern 2-bay Offset-sided Hopper	37 _____
3273	Reading Blue Coal 2-bay Offset-sided Hopper	37 _____
3274	Rock Island 2-bay Offset-sided Hopper	37 _____
3275	CNJ 2-bay Offset-sided Hopper	37 _____
3300	PS-2 CD 3-bay Hopper	50 _____
3301	ADM PS-2 CD 3-bay Hopper	50 _____
3302	BN PS-2 CD 3-bay Hopper	50 _____
3303	Cargill PS-2 CD 3-bay Hopper	50 _____
3304	C&NW PS-2 CD 3-bay Hopper	50 _____
3305	Conrail PS-2 CD 3-bay Hopper	50 _____
3306	GN PS-2 CD 3-bay Hopper	50 _____
3307	IC PS-2 CD 3-bay Hopper	50 _____
3308	PRR PS-2 CD 3-bay Hopper	50 _____
3309	Pillsbury PS-2 CD 3-bay Hopper	50 _____
3310	D&RGW PS-2 CD 3-bay Hopper	50 _____
3311	The Rock PS-2 CD 3-bay Hopper	50 _____
3312	ATSF PS-2 CD 3-bay Hopper	50 _____
3313	UP PS-2 CD 3-bay Hopper	50 _____
3351	Santa Fe 3-bay Offset-sided Hopper	40 _____
3352	Burlington 3-bay Offset-sided Hopper	40 _____
3353	B&M 3-bay Offset-sided Hopper	40 _____
3354	B&LE 3-bay Offset-sided Hopper	40 _____
3357	C&NW 3-bay Offset-sided Hopper	40 _____
3358	C&O 3-bay Offset-sided Hopper	40 _____
3359	CN 3-bay Offset-sided Hopper	40 _____

____	**3360**	CP 3-bay Offset-sided Hopper	40
____	**3362**	Erie 3-bay Offset-sided Hopper	40
____	**3364**	GTW 3-bay Offset-sided Hopper	40
____	**3365**	IC 3-bay Offset-sided Hopper, orange	40
____	**3366**	IC 3-bay Offset-sided Hopper	40
____	**3367**	MP 3-bay Offset-sided Hopper	40
____	**3368**	B&O 3-bay Offset-sided Hopper	40
____	**3369**	NYC 3-bay Offset-sided Hopper	40
____	**3370**	NKP 3-bay Offset-sided Hopper	40
____	**3371**	P&LE 3-bay Offset-sided Hopper	40
____	**3372**	Peabody 3-bay Offset-sided Hopper	40
____	**3373**	Reading Blue Coal 3-bay Offset-sided Hopper	40
____	**3375**	Rock Island 3-bay Offset-sided Hopper	40
____	**3377**	Southern 3-bay Offset-sided Hopper	40
____	**3378**	SP 3-bay Offset-sided Hopper	40
____	**3379**	UP 3-bay Offset-sided Hopper	40
____	**3400**	4-bay Offset-sided Hopper	37
____	**3401**	B&O 4-bay Offset-sided Hopper	37
____	**3402**	C&O 4-bay Offset-sided Hopper	37
____	**3403**	IC 4-bay Offset-sided Hopper	37
____	**3404**	NH 4-bay Offset-sided Hopper	37
____	**3405**	MP 4-bay Offset-sided Hopper	37
____	**3406**	Peabody Coal 4-bay Offset-sided Hopper	37
____	**3407**	Rock Island 4-bay Offset-sided Hopper	37
____	**3408**	ATSF 4-bay Offset-sided Hopper	37
____	**3409**	WM 4-bay Offset-sided Hopper	37
____	**3410**	NYC 4-bay Offset-sided Hopper	37
____	**3411**	NP 4-bay Offset-sided Hopper	37
____	**3412**	MKT 4-bay Offset-sided Hopper	37
____	**3414**	Reading Blue Coal 4-bay Offset-sided Hopper	37
____	**3415**	B&M 4-bay Offset-sided Hopper	37
____	**3451**	BN 4-bay Rib-sided Hopper	37
____	**3452**	CB&Q 4-bay Rib-sided Hopper	37
____	**3453**	C&NW 4-bay Rib-sided Hopper	37
____	**3454**	Conrail 4-bay Rib-sided Hopper	37
____	**3455**	CSX 4-bay Rib-sided Hopper	37
____	**3456**	D&RGW 4-bay Rib-sided Hopper	37
____	**3457**	GN 4-bay Rib-sided Hopper	37
____	**3458B**	GN 4-bay Rib-sided Hopper	37
____	**3458C**	PRR 4-bay Rib-sided Hopper, brown	37
____	**3458R**	PRR 4-bay Rib-sided Hopper	37
____	**3459**	UP 4-bay Rib-sided Hopper	37
____	**3460**	SP 4-bay Rib-sided Hopper	37
____	**3461**	Virginian 4-bay Rib-sided Hopper	37
____	**3463**	LV 4-bay Rib-sided Hopper	37
____	**4400**	Gondola	39

4401	Frisco Gondola	39 ____
4402	Wabash Gondola	39 ____
4403	Southern Gondola	39 ____
4404	PRR Gondola	39 ____
4405	GN Gondola	39 ____
4406	LV Gondola	39 ____
4407	B&O Gondola	39 ____
4408	C&O Gondola	39
4409	Milwaukee Road Gondola	39 ____
4410	SP Gondola	39 ____
4411	WM Gondola	39 ____
4412	Soo Line Gondola	39 ____
4413	Lackawanna Gondola	39 ____
4414	IC Gondola	39 ____
4415	NYC Gondola	39 ____
4416	NKP Gondola	39 ____
4417	N&W Gondola	39 ____
4418	UP Gondola	39 ____
4419	ATSF Gondola	39 ____
4420	BN Gondola	39 ____
4421	CP Gondola	39 ____
4422	NP Gondola	39 ____
4423	D&H Gondola	39 ____
4424	Reading Gondola	39 ____
4425	D&RGW Gondola	39 ____
4426	C&NW Gondola	39 ____
4427	Conrail Gondola	39 ____
4428	MP Gondola	39 ____
4429	CB&Q Gondola	39 ____
4430	NH Gondola	39 ____
4430B	NH Gondola, black	39 ____
4431	P&LE Gondola	39 ____
4432	Rock Island Gondola	39 ____
4433	NS Gondola, black	39 ____
4433R	NS Gondola, red	39 ____
4434	Virginian Gondola	39 ____
4435	IC Gondola	39 ____
4599	Chevron Tank Car (TCA)	90 ____
6000	USRA 46' Flatcar	40 ____
6001	B&O USRA 46' Flatcar	40 ____
6002	Burlington USRA 46' Flatcar	40 ____
6003	BN USRA 46' Flatcar	40 ____
6004	Conrail USRA 46' Flatcar	40 ____
6005	C&NW USRA 46' Flatcar	40 ____
6006	C&O USRA 46' Flatcar	40 ____
6007	CSX USRA 46' Flatcar	40 ____

____ **6008**	CP USRA 46' Flatcar	40
____ **6009**	D&RGW USRA 46' Flatcar	40
____ **6010**	GN USRA 46' Flatcar	40
____ **6011**	IC USRA 46' Flatcar	40
____ **6012**	NH USRA 46' Flatcar	40
____ **6013**	NYC USRA 46' Flatcar	40
____ **6014**	NP USRA 46' Flatcar	40
____ **6015**	N&W USRA 46' Flatcar	40
____ **6016**	MP USRA 46' Flatcar	40
____ **6017**	PRR USRA 46' Flatcar	40
____ **6018**	ATSF USRA 46' Flatcar	40
____ **6019**	Southern USRA 46' Flatcar	40
____ **6020**	SP USRA 46' Flatcar	40
____ **6021**	UP USRA 46' Flatcar	40
____ **6022**	Frisco USRA 46' Flatcar	40
____ **6023**	Milwaukee Road USRA 46' Flatcar	40
____ **6024**	Rock Island USRA 46' Flatcar	40
____ **6025**	B&M USRA 46' Flatcar	40
____ **6026**	MKT USRA 46' Flatcar	40
____ **7500**	Wood-sided Caboose	55
____ **7501**	ATSF Wood-sided Caboose	55
____ **7502**	ACL Wood-sided Caboose	55
____ **7503**	B&O Wood-sided Caboose	55
____ **7504**	CP Wood-sided Caboose	55
____ **7505**	CB&Q Wood-sided Caboose	55
____ **7506**	C&O Wood-sided Caboose	55
____ **7507**	C&NW Wood-sided Caboose	55
____ **7508**	D&RGW Wood-sided Caboose	55
____ **7509**	Erie Wood-sided Caboose	55
____ **7510**	Frisco Wood-sided Caboose	55
____ **7511**	GN Wood-sided Caboose	55
____ **7512**	GM&O Wood-sided Caboose	55
____ **7513**	IC Wood-sided Caboose	55
____ **7514**	Lackawanna Wood-sided Caboose	55
____ **7515**	Milwaukee Road Wood-sided Caboose	55
____ **7516**	MP Wood-sided Caboose	55
____ **7517**	NH Wood-sided Caboose	55
____ **7518**	NYC Wood-sided Caboose	55
____ **7519**	N&W Wood-sided Caboose	55
____ **7520**	NP Wood-sided Caboose	55
____ **7521**	PRR Wood-sided Caboose	55
____ **7522**	Rock Island Wood-sided Caboose	55
____ **7523**	Southern Wood-sided Caboose	55
____ **7524**	SP Wood-sided Caboose	55
____ **7525**	UP Wood-sided Caboose	55
____ **7526**	Rio Grande 4-stripe Wood-sided Caboose	55

Retail

7527	NYC Pacemaker Wood-sided Caboose	55 _____
7528	Pere Marquette Wood-sided Caboose	55 _____
7529	LV Wood-sided Caboose	55 _____
7530	Cotton Belt Wood-sided Caboose	55 _____
7531	WM Wood-sided Caboose	55 _____
7532	MKT Wood-sided Caboose	55 _____
7700	Bay Window Caboose	45 _____
7701	Chessie Bay Window Caboose	45 _____
7702	Erie Bay Window Caboose	45 _____
7703	Erie-Lackawanna Bay Window Caboose, red	45 _____
7704	Conrail Bay Window Caboose	45 _____
7705	C&NW Bay Window Caboose	45 _____
7706	Southern Bay Window Caboose	45 _____
7707	NYC Bay Window Caboose	45 _____
7708	PRR Bay Window Caboose	45 _____
7709	Norfolk & Western Bay Window Caboose	45 _____
7710	ATSF Bay Window Caboose	45 _____
7711	SP Bay Window Caboose	45 _____
7712	GN Bay Window Caboose	45 _____
7713	NP Bay Window Caboose	45 _____
7714	UP Bay Window Caboose	45 _____
7715	NH Bay Window Caboose	45 _____
7716	CP Bay Window Caboose	45 _____
7717	Virginian Bay Window Caboose, Premium	50 _____
7718	Erie-Lack. Bay Window Caboose, Premium	50 _____
7719	BN Bay Window Caboose	45 _____
7720	Burlington Bay Window Caboose, Premium	50 _____
7721	Milwaukee Road Bay Window Caboose	45 _____
7722	Frisco Bay Window Caboose, Premium	50 _____
7723	MP Bay Window Caboose	45 _____
7724	CSX Bay Window Caboose	45 _____
7725	NYC Bay Window Caboose	45 _____
7726	SP Bay Window Caboose	45 _____
7728	Virginian Bay Window Caboose	45 _____
7729	CNJ Bay Window Caboose	45 _____
7730	Wabash Bay Window Caboose	45 _____
7731	WP Bay Window Caboose	45 _____
46000-UndecAC	USRA 4-6-2 Pacific Locomotive, full sound	426 _____
46000-UndecHR	USRA 4-6-2 Pacific, hi-rail	380 _____
46000-UndecL	USRA 4-6-2 Pacific, limited sound	400 _____
46000-UndecS	USRA 4-6-2 Pacific, scale	380 _____
46000-ATSFAC	ATSF 4-6-2 Pacific Locomotive, full sound	426 _____
46000-ATSFHR	ATSF 4-6-2 Pacific, hi-rail	380 _____
46000-ATSFL	ATSF 4-6-2 Pacific, limited sound	400 _____
46000-ATSFS	ATSF 4-6-2 Pacific, scale	380 _____
46000-CBQAC	CB&Q 4-6-2 Pacific Locomotive, full sound	426 _____

____ 46000-CBQHR	CB&Q 4-6-2 Pacific Locomotive, hi-rail	380
____ 46000-CBQL	CB&Q 4-6-2 Pacific, limited sound	400
____ 46000-CBQS	CB&Q 4-6-2 Pacific, scale	380
____ 46000-GNAC	GN 4-6-2 Pacific Locomotive, full sound	426
____ 46000-GNHR	GN 4-6-2 Pacific, hi-rail	380
____ 46000-GNL	GN 4-6-2 Pacific, limited sound	400
____ 46000-GNS	GN 4-6-2 Pacific, scale	380
____ 46000-KATYAC	MKT 4-6-2 Pacific Locomotive, full sound	426
____ 46000-KATYHR	MKT 4-6-2 Pacific, hi-rail	380
____ 46000-KATYL	MKT 4-6-2 Pacific, limited sound	400
____ 46000-KATYS	MKT 4-6-2 Pacific, scale	380
____ 46000-NHAC	NH 4-6-2 Pacific Locomotive, full sound	426
____ 46000-NHHR	NH 4-6-2 Pacific, hi-rail	380
____ 46000-NHL	NH 4-6-2 Pacific, limited sound	400
____ 46000-NHS	NH 4-6-2 Pacific, scale	380
____ 46000-NYCAC	NYC 4-6-2 Pacific Locomotive, full sound	426
____ 46000-NYCHR	NYC 4-6-2 Pacific, hi-rail	380
____ 46000-NYCL	NYC 4-6-2 Pacific, limited sound	400
____ 46000-NYCS	NYC 4-6-2 Pacific, scale	380
____ 46000-PMAC	Pere Marquette 4-6-2 Pacific Locomotive, full sound	426
____ 46000-PMHR	Pere Marquette 4-6-2 Pacific, hi-rail	380
____ 46000-PML	Pere Marquette 4-6-2 Pacific, limited sound	400
____ 46000-PMS	Pere Marquette 4-6-2 Pacific, scale	380
____ 46000-PRRAC	PRR 4-6-2 Pacific Locomotive, full sound	426
____ 46000-PRRHR	PRR 4-6-2 Pacific, hi-rail	380
____ 46000-PRRL	PRR 4-6-2 Pacific, limited sound	400
____ 46000-PRRS	PRR 4-6-2 Pacific, scale	380
____ 46000-SPAC	SP 4-6-2 Pacific Locomotive, full sound	426
____ 46000-SPHR	SP 4-6-2 Pacific, hi-rail	380
____ 46000-SPL	SP 4-6-2 Pacific, limited sound	400
____ 46000-SPS	SP 4-6-2 Pacific, scale	380
____ 46000-UPAC	UP 4-6-2 Pacific Locomotive, full sound	426
____ 46000-UPHR	UP 4-6-2 Pacific, hi-rail	380
____ 46000-UPL	UP 4-6-2 Pacific, limited sound	400
____ 46000-UPS	UP 4-6-2 Pacific, scale	380
____ 46001	B&O USRA 4-6-2 Locomotive	350
____ 46003AC	MILW 4-6-2 Pacific Locomotive, full sound	426
____ 46003HR	MILW 4-6-2 Pacific, hi-rail	380
____ 46003L	MILW 4-6-2 Pacific, limited sound	400
____ 46003S	MILW 4-6-2 Pacific, scale	380
____ 46006AC	Southern 4-6-2 Pacific Locomotive, full sound	426
____ 46006HR	Southern 4-6-2 Pacific, hi-rail	380
____ 46006L	Southern 4-6-2 Pacific, limited sound	400
____ 46006S	Southern 4-6-2 Pacific, scale	380

46007AC	Rock Island 4-6-2 Pacific Locomotive, full sound	426 ____
46007HR	Rock Island 4-6-2 Pacific, hi-rail	380 ____
46007L	Rock Island 4-6-2 Pacific, limited sound	400 ____
46007S	Rock Island 4-6-2 Pacific, scale	380 ____
46200AC	LV 4-6-2 Pacific Locomotive, full sound	426 ____
46200HR	LV 4-6-2 Pacific, hi-rail	380 ____
46200L	LV 4-6-2 Pacific, limited sound	400 ____
46200S	LV 4-6-2 Pacific, scale	380 ____
46500	USRA 4-6-2 Locomotive	620 ____
46500AC	4-6-2 Pacific Steam Passenger Set	700 ____
46500HR	4-6-2 Pacific Steam Passenger Set, hi-rail	620 ____
46500S	4-6-2 Pacific Steam Passenger Set, scale	620 ____
46501	B&O USRA 4-6-2 Locomotive	620 ____
46502	Southern USRA 4-6-2 Locomotive	620 ____
46502AC	Southern 4-6-2 Pacific Steam Passenger Set	700 ____
46502HR	Southern 4-6-2 Pacific Steam Passenger Set, hi-rail	620 ____
46502S	Southern 4-6-2 Pacific Steam Passenger Set, scale	620 ____
46503AC	MILW 4-6-2 Pacific Steam Passenger Set	660 ____
46503HR	MILW 4-6-2 Pacific Steam Passenger Set, hi-rail	600 ____
46503S	MILW 4-6-2 Pacific Steam Passenger Set, scale	600 ____
46504AC	NH 4-6-2 Pacific Steam Passenger Set	700 ____
46504HR	NH 4-6-2 Pacific Steam Passenger Set, hi-rail	620 ____
46504S	NH 4-6-2 Pacific Steam Passenger Set, scale	620 ____
48400	4-8-4 Northern Locomotive	430 ____
48400-6	4-8-4 Northern Locomotive, coal tender	430 ____
48401	Santa Fe 4-8-4 Northern Locomotive	430 ____
48402	Rock Island 4-8-4 Northern Locomotive	430 ____
48403	LV 4-8-4 Northern Locomotive	430 ____
48404	CB&Q 4-8-4 Northern Locomotive	430 ____
48405	WM 4-8-4 Northern Locomotive	430 ____
48406	Cotton Belt 4-8-4 Northern Locomotive	430 ____
48407	SP 4-8-4 Northern Locomotive	430 ____
48408	C&O 4-8-4 Northern Locomotive	430 ____
48409	Lackawanna 4-8-4 Northern Locomotive	430 ____
48410	MILW 4-8-4 Northern Locomotive	430 ____
95247	CB&Q USRA 46' Flatcar with Burlington trailer (S Fest)	90 ____
547798	C&NW 4-bay Hopper (TCA)	85 ____
BD8RPO	Budd Railway Post Office Car	60 ____
BD8200	Budd Coach, silver	90 ____
BD8200C	Budd Coach, chrome	90 ____
BD8201	B&O Budd Coach	90 ____
BD8202	Southern Budd Coach	90 ____

____	**BD8203**	UP Budd Coach	90
____	**BD8204**	New Haven Budd Coach	90
____	**BD8205**	NYC Budd Coach	90
____	**BD8206**	ATSF Budd Coach	90
____	**BD8209**	PRR Budd Coach	90
____	**BD8214**	ACL Budd Coach	90
____	**BD8215**	Burlington Budd Coach	90
____	**BD8216**	Rock Island Budd Coach	90
____	**BD8217**	IC Budd Coach	90
____	**BD8218**	Central of Georgia Budd Coach	90
____	**BD8223**	MP Colorado Eagle Budd Coach	90
____	**BD8224**	SP Budd Coach	90
____	**BD8225**	Texas Special Budd Coach	90
____	**BDBS00**	Budd 4-Car Set, silver	290
____	**BDBS00C**	Budd 4-Car Set, chrome	320
____	**BDBS01**	B&O Budd 4-Car Set	320
____	**BDBS02**	Southern Budd 4-Car Set	320
____	**BDBS03**	UP Budd 4-Car Set	320
____	**BDBS04**	New Haven Budd 4-Car Set	320
____	**BDBS05**	NYC 4-Car Budd Set	320
____	**BDBS06**	ATSF Budd 4-Car Set	320
____	**BDBS09**	PRR Budd 4-Car Set	320
____	**BDBS14**	ACL Budd 4-Car Set	320
____	**BDBS15**	Burlington Budd 4-Car Set	320
____	**BDBS16**	Rock Island Budd 4-Car Set	320
____	**BDBS17**	IC Budd 4-Car Set	320
____	**BDBS18**	Central of Georgia Budd 4-Car Set	320
____	**BDBS23**	MP Colorado Eagle Budd 4-Car Set	320
____	**BDBS24**	SP Budd 4-Car Set	320
____	**BSSC1**	Conrail Trailer Hauler Freight Set	300
____	**BSSC4**	SP Trailer Hauler Freight Set	300
____	**CB208S**	Ground Throw	5
____	**DXF211AB**	B&O FA Diesel AB Set, sound	370
____	**DXF211ABA**	B&O FA Diesel ABA Set, sound	500
____	**DXF211ABPW**	B&O FA Diesel AB Set, powered B Unit	370
____	**DXF214AB**	RI FA Diesel AB Set, sound	370
____	**DXF214ABA**	RI FA Diesel ABA Set, sound	500
____	**DXF214ABPW**	RI FA Diesel AB Set, powered B Unit	370
____	**DXF710AB**	ACL FP7 Diesel AB Set, sound	370
____	**DXF710ABA**	ACL FP7 Diesel AB Set, sound	500
____	**DXF710ABPW**	ACL FP7 Diesel AB Set, powered B Unit	370
____	**DXF711AB**	B&O FP7 Diesel AB Set, sound	370
____	**DXF711ABA**	B&O FP7 Diesel ABA Set, sound	500
____	**DXF711ABPW**	B&O FP7 Diesel AB Set, powered B Unit	370
____	**DXF712AB**	C&O FP7 Diesel AB Set, sound	370
____	**DXF712ABA**	C&O FP7 Diesel ABA Set, sound	500

DXF712ABPW	C&O FP7 Diesel AB Set, powered B Unit	370 ____
DXF713AB	D&RGW FP7 Diesel AB Set, sound	370 ____
DXF713ABA	D&RGW FP7 Diesel ABA Set, sound	500 ____
DXF713ABPW	D&RGW FP7 Diesel AB Set, powered B Unit	370 ____
DXF714AB	RI FP7 Diesel AB Set, sound	370 ____
DXF714ABA	RI FP7 Diesel ABA Set, sound	500 ____
DXF714ABPW	RI FP7 Diesel AB Set, powered B Unit	370 ____
DXF715AB	Southern FP7 Diesel AB Set, sound	500 ____
DXF715ABA	Southern FP7 Diesel ABA Set, sound	370 ____
DXFA2011	B&O FA Diesel A Unit	250 ____
DXFA2014	Rock Island FA Diesel A Unit	250 ____
DXFA211DNS	B&O FA Diesel B Unit, sound	250 ____
DXFB211PW	B&O FA Diesel B Unit, powered	250 ____
DXFB214PW	Rock Island B Unit, powered	250 ____
DXFB214SND	Rock Island B Unit, sound	250 ____
DXFB710PW	ACL FP7 Diesel B Unit, powered	250 ____
DXFB711PW	B&O FP7 Diesel B Unit, powered	250 ____
DXFB711SND	B&O FP7 Diesel B Unit, sound	250 ____
DXFB712PW	C&O FP7 Diesel B Unit, powered	250 ____
DXFB712SND	C&O FP7 Diesel B Unit, sound	250 ____
DXFB713PW	D&RGW FP7 Diesel B Unit, powered	250 ____
DXFB713SND	D&RGW FP7 Diesel B Unit, sound	250 ____
DXFB714	Rock Island FP7 Diesel A Unit	250 ____
DXFB714PW	Rock Island FP7 Diesel B unit, powered	250 ____
DXFB714SND	Rock Island FP7 Diesel B Unit, sound	250 ____
DXFB715PW	Southern FP7 Diesel B Unit, powered	250 ____
DXFB715SND	Southern FP7 Diesel B Unit, sound	250 ____
DXFP7010	ACL FP7 Diesel A Unit	250 ____
DXFP7011	B&O FP7 Diesel A Unit	250 ____
DXFP7012	C&O FP7 Diesel A Unit	250 ____
DXFP7013	D&RGW FP7 Diesel A Unit	250 ____
DXFP715	Southern FP7 Diesel A Unit	250 ____
DXFP7B710SND	ACL FP7 Diesel B Unit, sound	250 ____
E800	E8 Diesel, DC scale or hi-rail	250 ____
E800AA	E8 Diesel AA Set, DC scale or hi-rail	470 ____
E803	NYC E8 Diesel, DC scale or hi-rail	250 ____
E803AA	NYC E8 Diesel AA Set, DC scale or hi-rail	470 ____
E805	PRR E8 Diesel, DC scale or hi-rail, red	250 ____
E805AA	PRR E8 Diesel AA Set, DC scale or hi-rail, red	470 ____
E806	PRR E8 Diesel, DC scale or hi-rail, green	250 ____
E806AA	PRR E8 Diesel AA Set, DC scale or hi-rail, green	470 ____
E808	UP E8 Diesel, DC scale or hi-rail	250 ____
E808AA	UP E8 Diesel AA Set, DC scale or hi-rail	470 ____
E811	B&O E8 Diesel, DC scale or hi-rail	250 ____
E811AA	B&O E8 Diesel AA Set, DC scale or hi-rail	470 ____
E818	ATSF E8 Diesel, DC scale or hi-rail	250 ____

____ E818AA	ATSF E8 Diesel AA Set, DC scale or hi-rail	470
____ E819	Burlington E8 Diesel, DC scale or hi-rail	250
____ E819AA	Burlington E8 Diesel AA Set, DC scale or hi-rail	470
____ E820	IC E8 Diesel, DC scale or hi-rail	250
____ E820AA	IC E8 Diesel AA Set, DC scale or hi-rail	470
____ E821	Central of Georgia E8 Diesel, DC scale or hi-rail	250
____ E821AA	Central of Georgia E8 Diesel AA Set, DC scale or hi-rail	470
____ E822	Lackawanna E8 Diesel, DC scale or hi-rail	250
____ E822AA	Lackawanna E8 Diesel AA Set, DC scale or hi-rail	470
____ E823	MP E8 Diesel, DC scale or hi-rail	250
____ E823AA	MP E8 Diesel AA Set, DC scale or hi-rail	470
____ E824	SP E8 Diesel, DC scale or hi-rail	250
____ E824AA	SP E8 Diesel AA Set, DC scale or hi-rail	470
____ ESE01	Empire State Express Set	700
____ F40PIIAC	Amtrak F40 Diesel, phase II	210
____ F40PIIIAC	Amtrak F40 Diesel, phase III	210
____ F200AB	FA2 Diesel AB Set, sound	350
____ F200ABA	FA2 Diesel ABA Set, sound	500
____ F200ABPW	FA2 Diesel AB Set, powered	350
____ F201AB	CP FA2 Diesel AB Set, sound	350
____ F201ABA	CP FA2 Diesel ABA Set, sound	500
____ F201ABPW	CP FA2 Diesel AB Set, powered	350
____ F202AB	GN FA2 Diesel AB Set, sound	350
____ F202ABA	GN FA2 Diesel ABA Set, sound	500
____ F202ABPW	GN FA2 Diesel AB Set, powered	350
____ F203AB	NH FA2 Diesel AB Set, sound	350
____ F203ABA	NH FA2 Diesel ABA Set, sound	500
____ F203ABPW	NH FA2 Diesel AB Set, powered	350
____ F204AB	NYC FA2 Diesel AB Set, sound	350
____ F204ABA	NYC FA2 Diesel ABA Set, sound	500
____ F204ABPW	NYC FA2 Diesel AB Set, powered	350
____ F205AB	UP FA2 Diesel AB Set, sound	350
____ F205ABA	UP FA2 Diesel ABA Set, sound	500
____ F205ABPW	UP FA2 Diesel AB Set, powered	350
____ F206AB	PRR FA2 Diesel AB Set, sound	350
____ F206ABA	PRR FA2 Diesel ABA Set, sound	500
____ F206ABPW	PRR FA2 Diesel AB Set, powered	350
____ F700AB	FP7 Diesel AB Set, sound	360
____ F700ABA	FP7 Diesel ABA Set, sound	500
____ F700ABPW	FP7 Diesel AB Set, powered	360
____ F701AB	BN FP7 Diesel AB Set, sound	360
____ F701ABA	BN FP7 Diesel ABA Set, sound	500
____ F701ABPW	BN FP7 Diesel AB Set, powered	360
____ F702AB	GN FP7 Diesel AB Set, sound	360

F702ABA	GN FP7 Diesel ABA Set, sound	500 ____
F702ABPW	GN FP7 Diesel AB Set, powered	360 ____
F703AB	NYC FP7 Diesel AB Set, sound	360 ____
F703ABA	NYC FP7 Diesel ABA Set, sound, gray	500 ____
F703ABPW	NYC FP7 Diesel AB Set, powered, gray	360 ____
F704AB	NP FP7 Diesel AB Set, sound	360 ____
F704ABA	NP FP7 Diesel ABA Set, sound	500 ____
F704ABPW	NP FP7 Diesel AB Set, powered	360 ____
F705AB	PRR FP7 Diesel AB Set, sound	360 ____
F705ABA	PRR FP7 Diesel ABA Set, sound, red	500 ____
F705ABPW	PRR FP7 Diesel AB Set, powered, red	360 ____
F706AB	PRR FP7 Diesel AB Set, sound	360 ____
F706ABA	PRR FP7 Diesel ABA Set, sound, green	500 ____
F706ABPW	PRR FP7 Diesel AB Set, powered, green	360 ____
F707AB	SP FP7 Diesel AB Set, sound	360 ____
F707ABA	SP FP7 Diesel ABA Set, sound	500 ____
F707ABPW	SP FP7 Diesel AB Set, powered	360 ____
F708AB	UP FP7 Diesel AB Set, sound	360 ____
F708ABA	UP FP7 Diesel ABA Set, sound	500 ____
F708ABPW	UP FP7 Dicscl AB Set, powered	360 ____
F709AB	NYC FP7 Diesel AB Set, sound	360 ____
F709ABA	NYC FP7 Diesel ABA Set, sound, black	500 ____
F709ABPW	NYC FP7 Diesel AB Set, powered, black	360 ____
F7B00PW	FP7 Diesel B Unit, powered	190 ____
F7B00SND	FP7 Diesel B Unit, sound	190 ____
F7B01PW	BN FP7 Diesel B Unit, powered	190 ____
F7B01SND	BN FP7 Diesel B Unit, sound	190 ____
F7B02PW	GN FP7 Diesel B Unit, powered	190 ____
F7B02SND	GN FP7 Diesel B Unit, sound	190 ____
F7B03PW	NYC FP7 Diesel B Unit, powered, gray	190 ____
F7B03SND	NYC FP7 Diesel B Unit, sound, gray	190 ____
F7B04PW	NP FP7 Diesel B Unit, powered	190 ____
F7B04SND	NP FP7 Diesel B Unit, sound	190 ____
F7B05PW	PRR FP7 Diesel B Unit, powered, red	190 ____
F7B05SND	PRR FP7 Diesel B Unit, sound, red	190 ____
F7B06PW	PRR FP7 Diesel B Unit, powered, green	190 ____
F7B06SND	PRR FP7 Diesel B Unit, sound, green	190 ____
F7B07PW	SP FP7 Diesel B Unit, powered	190 ____
F7B07SND	SP FP7 Diesel B Unit, sound	190 ____
F7B08PW	UP FP7 Diesel B Unit, powered	190 ____
F7B08SND	UP FP7 Diesel B Unit, sound	190 ____
F7B09PW	NYC FP7 Diesel B Unit, powered, black	190 ____
F7B09SND	NYC FP7 Diesel B Unit, sound, black	190 ____
FA2000	Alco FA2 Diesel	250 ____
FA2001	CP Alco FA2 Diesel	250 ____
FA2002	GN Alco FA2 Diesel	250 ____

____	**FA2003**	NH Alco FA2 Diesel	250
____	**FA2004**	NYC Alco Diesel FA2	250
____	**FA2005**	UP Alco Diesel FA2	250
____	**FA2006**	PRR Alco Diesel FB2	250
____	**FB200PW**	FA2 Diesel B Unit, powered	190
____	**FB200SND**	FA2 Diesel B Unit, sound	190
____	**FB201PW**	CP FA2 Diesel B Unit, powered	190
____	**FB201SND**	CP FA2 Diesel B Unit, sound	190
____	**FB202PW**	GN FA2 Diesel B Unit, powered	190
____	**FB202SND**	GN FA2 Diesel B Unit, sound	190
____	**FB203PW**	NH FA2 Diesel B Unit, powered	190
____	**FB203SND**	NH FA2 Diesel B Unit, sound	190
____	**FB204PW**	NYC FA2 Diesel B Unit, powered	190
____	**FB204SND**	NYC FA2 Diesel B Unit, sound	190
____	**FB205PW**	UP FA2 Diesel B Unit, powered	190
____	**FB205SND**	UP FA2 Diesel B Unit, sound	190
____	**FB206PW**	PRR FA2 Diesel B Unit, powered	190
____	**FB206SND**	PRR FA2 Diesel B Unit, sound	190
____	**FB2000**	Alco FB2 Diesel	190
____	**FB2001**	CP Alco FB2 Diesel	190
____	**FB2002**	GN Alco FB2 Diesel	190
____	**FB2003**	NH Alco FB2 Diesel	190
____	**FB2004**	NYC Alco FB2 Diesel	190
____	**FB2005**	UP Alco FB2 Diesel	190
____	**FB2006**	PRR Alco FB2 Diesel	190
____	**FB7000**	FB-7 Diesel	250
____	**FB7001**	BN FB-7 Diesel	250
____	**FB7002**	GN FB-7 Diesel	250
____	**FB7003**	NYC FB-7 Diesel	250
____	**FB7004**	NP FB-7 Diesel	250
____	**FB7005**	PRR FB-7 Diesel, tuscan	250
____	**FB7006**	PRR FB-7 Diesel, green	250
____	**FB7007**	SP FB-7 Diesel	250
____	**FB7008**	UP FB-7 Diesel	250
____	**FP7000**	FP7 Diesel	250
____	**FP7001**	BN FP7 Diesel	250
____	**FP7002**	GN FP7 Diesel	250
____	**FP7003**	NYC FP7 Diesel	250
____	**FP7004**	NP FP7 Diesel	250
____	**FP7005**	PRR FP7 Diesel, tuscan	250
____	**FP7006**	PRR FP7 Diesel, green	250
____	**FP7007**	SP FP7 Diesel	250
____	**FP7008**	UP FP7 Diesel	250
____	**GG1200**	GG1 Electric Locomotive	310
____	**GG1201**	PRR GG1 Electric Locomotive, green	310
____	**GG1202**	PRR GG1 Electric Locomotive, tuscan	310

GGCCAC	PRR Congressional GG1 Electric Locomotive, chrome	280 ____
GGCSAC	PRR Congressional GG1 Electric Locomotive, silver	280 ____
GGGIAC	PRR GG1 Electric Locomotive, green, 1-stripe	280 ____
GGGSAC	PRR GG1 Electric Locomotive, green, 5-stripe	280 ____
GGR6AC	PRR GG1 Electric Locomotive, tuscan, 5-stripe	280 ____
GGRIAC	PRR GG1 Electric Locomotive, tuscan, 1-stripe	280 ____
GP9000AC	GP9 Diesel	210 ____
GP9001AC	Conrail GP9 Diesel	210 ____
GP9002AC	Erie-Lackawanna GP9 Diesel	210 ____
GP9003AC	NH GP9 Diesel	210 ____
GP9004AC	NYC GP18 Diesel	210 ____
GP9005AC	N&W GP9 Diesel	210 ____
GP9006AC	PRR GP9 Diesel	210 ____
GP9007AC	ATSF GP9 Diesel	210 ____
GP9008AC	SP GP9 Diesel	210 ____
GP9009AC	UP GP9 Diesel	210 ____
GP9010AC	C&O GP9 Diesel	210 ____
GP35000AC	GP35 Diesel	210 ____
GP35001AC	C&O GP35 Diesel	210 ____
GP35002AC	C&NW GP35 Diesel	210 ____
GP35003AC	Conrail GP35 Diesel	210 ____
GP35004AC	Erie-Lackawanna GP35 Diesel	210 ____
GP35005AC	GN GP35 Diesel	210 ____
GP35006AC	MP GP35 Diesel	210 ____
GP35007AC	NYC GP35 Diesel	210 ____
GP35008AC	PRR GP35 Diesel	210 ____
GP35010AC	SP GP35 Diesel	210 ____
GP35011AC	UP GP35 Diesel	210 ____
GP35012AC	BN GP35 Diesel	210 ____
GP35013AC	CSX GP35 Diesel	210 ____
GP35014AC	ATSF GP35 Diesel, warbonnet	210 ____
GP35015AC	Soo Line GP35 Diesel	210 ____
GP35016AC	D&RGW GP35 Diesel	210 ____
GP35017AC	Ann Arbor GP35 Diesel	210 ____
HA8000	80' Passenger Lightweight Set	250 ____
HA8001	GN 80' Passenger Lightweight Set	250 ____
HA8002	NP 80' Passenger Lightweight Set	250 ____
HA8003	NYC 80' Passenger Lightweight Set	250 ____
HA8004	PRR 80' Passenger Lightweight Set	250 ____
HA8006	UP 80' Passenger Lightweight Set	250 ____
HA8100	Baggage-Dormitory Car	45 ____
HA8101	NP Baggage-Dormitory Car	45 ____
HA8103	NYC Baggage-Dormitory Car	45 ____
HA8104	PRR Baggage-Dormitory Car	45 ____

____ HA8106	UP Baggage-Dormitory Car	45
____ HA8111	GN Baggage-Dormitory Car	45
____ HA8200	60-seat Coach	45
____ HA8201	NP 60-seat Coach	45
____ HA8203	NYC 60-seat Coach	45
____ HA8204	PRR 60-seat Coach	45
____ HA8206	UP 60-seat Coach	45
____ HA8211	GN 60-seat Coach	45
____ HA8300	Vista Dome Car	45
____ HA8301	NP Vista Dome Car	45
____ HA8303	NYC Vista Dome Car	45
____ HA8304	PRR Vista Dome Car	45
____ HA8306	UP Vista Dome Car	45
____ HA8311	GN Vista Dome Car	45
____ HA8400	4-16 Duplex Sleeper Car	45
____ HA8401	NP 4-16 Duplex Sleeper Car	45
____ HA8403	NYC 4-16 Duplex Sleeper Car	45
____ HA8404	PRR 4-16 Duplex Sleeper Car	45
____ HA8406	UP 4-16 Duplex Sleeper Car	45
____ HA8411	GN 4-16 Duplex Sleeper Car	45
____ HA8500	Observation Lounge Car	45
____ HA8501	NP Observation Lounge Car	45
____ HA8503	NYC Observation Lounge Car	45
____ HA8504	PRR Observation Lounge Car	45
____ HA8506	UP Observation Lounge Car	45
____ HA8511	GN Observation Lounge Car	45
____ HW8000	72' Heavyweight Passenger Set	320
____ HW8001	C&NW 72' Heavyweight Passenger Set	320
____ HW8002	Southern Crescent 72' Heavyweight Passenger Set	320
____ HW8003	UP 72' Heavyweight Passenger Set	320
____ HW8004	NH 72' Heavyweight Passenger Set	320
____ HW8005	NYC 72' Heavyweight Passenger Set	320
____ HW8006	ATSF 72' Heavyweight Passenger Set	320
____ HW8007	D&RGW 72' Heavyweight Passenger Set	320
____ HW8008	C&NW 72' Heavyweight Passenger Set	320
____ HW8009	PRR 72' Heavyweight Passenger Set	290
____ HW8010	PRR 72' Heavyweight Passenger Set	320
____ HW8011	MILW 72' Heavyweight Passenger Set	320
____ HW8012	SP 72' Heavyweight Passenger Set	320
____ HW8013	Heavyweight Passenger Set, Pullman green, no lettering	320
____ HW8014	Heavyweight Passenger Set, Pullman green, green roof	320
____ HW8015	SP 72' Heavyweight Passenger Set, gray	320
____ HW8016	C&O 72' Heavyweight Passenger Set	320
____ HW8017	CNJ 72' Heavyweight Passenger Set	320

Retail

HW8018	NH 72' Heavyweight Passenger Set	320 ____
HW8019	Lackawanna 72' Heavyweight Passenger Set	320 ____
HW8020	MKT 72' Heavyweight Passenger Set	320 ____
HW8200	Heavyweight Coach	70 ____
HW8201	C&NW Heavyweight Coach	70 ____
HW8202	Southern Crescent Heavyweight Coach	70 ____
HW8203	UP Heavyweight Coach	70 ____
HW8204	NH Heavyweight Coach	70 ____
HW8205	NYC Heavyweight Coach	70 ____
HW8206	ATSF Heavyweight Coach	70 ____
HW8207	D&RGW Heavyweight Coach	70 ____
HW8208	C&NW Heavyweight Coach	70 ____
HW8209	PRR Heavyweight Coach	70 ____
HW8210	PRR Pullman Heavyweight Coach	70 ____
HW8211	MILW Heavyweight Coach	70 ____
HW8212	SP Heavyweight Coach	70 ____
HW8213	Heavweight Pullman, black roof	70 ____
HW8215	SP Heavyweight Passenger Coach, gray	70 ____
HW8216	C&O Heavyweight Passenger Coach	70 ____
HW8217	CNJ Heavyweight Coach	70 ____
HW8218	NH Heavyweight Coach	70 ____
HW8220	MKT Heavyweight Coach	70 ____
HX8100	80' Pullman Heavyweight 12-1 Sleeper Car	70 ____
HX8200	80' Pullman Heavyweight 10-1 Sleeper Car	70 ____
HX8300	80' Pullman Heavyweight Cafe	70 ____
HX8301	80' Pullman Heavyweight Cafe	70 ____
HX8302	NYC 80' Pullman Heavyweight Cafe	70 ____
HX8303	PRR 80' Pullman Heavyweight Cafe	70 ____
HX8304	CN 80' Pullman Heavyweight Cafe	70 ____
J3a	NYC J3a Class Hudson 4-6-4 Locomotive, tender	360 ____
K46201	PRR K4 4-6-2 Torpedo Locomotive, DC, bronze	400 ____
K46201AC	PRR K4 4-6-2 Torpedo Locomotive, AC, bronze	400 ____
K46202	PRR K4 4-6-2 Torpedo Locomotive, DC, green	400 ____
K46202AC	PRR K4 4-6-2 Torpedo Locomotive, AC, green	400 ____
PABA400	Alco PA1 Diesel ABA Set	565 ____
PABA401	PRR Alco PA1 Diesel ABA Set, freight scheme, green	565 ____
PABA402	ATSF Alco PA1 Diesel ABA Set, warbonnet, tuscan	565 ____
PABA403	NYC Alco PA1 Diesel ABA Set	565 ____
PABA404	NYC Alco PA2 Diesel ABA Set	565 ____
PABA405	NYC System Alco PA1 Diesel ABA Set	565 ____
PABA406	D&RGW Alco PA1 Diesel ABA Set	565 ____
PABA407	NH Alco PA1 Diesel ABA Set, McGuiness scheme	565 ____
PABA408	UP Alco PA1 Diesel ABA Set	565 ____

			Retail
____	**PABA409**	ATSF Alco PA1 Diesel ABA Set, warbonnet scheme	565
____	**PABA410**	ATSF Alco PA1 Diesel ABA Set, freight scheme	565
____	**PABA411**	D&H Alco PA1 Diesel ABA Set	565
____	**PABA412**	SP Daylight Alco PA1 Diesel ABA Set	585
____	**RS3000**	Alco RS3 Diesel	190
____	**RS3001**	Conrail Alco RS3 Diesel	190
____	**RS3002**	Cotton Belt Alco RS3 Diesel	190
____	**RS3003**	Erie-Lackawanna Alco RS3 Diesel	190
____	**RS3004**	GN Alco RS3 Diesel	190
____	**RS3005**	NH Alco RS3 Diesel	190
____	**RS3006**	NYC Alco RS3 Diesel	190
____	**RS3007**	PRR Alco RS3 Diesel	190
____	**RS3014**	Rock Island RS3 Diesel	190
____	**S1200**	Baldwin S12 Diesel	170
____	**S1201**	NH Baldwin S12 Diesel	170
____	**S1202**	C&NW Baldwin S12 Diesel	170
____	**S1203**	Conrail Baldwin S12 Diesel	170
____	**S1204**	Erie-Lackawanna Baldwin S12 Diesel	170
____	**S1205**	Erie-Lackawanna Baldwin S12 Diesel	170
____	**S1206**	Southern Baldwin S12 Diesel	180
____	**S1207**	NYC Baldwin S12 Diesel	170
____	**S1208**	PRR Baldwin S12 Diesel	170
____	**S1209**	ATSF Baldwin S12 Diesel	170
____	**S1210**	SP Baldwin S12 Diesel	170
____	**S1211**	UP Baldwin S12 Diesel	170
____	**S1212**	D&RGW Baldwin S12 Diesel	170
____	**S1213**	D&RGW Baldwin S12 Diesel	170
____	**S1214**	CB&Q Baldwin S12 Diesel	180
____	**S1215**	BN Baldwin S12 Diesel	170
____	**S1216**	BN Baldwin S12 Diesel	170
____	**S1217**	BN Baldwin S12 Diesel	170
____	**S1218**	BN Baldwin S12 Diesel	170
____	**S1219**	B&O Baldwin S12 Diesel	170
____	**S1220**	IC Baldwin S12 Diesel	170
____	**S1221**	IC Baldwin S12 Diesel	170
____	**S1222**	CP Baldwin S12 Diesel	170
____	**S1223**	CP Baldwin S12 Diesel	170
____	**S1224**	SP Baldwin S12 Diesel	170
____	**SC65T**	Trailer Train 5-Unit Spine Set	160
____	**SD60EMD**	SD60 Diesel, long nose	250
____	**SD60EMDAA**	SD60 Diesel AA Set, long nose	450
____	**SD6000**	SD60 Diesel, long nose	250
____	**SD6000AA**	SD60 Diesel AA Set, long nose	450
____	**SD6000Low**	SD60 Diesel, low nose	250
____	**SD6000LowAA**	SD60 Diesel AA Set, low nose	450

AMERICAN MODELS 1981-2015

Retail

SD6000M	SD60 Diesel, wide cab	250 ____
SD6000MAA	SD60 Diesel AA Set, wide cab	450 ____
SD6002	C&NW SD60 Diesel, long nose	250 ____
SD6002AA	C&NW SD60 Diesel AA Set, long nose	450 ____
SD6003M	Conrail SD60 Diesel, wide cab	250 ____
SD6003MAA	Conrail SD60 Diesel AA Set, wide cab	450 ____
SD6011	UP SD60 Diesel, long nose	250 ____
SD6011AA	UP SD60 Diesel AA Set, long nose	450 ____
SD6011M	UP SD60 Diesel, wide cab	250 ____
SD6011MAA	UP SD60 Diesel AA Set, wide cab	450 ____
SD6012	BN SD60 Diesel, long nose	250 ____
SD6012AA	BN SD60 Diesel AA Set, long nose	450 ____
SD6012M	BN SD60 Diesel, wide cab	250 ____
SD6012MAA	BN SD60 Diesel AA Set, wide cab	450 ____
SD6013	CSX SD60 Diesel, long nose	250 ____
SD6013AA	CSX SD60 Diesel AA Set, long nose	450 ____
SD6013M	CSX SD60 Diesel, wide cab	250 ____
SD6013MAA	CSX SD60 Diesel AA Set, wide cab	450 ____
SD6015	Soo Line SD60 Diesel, long nose	250 ____
SD6015AA	Soo Line SD60 Diesel AA Set, long nose	450 ____
SD6015M	Soo Line SD60 Diesel, wide cab	250 ____
SD6015MAA	Soo Line SD60 Diesel AA Set, wide cab	450 ____
SD6024	NS SD60 Diesel, long nose	250 ____
SD6024AA	NS SD60 Diesel AA Set, long nose	450 ____
SD6025M	BNSF SD60 Diesel, wide cab	250 ____
SD6025MAA	BNSF SD60 Diesel AA Set, wide cab	450 ____
SDK2053	Transformer	110 ____
SLBSP2	Amtrak Superliner Set, phase II	370 ____
SLBSP3	Amtrak Superliner Set, phase III	370 ____
T-1	UP 40' Semi Trailer	13 ____
T-2	Southern 40' Semi Trailer	13 ____
T-3	BN 40' Semi Trailer	13 ____
T-4	CSX 40' Semi Trailer	13 ____
T-5	D&RGW 40' Semi Trailer	13 ____
T-6	ATSF 40' Semi Trailer	13 ____
T-7	SP 40' Semi Trailer	13 ____
T-8	Quantum 40' Semi Trailer	13 ____
T-9	IC 40' Semi Trailer	13 ____
T-10	CN&W 40' Semi Trailer	13 ____
T-11	Conrail 40' Semi Trailer	13 ____
T-12	American President Line 40' Semi Trailer	13 ____
T-13	K-Line 40' Semi Trailer	13 ____
T-14	Evergreen 40' Semi Trailer	13 ____
T-15	N&W 40' Semi Trailer	13 ____
T-16	Transamerica 40' Semi Trailer	13 ____
T-17	MP 40' Semi Trailer	13 ____

____ T-18	SP 40' Semi Trailer	13
____ T148B	Bumper 2-pack	8
____ T148C30	30-degree Crossing	25
____ T148C75	75-degree Crossing	20
____ T148L	27"-radius Turnout, left hand, throw bar	33
____ T148L-HT	27"-radius Turnout, left hand, hand throw	38
____ T148L-PW	27"-radius Turnout, left hand, powered	48
____ T148R	27"-radius Turnout, right hand, throw bar	33
____ T148R-HT	27"-radius Turnout, right hand, hand throw	38
____ T148R-PW	27"-radius Turnout, right hand, powered	48
____ T148UNC	Electric Uncoupler	18
____ T710	Rail Joiners, 16 pieces	3
____ T710INS	Rail Joiners, insulated, 16 pieces	4
____ T711	Terminal with wire	2
____ T14812	12" Straight Track	4
____ T14821	21"-radius S-42 Track	4
____ T14824	24"-radius S-48 Track	5
____ T14827	27"-radius S-54 Track	5
____ T14836	3' Flex Track	11
____ TM00AC	FM H-24-66 Diesel	270
____ TM00DC	FM H-24-66 Diesel, scale or hi-rail	250
____ TM00AAAC	FM H-24-66 Diesel AA Set	500
____ TM00AADC	FM H-24-66 Diesel AA Set, scale or hi-rail	470
____ TM01AC	C&NW FM H-24-66 Diesel	270
____ TM01DC	C&NW FM H-24-66 Diesel, scale or hi-rail	250
____ TM01AAAC	C&NW FM H-24-66 Diesel AA Set	500
____ TM01AADC	C&NW FM H-24-66 Diesel AA Set, scale or hi-rail	470
____ TM02AC	Lackawanna FM H-24-66 Diesel	270
____ TM02DC	Lackawanna FM H-24-66 Diesel, scale or hi-rail	250
____ TM02AAAC	Lackawanna FM H-24-66 Diesel AA Set	500
____ TM02AADC	Lackawanna FM H-24-66 Diesel AA Set, scale or hi-rail	470
____ TM03AC	Pennsylvania FM H-24-66 Diesel	270
____ TM03DC	Pennsylvania FM H-24-66 Diesel, scale or hi-rail	250
____ TM03AAAC	Pennsylvania FM H-24-66 Diesel AA Set	500
____ TM03AADC	Pennsylvania FM H-24-66 Diesel AA Set, scale or hi-rail	470
____ TM04AC	Reading FM H-24-66 Diesel	270
____ TM04DC	Reading FM H-24-66 Diesel, scale or hi-rail	250
____ TM04AAAC	Reading FM H-24-66 Diesel AA Set	500
____ TM04AADC	Reading FM H-24-66 Diesel AA Set, scale or hi-rail	470
____ TM05AC	SP FM H-24-66 Diesel	270
____ TM05DC	SP FM H-24-66 Diesel, scale or hi-rail	250

Retail

TM05AAAC	SP FM H-24-66 Diesel AA Set	500	____
TM05AADC	SP FM H-24-66 Diesel AA Set, scale or hi-rail	470	____
TM06AC	Virginian FM H-24-66 Diesel	270	____
TM06DC	Virginian FM H-24-66 Diesel, scale or hi-rail	250	____
TM06AAAC	Virginian FM H-24-66 Diesel AA Set	500	____
TM06AADC	Virginian FM H-24-66 Diesel AA Set, scale or hi-rail	470	____
TM07AC	CNJ FM H-24-66 Diesel	270	____
TM07DC	CNJ FM H-24-66 Diesel, scale or hi-rail	250	____
TM07AAAC	CNJ FM H-24-66 Diesel AA Set	500	____
TM07AADC	CNJ FM H-24-66 Diesel AA Set, scale or hi-rail	470	____
TM08AC	CP FM H-24-66 Diesel	270	____
TM08DC	CP FM H-24-66 Diesel, scale or hi-rail	250	____
TM08AAAC	CP FM H-24-66 Diesel AA Set	500	____
TM08AADC	CP FM H-24-66 Diesel AA Set, scale or hi-rail	470	____
TM09AC	NH FM H-24-66 Diesel	270	____
TM09DC	NH FM H-24-66 Diesel, scale or hi-rail	250	____
TM09AAAC	NH FM H-24-66 Diesel AA Set	500	____
TM09AADC	NH FM H-24-66 Diesel AA Set, scale or hi-rail	470	____
TM10AC	Wabash FM H-24-66 Diesel	270	____
TM10DC	Wabash FM H-24-66 Diesel, scale or hi-rail	250	____
TM10AAAC	Wabash FM H-24-66 Diesel AA Set	500	____
TM10AADC	Wabash FM H-24-66 Diesel AA Set, scale or hi-rail	470	____
TMC-L	Left Hand Turnout Powering Kit	20	____
TMC-R	Right Hand Turnout Powering Kit	20	____
TMDAC	Demonstrator FM H-24-66 Diesel	270	____
TMDDC	Demonstrator FM H-24-66 Diesel, scale or hi-rail	250	____
TMDAAAC	Demonstrator FM H-24-66 Diesel AA Set	500	____
TMDAADC	Demonstrator FM H-24-66 Diesel AA Set, scale or hi-rail	470	____
TML	Turnout Motor Kit, left hand	14	____
TMR	Turnout Motor Kit, right hand	14	____
TSP	Throw Bar Spring	1	____
TWS103	Rail Weathering Solution, 3 oz.	11	____
U2500AC	U25B Diesel	230	____
U2500DC	U25B Diesel	190	____
U2500AC-DUAL	U25B Diesel Set	430	____
U2500DC-DUAL	U25B Diesel Set	370	____
U2501AC	Burlington U25B Diesel	230	____
U2501DC	Burlington U25B Diesel	190	____
U2501AC-DUAL	Burlington U25B Diesel Set	430	____
U2501DC-DUAL	Burlington U25B Diesel Set	370	____
U2502AC	C&O U25B Diesel	230	____
U2502DC	C&O U25B Diesel	190	____
U2502AC-DUAL	C&O U25B Diesel Set	430	____

____ **U2502DC-DUAL**	C&O U25B Diesel Set	370
____ **U2503AC**	Erie-Lack. U25B Diesel	230
____ **U2503DC**	Erie-Lack. U25B Diesel	190
____ **U2503AC-DUAL**	Erie-Lack. U25B Diesel Set	430
____ **U2503DC-DUAL**	Erie-Lack. U25B Diesel Set	370
____ **U2504AC**	Frisco U25B Diesel	230
____ **U2504DC**	Frisco U25B Diesel	190
____ **U2504AC-DUAL**	Frisco U25B Diesel Set	430
____ **U2504DC-DUAL**	Frisco U25B Diesel Set	370
____ **U2505AC**	GN U25B Diesel	230
____ **U2505DC**	GN U25B Diesel	190
____ **U2505AC-DUAL**	GN U25B Diesel Set	430
____ **U2505DC-DUAL**	GN U25B Diesel Set	370
____ **U2506AC**	NH U25B Diesel	230
____ **U2506DC**	NH U25B Diesel	190
____ **U2506AC-DUAL**	NH U25B Diesel Set	430
____ **U2506DC-DUAL**	NH U25B Diesel Set	370
____ **U2507AC**	RI U25B Diesel	230
____ **U2507DC**	RI U25B Diesel	190
____ **U2507AC-DUAL**	RI U25B Diesel Set	430
____ **U2507DC-DUAL**	RI U25B Diesel Set	370
____ **U2508AC**	Santa Fe U25B Diesel	230
____ **U2508DC**	Santa Fe U25B Diesel	190
____ **U2508AC-DUAL**	Santa Fe U25B Diesel Set	430
____ **U2508DC-DUAL**	Santa Fe U25B Diesel Set	370
____ **U2509AC**	SP U25B Diesel	230
____ **U2509DC**	SP U25B Diesel	190
____ **U2509AC-DUAL**	SP U25B Diesel Set	430
____ **U2509DC-DUAL**	SP U25B Diesel Set	370

Unnumbered Items

____ **Limited Run**	Wisconsin Central GP35 "728"	220

Retail

35-1001	15" Straight Track, 6-pack	40	____
35-1002	10" Straight Track, 6-pack	35	____
35-1003	5" Straight Track, 6-pack	30	____
35-1004	40" Flex Track, 6-pack	60	____
35-1005	40" Flex Track, 24-pack	220	____
35-1006	20" Radius 30 Degree Curved Track, 6-pack	35	____
35-1007	20" Radius 15 Degree Half Curved Track, 6-pack	30	____
35-1008	25" Radius 30 Degree Curved Track, 6-pack	38	____
35-1009	25" Radius 15 Degree Half Curved Track, 6-pack	33	____
35-1010	30" Radius 30 Degree Curved Track, 6-pack	40	____
35-1011	30" Radius 15 Degree Half Curved Track, 6-pack	35	____
35-1012	STrax Railjoiner, 36-pack	10	____
35-1013	STrax Railjoiner, insulated,36-pack	10	____
35-1014	Flex Track Railjoiner, 36-pack	8	____
35-1016	American Flyer Railjoiner Adapter, 36-pack	10	____
35-1017	STrax Railjoiner Feeder Wire,12-pack	10	____
35-1018	No. 3 Remote Control Switch, right hand	70	____
35-1019	No. 3 Remote Control Switch, left hand)	70	____
35-1020	Switch Controller with 40" harness extension	15	____
35-1021	5" Bumper with operating warning light	22	____
35-1022	5" Operating Uncoupler Track	25	____
35-1023	5" Operating Accessory Track	25	____
35-1101	AAR 70-Ton Friction Bearing Truck, hi-rail	20	____
35-1102	AAR 70-Ton Friction Bearing Truck, scale	20	____
35-1103	AAR Type Y Truck, hi-rail	20	____
35-1104	AAR Type Y Truck, scale	20	____
35-1105	Barber S2 70 Ton Roller Bearing Truck, hi-rail	20	____
35-1106	Barber S2 70 Ton Roller Bearing Truck, scale	20	____
35-1107	American Flyer Compatible Freight Car Coupler	5	____
35-1108	33" Insulated Wheel 4-pack, hi-rail	13	____
35-1109	Code 110 33" Insulated Wheel 4-pack, scale	13	____
35-1110	Kadee Compatible Freight Car Coupler, scale	7	____
35-90001	No. 23796 Saw Mill	120	____
35-90002	No. 23772 Water Tower with bubbling pipe	120	____
35-90003	No. 23769 Revolving Aircraft Beacon	120	____
35-90004	No. 23774 Floodlight Tower	120	____
35-90005	No. 787 Log Loader	200	____
35-90006	Lamplighter	180	____
35-20001-1	Jersey Central F3 Diesel A Unit "52"	380	____

____	**35-20002-1**	Jersey Central F3 Diesel A Unit "55"	380
____	**35-20003-3**	Jersey Central F3 Diesel A Unit "56," nonpowered	200
____	**35-20004-1**	Jersey Central F3 Diesel B Unit "D"	360
____	**35-20005-3**	Jersey Central F3 Diesel B Unit "B," nonpowered	190
____	**35-20006-1**	New York Central F3 Diesel A Unit "1608"	380
____	**35-20007-1**	New York Central F3 Diesel A Unit "1635"	380
____	**35-20008-3**	New York Central F3 Diesel A Unit "1616," nonpowered	200
____	**35-20009-1**	New York Central F3 Diesel B Unit "2413"	360
____	**35-20010-3**	New York Central F3 Diesel B Unit "2408," nonpowered	190
____	**35-20011-1**	Pennsylvania F3 Diesel A Unit "9508"	380
____	**35-20012-1**	Pennsylvania F3 Diesel A Unit "9509"	380
____	**35-20013-3**	Pennsylvania F3 Diesel A Unit "9517," nonpowered	200
____	**35-20014-1**	Pennsylvania F3 Diesel B Unit "9512B"	360
____	**35-20015-3**	Pennsylvania F3 Diesel B Unit "9508," nonpowered	190
____	**35-20016-1**	Seaboard F3 Diesel A Unit "4024"	380
____	**35-20017-1**	Seaboard F3 Diesel A Unit "4027"	380
____	**35-20018-3**	Seaboard F3 Diesel A Unit "4029," nonpowered	200
____	**35-20019-1**	Santa Fe F3 Diesel A Unit "18"	380
____	**35-20020-1**	Santa Fe F3 Diesel A Unit "19C"	380
____	**35-20021-3**	Santa Fe F3 Diesel A Unit "24," nonpowered	200
____	**35-20022-1**	Santa Fe F3 Diesel B Unit "18A"	360
____	**35-20023-3**	Santa Fe F3 Diesel B Unit "24B," nonpowered	190
____	**35-20024-1**	Union Pacific F3 Diesel A Unit "1404A"	380
____	**35-20025-1**	Union Pacific F3 Diesel A Unit "1407A"	380
____	**35-20026-3**	Union Pacific F3 Diesel A Unit "1441A," nonpowered	200
____	**35-20027-1**	Union Pacific F3 Diesel B Unit "1471B"	360
____	**35-20028-3**	Union Pacific F3 Diesel B Unit "1446B," nonpowered	190
____	**35-70001**	Milwaukee Road PS2 Hopper 6-Car Set	330
____	**35-70002**	Norfolk Southern PS2 Hopper 6-Car Set	330
____	**35-70003**	BNSF PS2 Hopper 6-Car Set	330
____	**35-70004**	Southern PS2 Hopper 6-Car Set	330
____	**35-70005**	Bessemer & Lake Erie PS2 Hopper 6-Car Set	330
____	**35-70006**	Detroit Toledo & Ironton PS2 Hopper 6-Car Set	330
____	**35-70007**	Lehigh Valley PS2 Hopper 6-Car Set	330
____	**35-70008**	Maryland Midland PS2 Hopper 6-Car Set	330
____	**35-70009**	Milwaukee Road Ore Car 6-Car Set	330
____	**35-70010**	Duluth Missabe & Iron Range Ore Car 6-Car Set	330
____	**35-70011**	Chicago Northwestern Ore Car 6-Car Set	330

Retail

35-70012	Canadian Pacific Ore Car 6-Car Set	330	____
35-70013	SOO Line Ore Car 6-Car Set	330	____
35-70014	Canadian National Ore Car 6-Car Set	330	____
35-70015	Bessemer & Lake Erie Ore Car 6-Car Set	330	____
35-70016	Great Northern Ore Car 6-Car Set	330	____
35-74000	Baltimore & Ohio Steel Rebuilt Boxcar "466013"	55	____
35-74001	Christmas Steel Rebuilt Boxcar "2013"	60	____
35-74002	Boston & Maine Steel Rebuilt Boxcar "73022"	60	____
35-74003	Boston & Maine Steel Rebuilt Boxcar "73025"	60	____
35-74004	New Haven Steel Rebuilt Boxcar "36454"	60	____
35-74005	New Haven Steel Rebuilt Boxcar "36450"	60	____
35-74006	New York Central Steel Rebuilt Boxcar "174992"	60	____
35-74007	New York Central Steel Rebuilt Boxcar "174995"	60	____
35-74008	Norfolk & Western Steel Rebuilt Boxcar "43628"	60	____
35-74009	Norfolk & Western Steel Rebuilt Boxcar "43630"	60	____
35-74010	Western Maryland Steel Rebuilt Boxcar "29076"	60	____
35-74011	Western Maryland Steel Rebuilt Boxcar "29083"	60	____
35-74012	Santa Fe Steel Rebuilt Boxcar "145002"	60	____
35-74013	Santa Fe Steel Rebuilt Boxcar "145005"	60	____
35-74014	Union Pacific Steel Rebuilt Boxcar "181679"	60	____
35-74015	Union Pacific Steel Rebuilt Boxcar "181680"	60	____
35-75001	Milwaukee Road PS2 Hopper "99618"	60	____
35-75002	Milwaukee Road PS2 Hopper "99614"	60	____
35-75003	Norfolk Southern PS2 Hopper "233548"	60	____
35-75004	Norfolk Southern PS2 Hopper "233635"	60	____
35-75005	Maryland Midland PS2 Hopper "5152"	60	____
35-75006	Maryland Midland PS2 Hopper "5186"	60	____
35-75007	Lehigh Valley PS2 Hopper "50835"	60	____
35-75008	Lehigh Valley PS2 Hopper "50879"	60	____
35-75009	Bessemer & Lake Erie PS2 Hopper "3732"	60	____
35-75010	Bessemer & Lake Erie PS2 Hopper "3735"	60	____
35-75011	Southern PS2 Hopper "95420"	60	____
35-75012	Southern PS2 Hopper "95462"	60	____
35-75013	Detroit Toledo & Ironton PS2 Hopper "11120"	60	____
35-75014	Detroit Toledo & Ironton PS2 Hopper "11135"	60	____
35-75015	BNSF PS2 Hopper "405600"	60	____
35-75016	BNSF PS2 Hopper "405619"	60	____
35-75017	Bessemer & Lake Erie Ore Car "20090"	60	____
35-75018	Bessemer & Lake Erie Ore Car "20093"	60	____
35-75019	Canadian National Ore Car "123060"	60	____
35-75020	Canadian National Ore Car "123064"	60	____
35-75021	Canadian Pacific Ore Car "377120"	60	____

___ 35-75022	Canadian Pacific Ore Car "377128"	60
___ 35-75023	Chicago Northwestern Ore Car "111542"	60
___ 35-75024	Chicago Northwestern Ore Car "111548"	60
___ 35-75025	Duluth Missabe & Iron Range Ore Car "31050"	60
___ 35-75026	Duluth Missabe & Iron Range Ore Car "31056"	60
___ 35-75027	Great Northern Ore Car "89001"	60
___ 35-75028	Great Northern Ore Car "89003"	60
___ 35-75029	Milwaukee Road Ore Car "76712"	60
___ 35-75030	Milwaukee Road Ore Car "76730"	60
___ 35-75031	SOO Line Ore Car "81950"	60
___ 35-75032	SOO Line Ore Car "81956"	60
35-78001 ___	Fairmont Creamery 40' Wood-sided Reefer "30210"	60
35-78002 ___	Fairmont Creamery 40' Wood-sided Reefer "30219"	60
___ 35-78003	Fulton Market 40' Wood-sided Reefer "10400"	60
___ 35-78004	Fulton Market 40' Wood-sided Reefer "10402"	60
35-78005 ___	Jelke Good Luck Margarine 40' Wood-sided Reefer "10803"	60
35-78006 ___	Jelke Good Luck Margarine 40' Wood-sided Reefer "10805"	60
35-78007 ___	Krey's Ham & Bacon 40' Wood-sided Reefer "873"	60
35-78008 ___	Krey's Ham & Bacon 40' Wood-sided Reefer "875"	60
35-78009 ___	M.K. Goetz Brewery 40' Wood-sided Reefer "14310"	60
35-78010 ___	M.K. Goetz Brewery 40' Wood-sided Reefer "14313"	60
35-78011 ___	Pacific Fruit Express 40' Wood-sided Reefer "74780"	60
35-78012 ___	Pacific Fruit Express 40' Wood-sided Reefer "74781"	60
___ 35-78013	Santa Fe 40' Wood-sided Reefer "25090"	60
___ 35-78014	Santa Fe 40' Wood-sided Reefer "25094"	60
___ 35-78015	Senate Beer 40' Wood-sided Reefer "100"	60
___ 35-78016	Senate Beer 40' Wood-sided Reefer "105"	60

Retail

00001	70-ton Truck, friction bearing, Code 110, pair	10 ___
00002	70-ton Truck, friction bearing, hi-rail, pair	10 ___
00003	70-ton Truck, roller bearing, Code 110, pair	10 ___
00004	70-ton Truck, roller bearing, hi-rail, pair	10 ___
00005	Freight Coupler, AF compatible, pair	3 ___
00006	B&M PS-2 2-bay Covered Hopper	50 ___
00007	NYC PS-2 2-bay Covered Hopper	50 ___
00008	PRR PS-2 2-bay Covered Hopper, scheme I	50 ___
00009	ATSF PS-2 2-bay Covered Hopper, scheme I #1	50 ___
00010	Wabash PS-2 2-bay Covered Hopper	50 ___
00011	WM PS-2 2-bay Covered Hopper	50 ___
00012	BN PS-2 2-bay Covered Hopper, scheme I	50 ___
00013	Chessie (WM) PS-2 2-bay Covered Hopper	50 ___
00014	C&NW (M&StL) PS-2 2-bay Covered Hopper, scheme I	50 ___
00015	Conrail PS-2 2-bay Covered Hopper, scheme I	50 ___
00016	Soo Line PS-2 2-bay Covered Hopper #1	50 ___
00017	SP PS-2 2-bay Covered Hopper, scheme I	50 ___
00018	CNJ PS-2 2-bay Covered Hopper, scheme I	50 ___
00019	MILW PS-2 2-bay Covered Hopper	50 ___
00020	Trona PS-2 2-bay Covered Hopper	50 ___
00021	PS-2 2-bay Covered Hopper, gray	50 ___
00022	PRR PS-2 2-bay Covered Hopper, scheme I	50 ___
00023	70-ton Truck, roller bearing, Code 110, 36" wheels, pair	7 ___
00024	33" Scale Wheel Set, Code 10, 4-pack	4 ___
00025	33" Wheel Set, hi-rail, 4-pack	4 ___
00026	PRR PS-2 2-bay Covered Hopper, scheme II	50 ___
00027	B&O PS-2 2-bay Covered Hopper	50 ___
00028	D&RGW PS-2 2-bay Covered Hopper	50 ___
00029	ATSF PS-2 2-bay Covered Hopper, scheme I #2	50 ___
00030	MEC PS-2 2-bay Covered Hopper	50 ___
00031	UP PS-2 2-bay Covered Hopper	50 ___
00032	Wisconsin Central PS-2 2-bay Covered Hopper	50 ___
00033	LV PS-2 2-bay Covered Hopper	50 ___
00034	Rock Island PS-2 2-bay Covered Hopper #1	50 ___
00035	Rock Island PS-2 2-bay Covered Hopper #2	50 ___
00036	DT&I PS-2 2-bay Covered Hopper (NASG)	50 ___
00037	CSX PS-2 2-bay Covered Hopper	50 ___
00038	C&NW PS-2 2-bay Covered Hopper, scheme I	50 ___
00039	C&NW (CGW) PS-2 2-bay Covered Hopper	50 ___
00040	BN PS-2 2-bay Covered Hopper, scheme II	50 ___
00041	DT&I PS-2 2-bay Covered Hopper #2 (NASG)	50 ___

____ **00042**	IMCO PS-2 2-bay Covered Hopper	50
____ **00043**	PS-2 2-bay Covered Hopper, roller bearing, gray	50
____ **00044**	Chessie (B&O) PS-2 2-bay Covered Hopper	50
____ **00045**	50-ton Truck, Code 110, pair	10
____ **00046**	50-ton Truck, hi-rail, pair	10
____ **00047**	50-ton Type Y Truck, Code 110, pair	10
____ **00048**	50-ton Type Y Truck, hi-rail, pair	10
____ **00049**	Stock Car, red	50
____ **00050**	UP Stock Car #1	50
____ **00051**	UP Stock Car #2	50
____ **00052**	D&RGW Stock Car	50
____ **00053**	C&NW Stock Car #1	50
____ **00054**	C&NW Stock Car #2	50
____ **00055**	ACL Stock Car	50
____ **00056**	GN Stock Car #1	50
____ **00057**	GN Stock Car #2	50
____ **00058**	PRR Stock Car #1	50
____ **00059**	PRR Stock Car #2	50
____ **00060**	ATSF Stock Car, scheme I #1	50
____ **00061**	ATSF Stock Car, scheme I #2	50
____ **00062**	NP Stock Car (Leventon Hobby)	50
____ **00063**	USRA Single-sheathed Boxcar, red	50
____ **00064**	NYC Stock Car	50
____ **00065**	WP Stock Car	50
____ **00066**	PRR USRA Single-sheathed Boxcar, scheme I #1	50
____ **00067**	PRR USRA Single-sheathed Boxcar, scheme I #2	50
____ **00068**	CB&Q (C&S) USRA Single-sheathed Boxcar	50
____ **00069**	CB&Q USRA Single-sheathed Boxcar	50
____ **00070**	MEC (PTM) USRA Single-sheathed Boxcar	50
____ **00071**	B&O USRA Single-sheathed Boxcar, scheme I	50
____ **00072**	SP USRA Single-sheathed Boxcar	50
____ **00073**	NYC USRA Single-sheathed Boxcar	50
____ **00074**	Yakima Valley USRA Single-sheathed Boxcar (NMRA)	50
____ **00075**	CP USRA Single-sheathed Boxcar	50
____ **00076**	GN PS-2 2-bay Covered Hopper	50
____ **00077**	NKP PS-2 2-bay Covered Hopper	50
____ **00078**	NYC (PL&E) PS-2 2-bay Covered Hopper	50
____ **00079**	Soo Line PS-2 2-bay Covered Hopper #2	50
____ **00080**	NYNH&H PS-2 2-bay Covered Hopper	50
____ **00081**	WP PS-2 2-bay Covered Hopper	50
____ **00082**	MKT PS-2 2-bay Covered Hopper	50
____ **00083**	BN PS-2 2-bay Covered Hopper, scheme II	50
____ **00084**	PC PS-2 2-bay Covered Hopper	50
____ **00085**	Chessie (CSXT) PS-2 2-bay Covered Hopper	50
____ **00086**	C&NW PS-2 2-bay Covered Hopper, scheme II	50

S-HELPER SERVICE 1994-2012

Retail

00087	Revere Sugar PS-2 2-bay Hopper (RSSVP Models)	75 ____
00088	Conrail PS-2 2-bay Covered Hopper, scheme II	50 ____
00089	GTW PS-2 2-bay Covered Hopper	50 ____
00090	Ready Mix Concrete PS-2 2-bay Covered Hopper	50 ____
00091	SP PS-2 2-bay Covered Hopper, scheme II	50 ____
00092	SW9 Diesel, black	200 ____
00093	ACL SW9 Diesel #1	200 ____
00094	ACL SW9 Diesel #2	200 ____
00097	B&O SW9 Diesel #1	200 ____
00098	B&O SW9 Diesel #2	200 ____
00099	B&M SW9 Diesel #1	200 ____
00100	B&M SW9 Diesel #2	200 ____
00101	BN SW9 Diesel #1	200 ____
00102	BN SW9 Diesel #2	200 ____
00103	CP SW9 Diesel #1	200 ____
00104	CP SW9 Diesel #2	200 ____
00105	CB&Q SW9 Diesel #1	200 ____
00106	CB&Q SW9 Diesel #2	200 ____
00107	Chessie (C&O) SW9 Diesel	200 ____
00108	Chessie (B&O) SW9 Diesel #1	200 ____
00109	C&NW SW9 Diesel #1	200 ____
00110	C&NW SW9 Diesel #2	200 ____
00111	Conrail SW9 Diesel, scheme I #1	200 ____
00112	Conrail SW9 Diesel, scheme I #2	200 ____
00113	Erie-Lackawanna SW9 Diesel #1	200 ____
00114	Erie-Lackawanna SW9 Diesel #2	200 ____
00115	NYC SW9 Diesel #1	200 ____
00116	NYC SW9 Diesel #2	200 ____
00117	PRR SW9 Diesel #1	200 ____
00118	PRR SW9 Diesel #2	200 ____
00119	ATSF SW9 Diesel #1	200 ____
00120	ATSF SW9 Diesel #2	200 ____
00121	UP SW9 Diesel, scheme I #1	200 ____
00122	UP SW9 Diesel, scheme I #2	200 ____
00123	UP Stock Car #3	50 ____
00124	40' Steel Rebuilt Boxcar, red	50 ____
00125	C&O 40' Steel Rebuilt Boxcar #1	50 ____
00126	C&NW 40' Steel Rebuilt Boxcar, scheme I	50 ____
00127	DL&W 40' Steel Rebuilt Boxcar	50 ____
00128	Frisco 40' Steel Rebuilt Boxcar, scheme I	50 ____
00129	NYC (PMKY) 40' Steel Rebuilt Boxcar #1	50 ____
00130	NYC (PMKY) 40' Steel Rebuilt Boxcar #2	50 ____
00131	PRR 40' Steel Rebuilt Boxcar, scheme I #1	50 ____
00132	PRR 40' Steel Rebuilt Boxcar, scheme I #2	50 ____
00133	ATSF "Scout" 40' Steel Rebuilt Boxcar	50 ____

_____ **00134**	ATSF "Grand Canyon" 40' Steel Rebuilt Boxcar	50
_____ **00135**	Vermont Central 40' Steel Rebuilt Boxcar	50
_____ **00136**	CN Stock Car #1	50
_____ **00137**	CB&Q Stock Car #1	50
_____ **00138**	MP Stock Car	50
_____ **00139**	MKT Stock Car	50
_____ **00140**	UP (Oregon Short Line) Stock Car, scheme I #1	40
_____ **00141**	Rutland USRA Single-sheathed Boxcar	50
_____ **00142**	Clinchfield USRA Single-sheathed Boxcar	50
_____ **00143**	Erie USRA Single-sheathed Boxcar	50
_____ **00144**	CMStP&P USRA Single-sheathed Boxcar	50
_____ **00145**	PRR USRA Single-sheathed Boxcar	50
_____ **00146**	Pacific Electric USRA Single-sheathed Boxcar	50
_____ **00147**	Wabash USRA Single-sheathed Boxcar	50
_____ **00148**	Chessie (B&O) SW9 Switcher #2	200
_____ **00149**	CN 40' Stock Car #2	50
_____ **00150**	CB&Q 40' Stock Car #2	50
_____ **00151**	MKT 40' Stock Car #2	50
_____ **00152**	UP (Oregon Short Line) 40' Stock Car, scheme I #2	40
_____ **00153**	C&O 40' Steel Rebuilt Boxcar #2	50
_____ **00154**	SLSF 40' Steel Rebuilt Boxcar, scheme I #2	50
_____ **00155**	Bulkhead Flatcar	56
_____ **00156**	BN Bulkhead Flatcar #1	56
_____ **00157**	BN Bulkhead Flatcar #2	56
_____ **00158**	CB&Q Bulkhead Flatcar #1	56
_____ **00159**	CB&Q Bulkhead Flatcar #2	56
_____ **00160**	D&RGW Bulkhead Flatcar	56
_____ **00161**	IC Bulkhead Flatcar #1	56
_____ **00162**	IC Bulkhead Flatcar #2	56
_____ **00163**	Southern Bulkhead Flatcar	56
_____ **00164**	UP Bulkhead Flatcar #1	56
_____ **00165**	UP Bulkhead Flatcar #2	56
_____ **00166**	Wabash Bulkhead Flatcar	56
_____ **00167**	Standard Flatcar, red	50
_____ **00168**	Standard Flatcar, black	50
_____ **00169**	BN Standard Flatcar	50
_____ **00170**	CB&Q Standard Flatcar	50
_____ **00171**	D&RGW Standard Flatcar	50
_____ **00172**	IC Standard Flatcar	50
_____ **00173**	Southern Standard Flatcar	50
_____ **00174**	UP Standard Flatcar, scheme I #1	50
_____ **00175**	Wabash Standard Flatcar	50
_____ **00176**	PRR Standard Flatcar #1	50
_____ **00177**	Flatcar with trailer	63
_____ **00178**	BAR Flatcar with trailer	63

00179	NKP Flatcar with trailer	63 ____
00180	Rock Island Flatcar with trailer	63 ____
00181	PRR Flatcar #1 with trailer	63 ____
00182	PRR Flatcar #2 with trailer	63 ____
00183	Seaboard Flatcar with trailer	63 ____
00184	UP Flatcar #1 with trailer	63 ____
00185	UP Flatcar #2 with trailer	63 ____
00186	Flatcar with trailer	63 ____
00187	C&NW Flatcar with trailer	63 ____
00188	C&NW Flatcar with trailer	63 ____
00189	NH Flatcar #1 with trailer	63 ____
00190	NH Flatcar #2 with trailer	63 ____
00191	NYC Flatcar #1 with trailer	63 ____
00192	NYC Flatcar #2 with trailer	63 ____
00193	TTX Flatcar with REA trailer, scheme I	63 ____
00194	TTX Flatcar with REA trailer, scheme II	63 ____
00195	35' Trailer, horizontal corrugations	16 ____
00196	35' Trailer, vertical ribs	16 ____
00197	B&A 35' Trailer, horizontal corrugations	16 ____
00198	NKP 35' Trailer, horizontal corrugations	16 ____
00199	Rock Island 35' Trailer, horizontal corrugations	16 ____
00200	PRR 35' Trailer, horizontal corrugations, scheme I	16 ____
00201	Seaboard 35' Trailer, horizontal corrugations	16 ____
00202	UP 35' Trailer, horizontal corrugations	16 ____
00203	C&NW 35' Trailer, vertical ribs	16 ____
00204	NYNH&H 35' Trailer, vertical ribs	16 ____
00205	NYC 35' Trailer, vertical ribs	16 ____
00206	REA 35' Trailer, vertical ribs, scheme I	16 ____
00207	REA 35' Trailer, vertical ribs, scheme II #1	16 ____
00208	B&A Standard Flatcar	50 ____
00209	C&NW Standard Flatcar	50 ____
00210	NH Standard Flatcar	50 ____
00211	NYC Standard Flatcar	50 ____
00212	NKP Standard Flatcar	50 ____
00213	PRR Standard Flatcar #1	50 ____
00214	Rock Island Standard Flatcar	50 ____
00215	Seaboard Standard Flatcar	50 ____
00216	UP Standard Flatcar, scheme II #1	50 ____
00217	Extended Vision Caboose	70 ____
00218	BN Extended Vision Caboose #1	70 ____
00219	BN Extended Vision Caboose #2	70 ____
00220	C&O Extended Vision Caboose #1	70 ____
00221	C&O Extended Vision Caboose #2	70 ____
00222	CB&Q Extended Vision Caboose, scheme I #1	70 ____
00223	CB&Q Extended Vision Caboose, scheme I #2	70 ____

____	00224	Chessie (B&O) Extended Vision Caboose #1	70
____	00225	Chessie (B&O) Extended Vision Caboose #2	70
____	00226	C&NW Extended Vision Caboose #1	70
____	00227	C&NW Extended Vision Caboose #2	70
____	00228	Conrail Extended Vision Caboose #1	70
____	00229	Conrail Extended Vision Caboose #2	70
____	00230	D&RGW Extended Vision Caboose #1	70
____	00231	D&RGW Extended Vision Caboose #2	70
____	00232	GN Extended Vision Caboose #1	70
____	00233	GN Extended Vision Caboose #2	70
____	00234	ICG Extended Vision Caboose #1	70
____	00235	ICG Extended Vision Caboose #2	70
____	00236	MP Extended Vision Caboose #1	70
____	00237	MP Extended Vision Caboose #2	70
____	00238	NP Extended Vision Caboose #1	70
____	00239	NP Extended Vision Caboose #2	70
____	00240	ATSF Extended Vision Caboose, scheme I #1	70
____	00241	ATSF Extended Vision Caboose, scheme I #2	70
____	00242	Seaboard Extended Vision Caboose #1	70
____	00243	Seaboard Extended Vision Caboose #2	70
____	00244	Soo Line Extended Vision Caboose #1	70
____	00245	Soo Line Extended Vision Caboose #2	70
____	00246	Evans Product Load for flatcar	10
____	00247	Gold Bond Product Load for flatcar, white	10
____	00248	Gold Bond Product Load for flatcar, red	10
____	00249	Johns Manville Product Load for flatcar	10
____	00250	Masonite Product Load for flatcar	10
____	00251	Plumb Creek Product Load for flatcar	10
____	00252	United States Gypsum Product Load for flatcar	10
____	00253	Rail Joiners, 12 pieces	5
____	00254	Insulated Rail Joiners, 12 pieces	3
____	00255	Rail Joiners with feeder wire, 12 pieces	8
____	00256	Track Starter Set, 16 pieces	75
____	00257	15" Straight Track, 6 pieces	40
____	00258	10" Straight Track, 6 pieces	33
____	00259	Curved Track, 20" radius, 30 degree, 6 pieces	33
____	00260	BN Standard Flatcar #2	50
____	00261	UP Standard Flatcar, scheme I #2	50
____	00262	B&M Flatcar with trailer (NASG)	63
____	00263	B&M Standard Flatcar (NASG)	50
____	00264	B&M 35' Trailer, vertical ribs (NASG)	16
____	00265	36" Scale Wheel Set, Code 110, 4-pack–99	4
____	00266	CMStP&P Extended Vision Caboose #1	70
____	00267	CMStP&P Extended Vision Caboose #2	70
____	00268	MEC Extended Vision Caboose, scheme I	78

00271	3-bay Covered Hopper	50 ___
00272	ATSF PS-2 3-bay Covered Hopper #1	50 ___
00273	BN PS-2 3-bay Covered Hopper #1	50 ___
00274	Chessie (B&O) PS-2 3-bay Covered Hopper #1	50 ___
00275	CB&Q PS-2 3-bay Covered Hopper, scheme I #1	50 ___
00276	C&NW PS-2 3-bay Covered Hopper, scheme I #2	50 ___
00277	Conrail PS-2 3-bay Covered Hopper #1	50 ___
00278	GN PS-2 3-bay Covered Hopper #1	50 ___
00279	Erie-Lackawanna PS-2 3-bay Covered Hopper #1	50 ___
00280	NYC PS-2 3-bay Covered Hopper #1	50 ___
00281	UP PS-2 3-bay Covered Hopper #1	50 ___
00282	C&NW (MStL) PS-2 2-bay Covered Hopper, scheme II #1	50 ___
00283	Jack Frost PS-2 2-bay Hopper #1 (RSSVP Models)	68 ___
00284	LNE PS-2 2-bay Covered Hopper #1	50 ___
00285	MStL PS-2 2-bay Covered Hopper #2	50 ___
00286	Central Soya PS-2 2-bay Covered Hopper #1	50 ___
00287	NAHX PS-2 2-bay Covered Hopper #1	50 ___
00288	NAHX PS-2 2-bay Covered Hopper #2	50 ___
00289	Diesel Engineer and Fireman Figure Set	6 ___
00290	AC/DC Reverse Unit with DCC socket	40 ___
00291	Curved Track, 20" radius, 15 degree, 6 pieces	27 ___
00292	Curved Track, 25" radius, 30 degree, 6 pieces	38 ___
00293	Curved Track, 25" radius, 15 degree, 6 pieces	28 ___
00294	Curved Track, 30" radius, 30 degree, 6 pieces	40 ___
00295	Locomotive Coupler, AF compatible, pair	4 ___
00297	5" Straight Track, 6 pieces	25 ___
00298	No. 3 Switch, right hand, remote control	55 ___
00299	No. 3 Switch, left hand, remote control	55 ___
00300	ATSF Flatcar with trailer, scheme I	70 ___
00301	B&O Flatcar with trailer	70 ___
00302	Maine Central Bulkhead Flatcar	56 ___
00303	CP Flatcar with Speedway trailer	70 ___
00304	GN Flatcar with trailer	70 ___
00305	NH Flatcar with Yale trailer	70 ___
00306	PRR Flatcar with trailer #3	70 ___
00307	TTX Flatcar with Carolina trailer	70 ___
00308	D&RGW Flatcar with trailer	70 ___
00309	UP Standard Flatcar #2	50 ___
00310	WM Flatcar with trailer	70 ___
00311	ATSF Standard Flatcar, scheme I	50 ___
00312	B&O Standard Flatcar	50 ___
00313	Maine Central Standard Flatcar	50 ___
00314	CP Standard Flatcar	50 ___
00315	GN Standard Flatcar, scheme I #1	50 ___
00316	NYNH&H Standard Flatcar #3	50 ___

		Retail
_____ **00317**	PRR Standard Flatcar #3	50
_____ **00318**	D&RGW Standard Flatcar	50
_____ **00319**	UP Standard Flatcar, scheme II #2	50
_____ **00320**	WM Standard Flatcar	50
_____ **00321**	ATSF 35' Trailer, horizontal corrugations, scheme I	16
_____ **00322**	B&O 35' Trailer, horizontal corrugations	16
_____ **00323**	Speedway 35' Trailer, horizontal corrugations	16
_____ **00324**	GN 35' Trailer "G322," horizontal corrugations	16
_____ **00325**	Yale 35' Trailer, vertical ribs	16
_____ **00326**	PRR 35' Trailer, vertical ribs, scheme II	16
_____ **00327**	Carolina 35' Trailer, vertical ribs	16
_____ **00328**	D&RGW 35' Trailer, horizontal corrugations	16
_____ **00329**	UP 35' Trailer #2, horizontal corrugations (NMRA)	16
_____ **00330**	WM 35' Trailer, vertical ribs	16
_____ **00331**	ATSF Bulkhead Flatcar #1	56
_____ **00332**	ATSF Bulkhead Flatcar #2	56
_____ **00333**	GN Bulkhead Flatcar #1	56
_____ **00334**	GN Bulkhead Flatcar #2	56
_____ **00335**	Soo Line Bulkhead Flatcar #1	56
_____ **00336**	Soo Line Bulkhead Flatcar #2	56
_____ **00337**	D&H Bulkhead Flatcar	56
_____ **00338**	Chessie (WM) Bulkhead Flatcar	56
_____ **00339**	ATSF Standard Flatcar, scheme II	50
_____ **00340**	GN Standard Flatcar, scheme I #2	50
_____ **00341**	Soo Line Standard Flatcar #2	50
_____ **00342**	Delaware & Hudson Standard Flatcar	50
_____ **00343**	Chessie (WM) Standard Flatcar	50
_____ **00344**	ATSF Set, 3 cars	100
_____ **00345**	C&NW Set, 3 cars	100
_____ **00346**	GN 40' Steel Rebuilt Boxcar, scheme 1 #1	50
_____ **00347**	GN 40' Steel Rebuilt Boxcar, scheme I #2	50
_____ **00348**	MP (IGN) "Eagle" 40' Steel Rebuilt Boxcar #1	50
_____ **00349**	MP (IGN) "Eagle" 40' Steel Rebuilt Boxcar #2	50
_____ **00350**	NYC Set, 3 cars	100
_____ **00351**	RS&P 40' Steel Rebuilt Boxcar	50
_____ **00352**	UP Set, 3 cars	100
_____ **00353**	Muncie & Western Ball Lines 40' Steel Rebuilt Boxcar #1	50
_____ **00354**	Truck with gear box, hi-rail wheels	10
_____ **00355**	Truck with gear box, Code 110 wheels	10
_____ **00356**	AC PCB/DCC Socket Harness Set, DC plug	40
_____ **00357**	Locomotive Coupler, AF compatible, pair	4
_____ **00358**	Caboose Conductor and Brakeman Figure Set	6
_____ **00359**	Caboose Coupler, AF compatible, pair	3
_____ **00362**	B&O F3 Diesel AB Set #1, phase II, sound	500
_____ **00363**	B&O F3 Diesel AB Set #2, phase II, sound	500

00364	CB&Q F3 Diesel AB Set #1, phase II, sound	500 ____
00365	CB&Q F3 Diesel AB Set #2, phase II, sound	500 ____
00366	C&NW F3 Diesel AB Set #1, phase II, sound	500 ____
00367	C&NW F3 Diesel AB Set #2, phase II, sound	500 ____
00368	DL&W F3 Diesel AB Set #1, phase II, sound	500 ____
00369	DL&W F3 Diesel AB Set #2, phase II, sound	500 ____
00370	Maine Central F3 Diesel AB Set #1, phase II, sound	500 ____
00371	Maine Central F3 Diesel AB Set #2, phase II, sound	500 ____
00372	NYC F3 Diesel AB Set #1, phase II, sound	500 ____
00373	NYC F3 Diesel A&B Set #2, phase II, sound	500 ____
00374	Southern F3 Diesel AB Set #1, phase II, sound	500 ____
00375	Southern F3 Diesel AB Set #2, phase II, sound	500 ____
00376	SP F3 Diesel AB Set #1, phase II, sound	500 ____
00377	SP F3 Diesel AB Set #2, phase II, sound	500 ____
00378	UP F3 Diesel AB Set #1, phase II, sound	500 ____
00379	UP F3 Diesel AB Set #2, phase II, sound	500 ____
00380	WP F3 Diesel AB Set #1, phase II, sound	500 ____
00381	WP F3 Diesel AB Set #2, phase II, sound	500 ____
00382	F3 Diesel AB Set, phase II, sound	500 ____
00383	Caboose Truck, roller bearing, Code 110, pair	10 ____
00384	Caboose Truck, roller bearing, hi-rail, pair	10 ____
00385	NYC F3 Diesel AB Freight Set #1, phase II, sound	500 ____
00386	NYC F3 Diesel AB Freight Set #2, phase II, sound	500 ____
00387	UP Flatcar with trailer (NMRA)	63 ____
00388	Boise Cascade Wrapped Lumber Load	10 ____
00389	Finlay Premium Wrapped Lumber Load	10 ____
00390	Western Carrier Wrapped Lumber Load	10 ____
00391	Weyerhauser Wrapped Lumber Load	10 ____
00392	Pulpwood Load	13 ____
00393	AF Track Adaptor, 8 pieces	5 ____
00394	Bulb, 2.5-volt, 2 pieces	2 ____
00395	Rail Joiner, insulated, yellow, 12 pieces	3 ____
00396	ATSF PS-2 3-bay Covered Hopper #2	50 ____
00397	BN PS-2 3-bay Covered Hopper #2	50 ____
00398	Chessie (B&O) PS-2 3-bay Covered Hopper #2	50 ____
00399	CB&Q PS-2 3-bay Covered Hopper, scheme I #2	50 ____
00400	C&NW PS-2 3-bay Covered Hopper, scheme I #2	50 ____
00401	Conrail PS-2 3-bay Covered Hopper #2	50 ____
00402	GN PS-2 3-bay Covered Hopper #2	50 ____
00403	Erie-Lackawanna PS-2 3-bay Covered Hopper #2	50 ____
00404	NYC PS-2 3-bay Covered Hopper #2	50 ____
00405	UP PS-2 3-bay Covered Hopper #2	50 ____
00407	C&NW (M&StL) PS-2 2-bay Hopper, scheme II #2	50 ____
00408	LNE PS-2 2-bay Covered Hopper #2	50 ____
00409	Central Soya PS-2 2-bay Covered Hopper #2	50 ____

Retail

00410	Roscoe, Snyder & Pacific 40' Steel Rebuilt Boxcar #2	50
00411	Muncie & Western Ball Lines 40' Steel Rebuilt Boxcar #2	50
00412	CB&Q PS-2 3-bay Covered Hopper, scheme II #1	50
00413	Jack Frost PS-2 2-bay Hopper #2 (RSSVP Models)	50
00414	Cedar Heights Clay PS-2 3-bay Covered Hopper	55
00415	Ann Arbor PS-2 2-bay Covered Hopper #1 (TCA)	50
00416	Ann Arbor PS-2 2-bay Covered Hopper #2 (TCA)	50
00417	M&StL PS-2 3-bay Covered Hopper #1	50
00418	M&StL PS-2 3-bay Covered Hopper #2	50
00419	M&StL PS-2 2-bay Covered Hopper #2	50
00420	CB&Q PS-2 3-bay Covered Hopper, scheme II #2	50
00421	Conrail SW9 Diesel Set, 4 cars	300
00422	BN SW9 Diesel Set, 5 cars	370
00423	ATSF SW9 Diesel Set, 6 cars	430
00425	Glencoe Skokie Valley Single-sheathed Boxcar (NMRA)	63
00426	Chesapeake & Ohio SW9 Diesel #1	200
00427	Chesapeake & Ohio SW9 Diesel #2	200
00428	Great Northern SW9 Diesel #1	200
00429	Great Northern SW9 Diesel #2	200
00430	D&RGW SW9 Diesel #1	200
00431	D&RGW SW9 Diesel #2	200
00432	ICG SW9 Diesel #1	200
00433	ICG SW9 Diesel #2	200
00434	Northern Pacific SW9 Diesel #1	200
00435	Northern Pacific SW9 Diesel #2	200
00436	UP SW9 Diesel, scheme II #1	200
00437	UP SW9 Diesel, scheme II #2	200
00438	SW1 Diesel	200
00439	Boston & Maine SW1 Diesel #1	200
00440	Boston & Maine SW1 Diesel #2	200
00441	Chessie (B&O) SW1 Diesel #1	200
00442	Chessie (B&O) SW1 Diesel #2	200
00443	C&NW SW1 Diesel #1	200
00444	C&NW SW1 Diesel #2	200
00445	WP SW1 Diesel #1	200
00446	WP SW1 Diesel #2	200
00447	CMStP&P SW1 Diesel #1	200
00448	CMStP&P SW1 Diesel #2	200
00449	PRR SW1 Diesel #1	200
00450	PRR SW1 Diesel #2	200
00451	Seaboard SW1 Diesel	200
00452	Soo Line SW1 Diesel	200
00453	Lehigh Valley SW1 Diesel #1	200
00454	Lehigh Valley SW1 Diesel #2	200
00455	SP SW1 Diesel #1	200

00456	SP SW1 Diesel #2	200 ___
00457	C&O SW9 Diesel Set, 6 cars	370 ___
00458	Conrail SW9 Diesel Set, 4 cars	300 ___
00459	D&RGW SW9 Diesel Set, 6 cars	430 ___
00460	GN SW9 Diesel Set, 6 cars	430 ___
00461	ICG SW9 Diesel Set, 5 cars	370 ___
00462	NP SW9 Diesel Set, 5 cars	370 ___
00463	No. 3 Manual Switch, right hand	40 ___
00464	No. 3 Manual Switch, left hand	40 ___
00465	40" Flextrack, 6 pieces	51 ___
00466	40" Flextrack, 24 pieces	186 ___
00468	5" Straight Track with lighted bumper	22 ___
00469	Flatcar with John Deere combine	55 ___
00470	Flatcar with IH Harvestor combine	55 ___
00471	Flatcar with John Deere log skidder	50 ___
00472	Flatcar with John Deere backhoe and front-end loader	60 ___
00473	Flatcar with 2 John Deere bulldozers	60 ___
00474	PRR PS-2 2-bay Covered Hopper, scheme II #1	50 ___
00475	PRR PS-2 2-bay Covered Hopper, scheme II #2	50 ___
00476	Wooden Billboard Reefer	53 ___
00477	Wooden Billboard Reefer, yellow	53 ___
00478	Wooden Billboard Reefer, orange	53 ___
00479	ART Wooden Billboard Reefer #1	53 ___
00480	ART Wooden Billboard Reefer #2	53 ___
00481	ATSF "Grand Canyon" Wooden Billboard Reefer	53 ___
00482	ATSF "El Capitan" Wooden Billboard Reefer	53 ___
00483	Burlington Wooden Billboard Reefer #1	53 ___
00484	Burlington Wooden Billboard Reefer #2	53 ___
00485	Robin Hood Beer Wooden Billboard Reefer #1	53 ___
00486	Robin Hood Beer Wooden Billboard Reefer #2	53 ___
00487	Gerber Wooden Billboard Reefer #1	53 ___
00489	LV Wooden Billboard Reefer #1	53 ___
00490	LV Wooden Billboard Reefer #2	53 ___
00491	North Western Wooden Billboard Reefer, scheme I #1	53 ___
00492	North Western Wooden Billboard Reefer, scheme I #2	53 ___
00493	North Western Wooden Billboard Reefer, scheme II #1	53 ___
00494	North Western Wooden Billboard Reefer, scheme II #2	53 ___
00495	Merchants Despatch Wooden Billboard Reefer #1	53 ___
00496	Merchants Despatch Wooden Billboard Reefer #2	53 ___
00497	Pacific Great Eastern Wooden Billboard Reefer	74 ___
00498	PFE Wooden Billboard Reefer #1	53 ___
00499	PFE Wooden Billboard Reefer #2	53 ___
00500	Tivoli Beer Wooden Billboard Reefer #1	53 ___
00501	Tivoli Beer Wooden Billboard Reefer #2	53 ___
00502	A&P Wooden Billboard Reefer #1	53 ___

_____ 00503	A&P Wooden Billboard Reefer #2	53
_____ 00504	Old Heidelberg Beer Wooden Billboard Reefer #1	53
_____ 00505	Old Heidelberg Beer Wooden Billboard Reefer #2	53
_____ 00506	Chateau Martin Wooden Billboard Reefer #1 (NASG)	53
_____ 00507	Chateau Martin Wooden Billboard Reefer #2 (NASG)	53
_____ 00508	Chateau Martin Wooden Billboard Reefer #3 (NASG)	53
_____ 00509	CUVA PS-2 2-bay Covered Hopper #1 (CVSG)	50
_____ 00510	CUVA PS-2 2-bay Covered Hopper #2 (CVSG)	50
_____ 00511	Flatcar with John Deere excavator	50
_____ 00512	Flatcar with 3 Bobcats	55
_____ 00513	Berghoff Beer Billboard Reefer (Scenery Unlimited)	53
_____ 00514	Wilson Car Lines Billboard Reefer (Scenery Unlimited)	53
_____ 00515	Zion Figs Wooden Billboard Reefer	53
_____ 00516	Ballantine Beer Wooden Billboard Reefer #1	53
_____ 00517	Ballantine Beer Wooden Billboard Reefer #2	53
_____ 00518	Parrot Potatoes Wooden Billboard Reefer	53
_____ 00519	40' Steel Rebuilt Boxcar, S Gaugian 40th Anniversary	50
_____ 00520	B&O 40' Steel Rebuilt Boxcar #1 (Boys RR Club)	50
_____ 00521	PRR Merchandise Service Rebuilt Boxcar, scheme I	50
_____ 00522	GN 40' Steel Rebuilt Boxcar, scheme II #1	50
_____ 00523	GN 40' Steel Rebuilt Boxcar, scheme II #2	50
_____ 00524	B&O 40' Steel Rebuilt Boxcar #2 (Boys RR Club)	50
_____ 00525	IGA Wooden Billboard Reefer #1 (RSSVP Models)	53
_____ 00526	IGA Wooden Billboard Reefer #2 (RSSVP Models)	53
_____ 00527	Narragansett Billboard Reefer #1 (RSSVP Models)	53
_____ 00528	Narragansett Billboard Reefer #2 (RSSVP Models)	53
_____ 00529	Flatcar with 3 New Holland grinder mixers	55
_____ 00530	Flatcar with Terra Gator dry fertilizer spreader	55
_____ 00531	Flatcar with Terra Gator liquid fertilizer spreader	55
_____ 00532	Flatcar with 4 John Deere skid loaders	60
_____ 00533	Switch Controller with 42" wire and extension	10
_____ 00534	Switch Controller with extension wire, 3 pieces	8
_____ 00535	IC Bulkhead Flatcar with pipe load	56
_____ 00536	ICG Switcher Set, 4 cars	300
_____ 00537	Soo Switcher Set, 5 cars	370
_____ 00538	CMStP&P Switcher Set, 5 cars	370
_____ 00539	GN Switcher Set, 6 cars	400
_____ 00540	Seaboard Switcher Set, 6 cars	400
_____ 00541	CB&Q F3 Diesel Freight Set, 6 cars	430
_____ 00542	USRA Double-sheathed Boxcar	50
_____ 00543	ACL USRA Double-sheathed Boxcar	50
_____ 00544	B&M USRA Double-sheathed Boxcar	50
_____ 00545	C&NW USRA Double-sheathed Boxcar	50
_____ 00546	D&LW USRA Double-sheathed Boxcar	50
_____ 00547	GN USRA Double-sheathed Boxcar	50

00548	NYC USRA Double-sheathed Boxcar	50 ____
00549	Toronto, Hamilton & Buffalo Double-sheathed Boxcar #1	50 ____
00550	Union Pacific USRA Double-sheathed Boxcar	50 ____
00551	Flatcar with IH Harvestor and corn load	55 ____
00552	LocoMatic 10-button Controller	70 ____
00554	C&NW MOW Flatcar	50 ____
00555	C&NW (M&StL) MOW Flatcar	50 ____
00556	Conrail Standard Flatcar #1	50 ____
00557	Conrail Standard Flatcar #2	50 ____
00558	Grand Truck Western Standard Flatcar #1	50 ____
00559	Grand Truck Western Standard Flatcar #2	50 ____
00560	Reading Standard Flatcar #1	50 ____
00561	Reading Standard Flatcar #2	50 ____
00562	Union Pacific Standard Flatcar, scheme II #1	50 ____
00563	Union Pacific Standard Flatcar, scheme II #2	50 ____
00564	NP USRA Double-sheathed Boxcar	70 ____
00565	Bulb 12-volt, 2 pieces	2 ____
00566	PFE Wooden Billboard Reefer, scheme II #1	53 ____
00567	PFE Wooden Billboard Reefer, scheme II #2	53 ____
00568	Lackawanna Wooden Billboard Reefer #1 (NASG)	53 ____
00569	Lackawanna Wooden Billboard Reefer #2 (NASG)	53 ____
00570	Baby Ruth Wooden Billboard Reefer #1	53 ____
00571	Baby Ruth Wooden Billboard Reefer #2	56 ____
00572	Ralston Purina Wooden Billboard Reefer	53 ____
00573	BAR Wooden Billboard Reefer #1	53 ____
00574	BAR Wooden Billboard Reefer #2	53 ____
00575	MP (NOT&M) "Eagle" 40' Steel Rebuilt Boxcar #1	50 ____
00576	MP (NOT&M) "Eagle" 40' Steel Rebuilt Boxcar #2	50 ____
00577	CStP&O 40' Steel Rebuilt Boxcar #1	50 ____
00578	CStP&O 40' Steel Rebuilt Boxcar #2	50 ____
00579	CGW "C" 40' Steel Rebuilt Boxcar	50 ____
00580	CGW "SL" 40' Steel Rebuilt Boxcar	50 ____
00581	CGW "DF" 40' Steel Rebuilt Boxcar	50 ____
00582	CGW "DFb" 40' Steel Rebuilt Boxcar	50 ____
00583	Dutch Cleanser Wooden Billboard Reefer #1	53 ____
00584	Land O' Lakes Wooden Billboard Reefer #1	53 ____
00585	Land O' Lakes Billboard Reefer #2 (Scenery Unlimited)	53 ____
00586	Flatcar with 4 John Deere 430 Crawlers	60 ____
00587	Switch Stand with marker light	6 ____
00588	Coupler, F3 mount, Kadee style, pair	3 ____
00589	Flatcar with 4 New Holland skid steers	60 ____
00590	Flatcar with John Deere wheel loader	50 ____
00591	Flatcar with John Deere grader	50 ____
00592	Dutch Cleanser Wooden Billboard Reefer #2	53 ____
00593	Chessie Extended Vision Caboose #1	70 ____

_____ **00594**	Chessie Extended Vision Caboose #2	70
_____ **00595**	Chessie Safety Special Extended Vision Caboose	70
_____ **00596**	C&NW Extended Vision Caboose #3	70
_____ **00597**	C&NW Extended Vision Caboose #4	70
_____ **00598**	MEC Extended Vision Caboose, scheme II	70
_____ **00599**	Reading Extended Vision Caboose #1	70
_____ **00600**	Reading Extended Vision Caboose #2	70
_____ **00601**	Rock Island Extended Vision Caboose #1	70
_____ **00602**	Rock Island Extended Vision Caboose #2	70
_____ **00603**	ATSF Extended Vision Caboose, scheme II #1	70
_____ **00604**	ATSF Extended Vision Caboose, scheme II #2	70
_____ **00605**	CGW "C" 40' Steel Boxcar, scheme II (State Line)	50
_____ **00606**	CGW "SL" 40' Steel Boxcar, scheme II (State Line)	50
_____ **00607**	CGW "DF" 40' Steel Boxcar, scheme II (State Line)	50
_____ **00608**	CGW "DFb" 40' Steel Boxcar, scheme II (State Line)	50
_____ **00609**	Flatcar with Caterpillar 609 Scraper	50
_____ **00610**	Kahn's Wooden Billboard Reefer #1 (Scenery Unlimited)	53
_____ **00611**	Kahn's Wooden Billboard Reefer #2 (Scenery Unlimited)	53
_____ **00612**	B&O F3 Diesel A Unit #1, phase II, sound	300
_____ **00613**	B&O F3 Diesel A Unit #2, phase II, sound	300
_____ **00614**	CB&Q F3 Diesel A Unit #1, phase II, sound	300
_____ **00615**	CB&Q F3 Diesel A Unit #2, phase II, sound	300
_____ **00616**	C&NW F3 Diesel A Unit #1, phase II, sound	300
_____ **00617**	C&NW F3 Diesel #2, phase II, sound	300
_____ **00618**	DL&W F3 Diesel A Unit #1, phase II, sound	300
_____ **00619**	DL&W F3 Diesel A Unit #2, phase II, sound	300
_____ **00620**	MEC F3 Diesel A Unit #1, phase II, sound	300
_____ **00621**	MEC F3 Diesel A Unit #2, phase II, sound	300
_____ **00622**	NYC Passenger F3 Diesel A Unit #1, phase II, sound	300
_____ **00623**	NYC Passenger F3 Diesel A Unit #2, phase II, sound	300
_____ **00624**	Southern F3 Diesel A Unit #1, phase II, sound	300
_____ **00625**	Southern F3 Diesel A Unit #2, phase II, sound	300
_____ **00626**	SP F3 Diesel A Unit #1, phase II, sound	300
_____ **00627**	SP F3 Diesel A Unit #2, phase II, sound	300
_____ **00628**	UP F3 Diesel A Unit #1, phase II, sound	300
_____ **00629**	UP F3 Diesel A Unit #2, phase II, sound	300
_____ **00630**	WP F3 Diesel A Unit #1, phase II, sound	300
_____ **00631**	WP F3 Diesel A Unit #2, phase II, sound	300
_____ **00632**	F3 Diesel A Unit, phase II, sound	300
_____ **00633**	NYC Freight F3 Diesel A Unit #1, phase II, sound	300
_____ **00634**	NYC Freight F3 Diesel A Unit #2, phase II, sound	300
_____ **00635**	B&O F3 Diesel B Unit #1, phase II, sound	290
_____ **00636**	B&O F3 Diesel B Unit #2, phase II, sound	290
_____ **00637**	CB&Q F3 Diesel B Unit #1, phase II, sound	290
_____ **00638**	CB&Q F3 Diesel B Unit #2, phase II, sound	290

S-HELPER SERVICE 1994-2012

Retail

00639	C&NW F3 Diesel B Unit #1, phase II, sound	290 ____
00640	C&NW F3 Diesel B Unit #2, phase II, sound	290 ____
00641	D&LW F3 Diesel B Unit #1, phase II, sound	290 ____
00642	D&LW F3 Diesel B Unit #2, phase II, sound	290 ____
00643	MEC F3 Diesel B Unit #1, phase II, sound	290 ____
00644	MEC F3 Diesel B Unit #2, phase II, sound	290 ____
00645	NYC Passenger F3 Diesel B Unit #1, phase II, sound	290 ____
00646	NYC Passenger F3 Diesel B Unit #2, phase II, sound	290 ____
00647	Southern F3 Diesel B Unit #1, phase II, sound	290 ____
00648	Southern F3 Diesel B Unit #2, phase II, sound	290 ____
00649	SP F3 Diesel B Unit #1, phase II, sound	290 ____
00650	SP F3 Diesel B Unit #2, phase II, sound	290 ____
00651	UP F3 Diesel B Unit #1, phase II, sound	290 ____
00652	UP F3 Diesel B Unit #2, phase II, sound	290 ____
00653	WP F3 Diesel B Unit #1, phase II, sound	290 ____
00654	WP F3 Diesel B Unit #2, phase II, sound	290 ____
00655	F3 Diesel B Unit, phase II, sound	290 ____
00656	NYC F3 Diesel B Unit #1, phase II, sound	290 ____
00657	NYC F3 Diesel B Unit #2, phase II, sound	290 ____
00658	Brookside Milk Wooden Billboard Reefer (Port Lines)	53 ____
00659	Saval Foods Wooden Billboard Reefer #1 (Port Lines)	53 ____
00660	Metal Rail Joiners for flex track, 36 pieces	4 ____
00661	PRR 40' Steel Rebuilt Boxcar, scheme II	50 ____
00662	GN 40' Steel Rebuilt Boxcar, scheme III #1	50 ____
00663	GN 40' Steel Rebuilt Boxcar, scheme III #2	50 ____
00664	33" Scale Caboose Wheel Set, Code 110, 4-pack	4 ____
00665	Speaker, 36mm diameter	3 ____
00666	Chessie SW1 Diesel Freight Set, 6 cars	370 ____
00667	MU Cables, pair	2 ____
00670	5" Uncoupler Track	22 ____
00671	5" Accessory Track	22 ____
00672	Flatcar with 2 Caterpillar D6R XL Bulldozers	60 ____
00673	Flatcar with Caterpillar D25D Articulated Truck	55 ____
00674	Flatcar with Caterpillar 950F Wheel Loader	50 ____
00675	Flatcar with Caterpillar 12G Grader	50 ____
00676	Flatcar with 2 Caterpillar Challenger Tractors	60 ____
00677	Flatcar with Caterpillar tractor and boom sprayer	55 ____
00678	Flatcar with Caterpillar tractor and spreader	55 ____
00679	Flatcar with Caterpillar tractor and Knight Slinger	55 ____
00680	Flatcar with 2 Caterpillar D6R Bulldozers	60 ____
00681	Flatcar with Caterpillar 611 Scraper	55 ____
00682	PFE Wooden Billboard Reefer Set, 3 cars	110 ____
00683	Burlington Wooden Billboard Reefer Set, 3 cars	110 ____
00684	North Western Wooden Billboard Reefer Set, 3 cars	110 ____
00685	FGE Wooden Billboard Reefer Set #1, 3 cars	110 ____

____ **00686**	NP Wooden Billboard Reefer #1	53
____ **00687**	NP Wooden Billboard Reefer #2	53
____ **00688**	Knickerbocker Billboard Reefer #1 (Port Lines)	53
____ **00689**	Knickerbocker Billboard Reefer #2 (Port Lines)	53
____ **00690**	Carling Black Label Billboard Reefer #1 (Port Lines)	53
____ **00691**	Carling Black Label Billboard Reefer #2 (Port Lines)	53
____ **00692**	C&NW SW9 Diesel Set, 5 cars	370
____ **00693**	C&NW Diesel F Unit Set, 6 cars	430
____ **00694**	MEC Diesel F Unit Set, 5 cars	370
____ **00697**	Edelweiss Beer Wooden Billboard Reefer	53
____ **00698**	Kraft Cheese Wooden Billboard Reefer	53
____ **00699**	CN Wooden Billboard Reefer #1	53
____ **00700**	CN Wooden Billboard Reefer #2	53
____ **00701**	B&M 40' Steel Rebuilt Boxcar #1 (Boys RR Club)	50
____ **00702**	B&M 40' Steel Rebuilt Boxcar #2 (Boys RR Club)	50
____ **00703**	ATSF 40' Steel Rebuilt Boxcar #1 (Boys RR Club)	50
____ **00704**	ATSF 40' Steel Rebuilt Boxcar #2 (Boys RR Club)	50
____ **00705**	D&RGW 40' Steel Boxcar #1, white (Boys RR Club)	50
____ **00706**	D&RGW 40' Steel Boxcar #2, white (Boys RR Club)	50
____ **00707**	D&RGW 40' Steel Boxcar #1, silver (Boys RR Club)	50
____ **00708**	D&RGW 40' Steel Boxcar #2, silver (Boys RR Club)	50
____ **00709**	Central of Georgia Boxcar, black #1 (Boys RR Club)	50
____ **00710**	Central of Georgia Boxcar, maroon (Boys RR Club)	50
____ **00711**	Central of Georgia Boxcar, black #2 (Boys RR Club)	50
____ **00712**	Central of Georgia Boxcar, black #3 (Boys RR Club)	50
____ **00713**	NP SW9 Diesel Freight Set, 4 cars	300
____ **00714**	CMStP&P SW1 Diesel Freight Set, 5 cars	370
____ **00715**	CB&Q F3 Diesel Freight Set, 6 cars	430
____ **00716**	Santa Fe "The Scout" Wooden Billboard Reefer	53
____ **00717**	Wooden Billboard Reefer, red	53
____ **00720**	Saval Foods Billboard Reefer #2 (Port Lines)	53
____ **00721**	B&O 40' Steel Rebuilt Boxcar #3 (Boys RR Club)	50
____ **00722**	B&O 40' Steel Rebuilt Boxcar #4 (Boys RR Club)	50
____ **00723**	Ore Car, black	40
____ **00724**	Ore Car, red	40
____ **00725**	DM&IR Ore Car	40
____ **00726**	DM&IR Ore Car 5-pack Set A	180
____ **00727**	B&LE Ore Car	40
____ **00728**	B&LE Ore Car 5-pack Set A	180
____ **00729**	CN Ore Car	40
____ **00730**	CN Ore Car 5-pack	180
____ **00731**	CP Ore Car	40
____ **00732**	CP Ore Car 5-pack	180
____ **00735**	GN Ore Car, scheme I	40
____ **00736**	GN Ore Car 5-pack Set A, scheme I	180

00737	CMStP&P Ore Car, scheme I	40 ____
00738	CMStP&P Ore Car 5-pack Set A, scheme I	180 ____
00741	SP Ore Car	40 ____
00742	SP Ore Car 5-pack	180 ____
00743	UP Ore Car	40 ____
00744	UP Ore Car 5-pack	180 ____
00745	DCC Sound Decoder, F Unit	160 ____
00746	ATSF 40' Steel Rebuilt Boxcar	50 ____
00747	C&NW 40' Steel Rebuilt Boxcar	50 ____
00748	NYC (P&LE) 40' Steel Rebuilt Boxcar #1	50 ____
00749	UP 40' Steel Rebuilt Boxcar	50 ____
00750	ATSF USRA Single-sheathed Boxcar	50 ____
00751	C&NW USRA Single-sheathed Boxcar	50 ____
00752	NYC USRA Single-sheathed Boxcar	50 ____
00753	UP USRA Single-sheathed Boxcar	50 ____
00754	ATSF Stock Car, scheme II	50 ____
00755	C&NW Stock Car #3	50 ____
00756	NYC Stock Car	50 ____
00757	UP (OSL) Stock Car, scheme II #3	50 ____
00758	Composite Side Hopper, black	50 ____
00759	Composite Side Hopper, red	50 ____
00760	Ann Arbor Composite Side Hopper 3-pack	100 ____
00761	Ann Arbor Composite Side Hopper	50 ____
00762	ATSF Composite Side Hopper 3-pack	100 ____
00763	ATSF Composite Side Hopper	50 ____
00764	B&O Composite Side Hopper 3-pack	100 ____
00765	B&O Composite Side Hopper	50 ____
00766	C&O Composite Side Hopper 3-pack	100 ____
00767	C&O Composite Side Hopper	50 ____
00768	CB&Q Composite Side Hopper 3-pack	100 ____
00769	CB&Q Composite Side Hopper	50 ____
00770	Clinchfield Composite Side Hopper 3-pack	100 ____
00771	Clinchfield Composite Side Hopper	50 ____
00772	LV Composite Side Hopper 3-pack	100 ____
00773	LV Composite Side Hopper	50 ____
00774	L&N Composite Side Hopper 3-pack	100 ____
00775	L&N Composite Side Hopper	50 ____
00776	NKP Composite Side Hopper 3-pack	100 ____
00777	NKP Composite Side Hopper	50 ____
00778	PRR Composite Side Hopper 3-pack	100 ____
00779	PRR Composite Side Hopper #4	50 ____
00780	Virginian Composite Side Hopper 3-pack	100 ____
00781	Virginian Composite Side Hopper	50 ____
00782	Wabash Composite Side Hopper 3-pack	100 ____
00783	Wabash Composite Side Hopper	50 ____

____	**00788** Feeder Wire Terminal, 12 pieces	4
____	**00796** NKP Wooden Billboard Reefer (CVSG)	53
____	**00797** NKP Wooden Billboard Reefer (CVSG)	53
____	**00798** NYNH&H Wooden Billboard Reefer #1 (Port Lines)	53
____	**00799** NYNH&H Wooden Billboard Reefer #2 (Port Lines)	53
____	**00800** Grand Union Wooden Billboard Reefer	53
____	**00801** Borden's Cheese Wooden Billboard Reefer	53
____	**00802** Pabst Blue Ribbon Wooden Billboard Reefer	53
____	**00803** Mexene Chili Powder Wooden Billboard Reefer	53
____	**00804** Swift Wooden Billboard Reefer 3-pack	110
____	**00805** B&O 40' Steel Rebuilt Boxcar #5 (Boys RR Club)	50
____	**00806** North Stratford 40' Steel Boxcar (Bristol S Gauge)	50
____	**00807** North Stratford 40' Steel Boxcar (Bristol S Gauge)	50
____	**00808** Frisco 40' Steel Rebuilt Boxcar 3-pack	100
____	**00809** F7 Diesel A Unit, phase I, AC/DC LocoMatic sound	300
____	**00810** ATSF Passenger F7 Diesel A Unit #1, phase I	300
____	**00811** ATSF Passenger F7 Diesel A Unit #2, phase I	300
____	**00812** ATSF Freight F7 Diesel A Unit #1, phase I	300
____	**00813** ATSF Freight F7 Diesel A Unit #2, phase I	300
____	**00814** B&M F7 Diesel A Unit #1, phase I	300
____	**00815** B&M F7 Diesel A Unit #2, phase I	300
____	**00816** D&RGW F7 Diesel A Unit #1, phase I	300
____	**00817** D&RGW F7 Diesel A Unit #2, phase I	300
____	**00818** GN F7 Diesel A Unit #1, phase I	300
____	**00819** GN F7 Diesel A Unit #2, phase I	300
____	**00820** MP F7 Diesel A Unit #1, phase I	300
____	**00821** MP F7 Diesel A Unit #2, phase I	300
____	**00822** PRR F7 Diesel A Unit #1, phase I	300
____	**00823** PRR F7 Diesel A Unit #2, phase I	300
____	**00824** F7 Diesel B Unit, phase I, AC/DC LocoMatic sound	290
____	**00825** ATSF Passenger F7 Diesel B Unit #1, phase I	290
____	**00826** ATSF Passenger F7 Diesel B Unit #2, phase I	290
____	**00827** ATSF Freight F7 Diesel B Unit #1, phase I	290
____	**00828** ATSF Freight F7 Diesel B Unit #2, phase I	290
____	**00829** B&M F7 Diesel B Unit #1, phase I	290
____	**00830** B&M F7 Diesel B Unit #2, phase I	290
____	**00831** D&RGW F7 Diesel B Unit #1, phase I	290
____	**00832** D&RGW F7 Diesel B Unit #2, phase I	290
____	**00833** GN F7 Diesel B Unit #1, phase I	290
____	**00834** GN F7 Diesel B Unit #2, phase I	290
____	**00835** MP F7 Diesel B Unit #1, phase I	290
____	**00836** MP F7 Diesel B Unit #2, phase II	290
____	**00837** PRR F7 Diesel B Unit #1, phase I	290
____	**00838** PRR F7 Diesel B Unit #2, phase I	290
____	**00839** F7 Diesel A Unit, phase I, DCC sound	300

00840	ATSF Passenger F7 Diesel A Unit #1, phase I	300 ____
00841	ATSF Passenger F7 Diesel A Unit #2, phase I	300 ____
00842	ATSF Freight F7 Diesel A Unit #1, phase I	300 ____
00843	SF Freight F7 Diesel A Unit #2, phase I	300 ____
00844	B&M F7 Diesel A Unit #1, phase I	300 ____
00845	B&M F7 Diesel A Unit #2, phase I	300 ____
00846	D&RGW F7 Diesel A Unit #1, phase I	300 ____
00847	D&RGW F7 Diesel A Unit #2, phase I	300 ____
00848	GN F7 Diesel A Unit #1, phase I	300 ____
00849	GN F7 Diesel A Unit #2, phase I	300 ____
00850	MP F7 Diesel A Unit #1, phase I	300 ____
00851	MP F7 Diesel A Unit #2, phase I	300 ____
00852	PRR F7 Diesel A Unit #1, phase I	300 ____
00853	PRR F7 Diesel A Unit #2, phase I	300 ____
00854	F7 Diesel B Unit, phase I, DCC sound	290 ____
00855	ATSF Passenger F7 Diesel B Unit #1, phase I	290 ____
00856	ATSF Passenger F7 Diesel B Unit #2, phase I	290 ____
00857	ATSF Freight F7 Diesel B Unit #1, phase I	290 ____
00858	SF Freight F7 Diesel B Unit #2, phase I	290 ____
00859	B&M F7 Diesel B Unit #1, phase I	290 ____
00860	B&M F7 Diesel B Unit #2, phase I	290 ____
00861	D&RGW F7 Diesel B Unit #1, phase I	290 ____
00862	D&RGW F7 Diesel B Unit #2, phase I	290 ____
00863	GN F7 Diesel B Unit #1, phase I	290 ____
00864	D&RGW F7 Diesel B Unit #2, phase I	290 ____
00865	MP F7 Diesel B Unit #1, phase I	290 ____
00866	MP F7 Diesel B Unit #2, phase I	290 ____
00867	PRR F7 Diesel B Unit #1, phase I	290 ____
00868	PRR F7 Diesel B Unit #2, phase I	290 ____
00869	F7 Diesel A Unit, phase I, DC no sound	200 ____
00870	ATSF Passenger F7 Diesel A Unit #1, phase I	200 ____
00871	ATSF Passenger F7 Diesel A Unit #2, phase I	200 ____
00872	ATSF Freight F7 Diesel A Unit #1, phase I	200 ____
00873	SF Freight F7 Diesel A Unit #2, phase I	200 ____
00874	B&M F7 Diesel A Unit #1, phase I	200 ____
00875	B&M F7 Diesel A Unit #2, phase I	200 ____
00876	D&RGW F7 Diesel A Unit #1, phase I	200 ____
00877	D&RGW F7 Diesel A Unit #2, phase I	200 ____
00878	GN F7 Diesel A Unit #1, phase I	200 ____
00879	GN F7 Diesel A Unit #1, phase I	200 ____
00880	MP F7 Diesel A Unit #1, phase I	200 ____
00881	MP F7 Diesel A Unit #2, phase I	200 ____
00882	PRR F7 Diesel A Unit #1, phase I	200 ____
00883	PRR F7 Diesel A Unit #2, phase I	200 ____
00884	F7 Diesel B Unit, phase I, DC no sound	190 ____

_____ **00885**	ATSF Passenger F7 Diesel B Unit #1, phase I	190
_____ **00886**	ATSF Passenger F7 Diesel B Unit #2, phase I	190
_____ **00887**	ATSF Freight F7 Diesel B Unit #1, phase I	190
_____ **00888**	ATSF Freight F7 Diesel B Unit #2, phase I	190
_____ **00889**	B&M F7 Diesel B Unit #1, phase I	190
_____ **00890**	B&M F7 Diesel B Unit #2, phase I	190
_____ **00891**	D&RGW F7 Diesel B Unit #1, phase I	190
_____ **00892**	D&RGW F7 Diesel B Unit #2, phase I	190
_____ **00893**	GN F7 Diesel B Unit #1, phase I	190
_____ **00894**	GN F7 Diesel B Unit #2, phase I	190
_____ **00895**	MP F7 Diesel B Unit #1, phase I	190
_____ **00896**	MP F7 Diesel B Unit #2, phase I	190
_____ **00897**	PRR F7 Diesel B Unit #1, phase I	190
_____ **00898**	PRR F7 Diesel B Unit #2, phase I	190
_____ **00899**	F7 Diesel ABA Set, phase I, DC LocoMatic sound	680
_____ **00900**	ATSF Passenger F7 Diesel ABA, phase I	680
_____ **00901**	ATSF Freight F7 Diesel ABA Set, phase I	680
_____ **00902**	B&M F7 Diesel ABA Set, phase I	680
_____ **00903**	D&RGW F7 Diesel ABA Set, phase I	680
_____ **00904**	GN F7 Diesel ABA Set, phase I	680
_____ **00905**	MP F7 Diesel ABA Set, phase I	680
_____ **00906**	PRR F7 Diesel ABA Set, phase I	680
_____ **00907**	F7 Diesel ABA Set, phase I, DCC sound	680
_____ **00908**	ATSF Passenger F7 Diesel ABA Set, phase I	680
_____ **00909**	ATSF Freight F7 Diesel ABA Set, phase I	680
_____ **00910**	B&M F7 Diesel ABA Set, phase I	680
_____ **00911**	D&RGW F7 Diesel ABA Set, phase I	680
_____ **00912**	GN F7 Diesel ABA Set, phase I	680
_____ **00913**	MP F7 Diesel ABA Set, phase I	680
_____ **00914**	PRR F7 Diesel ABA Set, phase I	680
_____ **00915**	F7 Diesel ABA Set, phase I, DC no sound	680
_____ **00916**	ATSF Passenger F7 Diesel ABA Set, phase I	680
_____ **00917**	ATSF Freight F7 Diesel ABA Set, phase I	680
_____ **00918**	B&M F7 Diesel ABA Set, phase I	680
_____ **00919**	D&RGW F7 Diesel ABA Set, phase I	680
_____ **00920**	GN F7 Diesel ABA Set, phase I	680
_____ **00921**	MP F7 Diesel ABA Set, phase I	680
_____ **00922**	PRR F7 Diesel ABA Set, phase I	680
_____ **00923**	Kahn's Wooden Billboard Reefer, scheme II #1	53
_____ **00924**	Kahn's Wooden Billboard Reefer, scheme II #2	53
_____ **00925**	Accessory Control Button	10
_____ **00926**	5" Straight Track with unlighted bumper	15
_____ **00927**	F7 Diesel AB Set, phase I, DC LocoMatic sound	490
_____ **00928**	ATSF Passenger F7 Diesel AB Set #1, phase I	490
_____ **00929**	ATSF Passenger F7 Diesel AB Set #2, phase I	490

00930	ATSF Freight F7 Diesel AB Set #1, phase I	490	___
00931	ATSF Freight F7 Diesel AB Set #2, phase I	490	___
00932	B&M F7 Diesel AB Set #1, phase I	490	___
00933	B&M F7 Diesel AB Set #2, phase I	490	___
00934	D&RGW F7 Diesel AB Set #1, phase I	490	___
00935	D&RGW F7 Diesel AB Set #2, phase I	490	___
00936	GN F7 Diesel AB Set #1, phase I	490	___
00937	GN F7 Diesel AB Set #2, phase I	490	___
00938	MP F7 Diesel AB Set #1, phase I	490	___
00939	MP F7 Diesel AB Set #2, phase I	490	___
00940	PRR F7 Diesel AB Set #1, phase I	490	___
00941	PRR F7 Diesel AB Set #2, phase I	490	___
00942	F7 Diesel AA Set, phase I, AC/DC LocoMatic sound	490	___
00943	ATSF Passenger F7 Diesel AA Set, phase I	490	___
00944	ATSF Freight F7 Diesel AA Set, phase I	490	___
00945	B&M F7 Diesel AA Set, phase I	490	___
00946	D&RGW F7 Diesel AA Set, phase I	490	___
00947	GN F7 Diesel AA Set, phase I	490	___
00948	MP F7 Diesel AA Set, phase I	490	___
00949	PRR F7 Diesel AA Set, phase I	490	___
00950	F7 Diesel ABB Set, phase I, AC/DC LocoMatic sound	680	___
00951	ATSF Passenger F7 Diesel ABB Set, phase I	680	___
00952	ATSF Freight F7 Diesel ABB Set, phase I	680	___
00953	B&M F7 Diesel ABB Set, phase I	680	___
00954	D&RGW F7 Diesel ABB Set, phase I	680	___
00955	GN F7 Diesel ABB Set, phase I	680	___
00956	MP F7 Diesel ABB Set, phase I	680	___
00957	PRR F7 Diesel ABB Set, phase I	680	___
00958	F7 Diesel ABBA Set, phase I, AC/DC LocoMatic sound	880	___
00959	ATSF Passenger F7 Diesel ABBA Set, phase I	880	___
00960	ATSF Freight F7 Diesel ABBA Set, phase I	880	___
00961	B&M F7 Diesel ABBA Set, phase I	880	___
00962	D&RGW F7 Diesel ABBA Set, phase I	880	___
00963	GN F7 Diesel ABBA Set, phase I	880	___
00964	MP F7 Diesel ABBA Set, phase I	880	___
00965	PRR F7 Diesel ABBA Set, phase I	880	___
00966	CNJ PS-2 2-bay Covered Hopper, scheme II	50	___
00967	33" Wheel Set, AF, single insulated, 4-pack	5	___
00968	Brachs PS-2 2-bay Hopper, scheme I #1 (RSSVP Models)	50	___
00969	Brachs PS-2 2-bay Hopper, scheme I #2 (RSSVP Models)	50	___
00970	Brachs PS-2 2-bay Hopper, scheme II #1 (RSSVP Models)	50	___
00971	Brachs PS-2 2-bay Hopper, scheme II #2 (RSSVP Models)	50	___
00972	Jack Frost PS-2 2-bay Hopper #2 (RSSVP Models)	58	___
00973	G&W PS-2 3-bay Covered Hopper #1	50	___
00974	G&W PS-2 3-bay Covered Hopper #2	50	___

____ **00975**	Reading PS-2 3-bay Covered Hopper #1	50
____ **00976**	Reading PS-2 3-bay Covered Hopper #2	50
____ **00977**	Wabash PS-2 3-bay Covered Hopper #1	50
____ **00978**	Wabash PS-2 3-bay Covered Hopper #2	50
____ **00979**	33" Wheel Set, AF, double insulated, 4-pack	5
____ **00980**	Panel Side Hopper, black	50
____ **00981**	Panel Side Hopper, red	50
____ **00982**	Anderson Panel Side Hopper 3-pack Set A	100
____ **00983**	Anderson Panel Side Hopper #4	50
____ **00984**	Ann Arbor Panel Side Hopper 3-pack	100
____ **00985**	Ann Arbor Panel Side Hopper	50
____ **00986**	C&O Panel Side Hopper 3-pack	100
____ **00987**	C&O Panel Side Hopper	50
____ **00988**	SLSF Panel Side Hopper 3-pack	100
____ **00989**	SLSF Panel Side Hopper	50
____ **00990**	D&H Panel Side Hopper 3-pack	100
____ **00991**	D&H Panel Side Hopper	50
____ **00992**	NYC Panel Side Hopper Car 3-pack, scheme I	100
____ **00993**	NYC Panel Side Hopper Car, scheme I	50
____ **00994**	NYC Panel Side Hopper 3-pack, scheme II	100
____ **00995**	NYC Panel Side Hopper, scheme I	50
____ **00996**	NYNH&H Panel Side Hopper	50
____ **00997**	PRR Panel Side Hopper	50
____ **00998**	Wabash Panel Side Hopper 3-pack	100
____ **00999**	Wabash Panel Side Hopper	50
____ **01000**	PFE Wooden Billboard Reefer, scheme I #1	53
____ **01001**	PFE Wooden Billboard Reefer, scheme I #2	53
____ **01002**	ART Wooden Billboard Reefer #3	53
____ **01003**	ART Wooden Billboard Reefer #4	53
____ **01004**	CNW Wooden Billboard Reefer #1 (Chicagoland)	53
____ **01005**	CNW Wooden Billboard Reefer #2 (Chicagoland)	59
____ **01006**	Northern "Bananas" Wooden Billboard Reefer	53
____ **01007**	Schlitz Beer Wooden Billboard Reefer	53
____ **01008**	MP "Eagle" 40' Steel Rebuilt Boxcar #1	50
____ **01009**	MP "Eagle" 40' Steel Rebuilt Boxcar #2	50
____ **01010**	CN 40' Steel Rebuilt Boxcar #1	50
____ **01011**	CN 40' Steel Rebuilt Boxcar #2	50
____ **01012**	Seaboard "Orange Blossom Special" Rebuilt Boxcar	50
____ **01013**	Seaboard "Silver Meteor" 40' Steel Rebuilt Boxcar	50
____ **01014**	ATSF "Super Chief" 40' Steel Rebuilt Boxcar	50
____ **01015**	FGE Wooden Billboard Reefer #1	53
____ **01016**	FGE Wooden Billboard Reefer #2	53
____ **01017**	Century Beer Wooden Billboard Reefer	53
____ **01018**	Burlington Route 40' Steel Boxcar #1 (Boys RR Club)	53
____ **01019**	Burlington Route 40' Steel Boxcar #2 (Boys RR Club)	53

01020	State of Maine BAR 40' Steel Boxcar (Boys RR Club)	53 ___
01021	State of Maine NYNH&H 40' Steel Boxcar (Boys RR Club)	53 ___
01022	L&N "Dixie" 40' Steel Rebuilt Boxcar #1 (Boys RR Club)	53 ___
01023	L&N "Dixie" 40' Steel Rebuilt Boxcar #2 (Boys RR Club)	53 ___
01024	WP 40' Steel Rebuilt Boxcar #1 (Boys RR Club)	53 ___
01025	WP 40' Steel Rebuilt Boxcar #2 (Boys RR Club)	53 ___
01026	PRR 40' Steel Rebuilt Boxcar #1 (Boys RR Club)	53 ___
01027	PRR 40' Steel Rebuilt Boxcar #2 (Boys RR Club)	53 ___
01028	NYC 40' Steel Rebuilt Boxcar #1 (Boys RR Club)	53 ___
01029	NYC 40' Steel Rebuilt Boxcar #2 (Boys RR Club)	53 ___
01030	NYC 40' Steel Rebuilt Boxcar #3 (Boys RR Club)	53 ___
01031	40' Steel Rebuilt Boxcar (CVSG)	53 ___
01032	Tipo Wine Billboard Reefer #1 (Scenery Unlimited)	53 ___
01033	Tipo Wine Billboard Reefer #2 (Scenery Unlimited)	53 ___
01034	ATSF F7 Diesel Freight Set, 6 cars	430 ___
01036	MP F7 Diesel Freight Set, 6 cars	430 ___
01037	S-Trax Bumper, yellow, 2-pack	6 ___
01038	S-Trax Bumper, red, 2-pack	6 ___
01043	ICG SW9 Diesel Freight Set, 4 cars	300 ___
01044	D&RGW SW9 Diesel Freight Set, 5 cars	370 ___
01045	Seaboard SW1 Diesel Freight Set, 5 cars	370 ___
01046	MEC F3 Diesel Freight Set, 5 cars	400 ___
01047	D&RGW Extended Vision Caboose #3	70 ___
01048	D&RGW Extended Vision Caboose #4	70 ___
01049	GTW Panel Side Hopper 3-pack	100 ___
01050	GTW Panel Side Hopper	50 ___
01051	2-8-0 Locomotive, hi-rail wheels, AC/DC LocoMatic sound	600 ___
01052	B&O 2-8-0 Locomotive #1	600 ___
01053	B&O 2-8-0 Locomotive #2	600 ___
01054	ATSF 2-8-0 Locomotive #1	600 ___
01055	ATSF 2-8-0 Locomotive #2	600 ___
01056	C&NW 2-8-0 Locomotive #1	600 ___
01057	C&NW 2-8-0 Locomotive #2	600 ___
01058	Erie 2-8-0 Locomotive #1	600 ___
01059	Erie 2-8-0 Locomotive #2	600 ___
01060	MEC 2-8-0 Locomotive #1	600 ___
01061	MEC 2-8-0 Locomotive #2	600 ___
01062	NYC 2-8-0 Locomotive #1	600 ___
01063	NYC 2-8-0 Locomotive #2	600 ___
01064	Southern 2-8-0 Locomotive #1	600 ___
01066	UP 2-8-0 Locomotive #1	600 ___
01067	UP 2-8-0 Locomotive #2	600 ___
01068	WM 2-8-0 Locomotive #1	600 ___
01069	WM 2-8-0 Locomotive #2	600 ___
01070	Flatcar with Oliver corn picker	55 ___

___ **01071**	2-8-0 Locomotive, hi-rail wheels, DCC sound	600
___ **01072**	B&O 2-8-0 Locomotive #1	600
___ **01073**	B&O 2-8-0 Locomotive #2	600
___ **01074**	ATSF 2-8-0 Locomotive #1	600
___ **01075**	ATSF 2-8-0 Locomotive #2	600
___ **01076**	C&NW 2-8-0 Locomotive #1	600
___ **01077**	C&NW 2-8-0 Locomotive #2	600
___ **01078**	Erie 2-8-0 Locomotive #1	600
___ **01079**	Erie 2-8-0 Locomotive #2	600
___ **01080**	MEC 2-8-0 Locomotive #1	600
___ **01081**	MEC 2-8-0 Locomotive #2	600
___ **01082**	NYC 2-8-0 Locomotive #1	600
___ **01083**	NYC 2-8-0 Locomotive #2	600
___ **01084**	Southern 2-8-0 Locomotive #1	600
___ **01086**	UP 2-8-0 Locomotive #1	600
___ **01087**	UP 2-8-0 Locomotive #2	600
___ **01088**	WM 2-8-0 Locomotive #1	600
___ **01089**	WM 2-8-0 Locomotive #2	600
___ **01090**	Flatcar with IH Farmall corn picker	55
___ **01091**	2-8-0 Locomotive, hi-rail wheels, DC no sound	450
___ **01092**	B&O 2-8-0 Locomotive #1	450
___ **01093**	B&O 2-8-0 Locomotive #2	450
___ **01094**	ATSF 2-8-0 Locomotive #1	450
___ **01095**	ATSF 2-8-0 Locomotive #2	450
___ **01096**	C&NW 2-8-0 Locomotive #1	450
___ **01097**	C&NW 2-8-0 Locomotive #2	450
___ **01098**	Erie 2-8-0 Locomotive #1	450
___ **01099**	Erie 2-8-0 Locomotive #2	450
___ **01100**	MEC 2-8-0 Locomotive #1	450
___ **01101**	MEC 2-8-0 Locomotive #2	450
___ **01102**	NYC 2-8-0 Locomotive #1	450
___ **01103**	NYC 2-8-0 Locomotive #2	450
___ **01104**	Southern 2-8-0 Locomotive #1	450
___ **01106**	UP 2-8-0 Locomotive #1	450
___ **01107**	UP 2-8-0 Locomotive #2	450
___ **01108**	WM 2-8-0 Locomotive #1	450
___ **01109**	WM 2-8-0 Locomotive #2	450
___ **01110**	GN Offset Hopper	50
___ **01111**	Green Bay & Western Offset Hopper 3-pack	100
___ **01112**	Green Bay & Western Offset Hopper	50
___ **01113**	IC Offset Hopper 3-pack	100
___ **01114**	IC Offset Hopper	50
___ **01115**	LNE Offset Hopper 3-pack	100
___ **01116**	LNE Offset Hopper	50
___ **01117**	NYC Offset Hopper 3-pack	100

Retail

Item	Description	Retail
01118	NYC Offset Hopper	50
01119	Peabody Offset Hopper 3-pack	100
01120	Peabody Offset Hopper	50
01121	Detroit & Mackinac Offset Hopper 3-pack	100
01122	S-Trax Track Planning Guide	8
01123	Detroit & Mackinac Offset Hopper	50
01124	TP&W Offset Hopper 3-pack	100
01125	TP&W Offset Hopper	50
01126	DT&I 40' Steel Rebuilt Boxcar #1	50
01127	DT&I 40' Steel Rebuilt Boxcar #2	50
01128	GN 40' Steel Rebuilt Boxcar, scheme IV #1	50
01129	GN 40' Steel Rebuilt Boxcar, scheme IV #2	50
01130	Swift Wooden Billboard Reefer, scheme I	53
01131	Swift Wooden Billboard Reefer, scheme II	53
01132	Swift Wooden Billboard Reefer, scheme III	53
01133	SLSF 40' Steel Rebuilt Boxcar, scheme II	50
01134	SLSF 40' Steel Rebuilt Boxcar, scheme III	50
01135	SLSF 40' Steel Rebuilt Boxcar, scheme I #2	50
01136	Armour Stock Express 40' Stock Car #1	50
01137	Armour Stock Express 40' Stock Car #2	50
01138	GN 40' Stock Car	73
01139	Nickel Plate Road 40' Stock Car #1	50
01140	Nickel Plate Road 40' Stock Car #2	50
01141	UP 40' Stock Car, scheme II #1	50
01142	UP 40' Stock Car, scheme II #2	50
01143	BN PS-2 2-bay Covered Hopper, scheme III #1	50
01144	BN PS-2 2-bay Covered Hopper, scheme III #2	50
01145	Chessie (C&O) PS-2 2-bay Covered Hopper #1	50
01146	Chessie (C&O) PS-2 2-bay Covered Hopper #2	50
01147	D&H PS-2 2-bay Covered Hopper #1	50
01148	D&H PS-2 2-bay Covered Hopper #2	50
01149	Boraxo PS-2 2-bay Covered Hopper	50
01150	Susquehanna 40' Steel Rebuilt Boxcar #1	50
01151	Susquehanna 40' Steel Rebuilt Boxcar #2	50
01152	PRR 40' Steel Rebuilt Boxcar, scheme II #1	50
01153	Offset Hopper, black	50
01154	Offset Hopper, red	50
01155	CNJ Offset Hopper 3-pack	100
01156	CNJ Offset Hopper	50
01157	DL&W Offset Hopper 3-pack	100
01158	DL&W Offset Hopper	50
01159	GN Offset Hopper 3-pack	100
01160	PRR 40' Steel Rebuilt Boxcar, scheme II #2	50
01161	GN Standard Flatcar, scheme II #1	50
01162	GN Standard Flatcar, scheme II #2	50

____ **01163**	NP Standard Flatcar #1	50
____ **01164**	NP Standard Flatcar #2	50
____ **01165**	SLSF Standard Flatcar #1	50
____ **01166**	SLSF Standard Flatcar #2	50
____ **01167**	SP Standard Flatcar, scheme I #1	50
____ **01168**	SP Standard Flatcar, scheme I #2	50
____ **01170**	Anderson Panel Side Hopper 3-pack Set B	100
____ **01171**	Anderson Panel Side Hopper Car #8	50
____ **01172**	CN Panel Side Hopper 3-pack	100
____ **01173**	CN Panel Side Hopper Car	50
____ **01174**	Rock Island Panel Side Hopper 3-pack	100
____ **01175**	Rock Island Panel Side Hopper Car	50
____ **01176**	USRA Rib Side Hopper, black	50
____ **01177**	USRA Rib Side Hopper, red	50
____ **01178**	B&O USRA Rib Side Hopper 3-pack	100
____ **01179**	B&O USRA Rib Side Hopper	50
____ **01180**	CNJ USRA Rib Side Hopper 3-pack	100
____ **01181**	CNJ USRA Rib Side Hopper	50
____ **01182**	CB&Q USRA Rib Side Hopper 3-pack	100
____ **01183**	CB&Q USRA Rib Side Hopper	50
____ **01184**	IH USRA Rib Side Hopper 3-pack	100
____ **01185**	IH USRA Rib Side Hopper	50
____ **01186**	L&N USRA Rib Side Hopper 3-pack	100
____ **01187**	L&N USRA Rib Side Hopper	50
____ **01188**	NYNH&H USRA Rib Side Hopper 3-pack	100
____ **01189**	NYNH&H USRA Rib Side Hopper	50
____ **01190**	NYC USRA Rib Side Hopper 3-pack	100
____ **01191**	NYC USRA Rib Side Hopper	50
____ **01192**	NYO&W USRA Rib Side Hopper 3-pack	100
____ **01193**	NYO&W USRA Rib Side Hopper	50
____ **01194**	PRR USRA Rib Side Hopper 3-pack	100
____ **01195**	PRR USRA Rib Side Hopper	50
____ **01196**	Reading USRA Rib Side Hopper 3-pack	100
____ **01197**	Reading USRA Rib Side Hopper	50
____ **01198**	32" Pipe Load	13
____ **01199**	F7 DCC Sound Decoder	180
____ **01200**	F3 AC/DC LocoMatic Sound Unit	160
____ **01201**	F7 AC/DC LocoMatic Sound Unit	160
____ **01202**	N&W USRA Rib Side Hopper 3-pack	100
____ **01203**	N&W USRA Rib Side Hopper #4	50
____ **01204**	N&W USRA Rib Side Hopper #5	50
____ **01205**	Control Button, slide switch	8
____ **01206**	Peabody USRA Rib Side Hopper 3-pack	100
____ **01207**	Peabody USRA Rib Side Hopper	50
____ **01208**	Andrews Tender Truck, 33" Code 110 wheels	11

Code	Description	Retail	
01209	Andrews Tender Truck, 33" hi-rail wheels	11	___
01210	Flatcar with Case IH grinder mixers	60	___
01211	Track-cleaning USRA Double-sheathed Boxcar	150	___
01212	Track-cleaning Standard Flatcar	150	___
01214	Custom Trax No. 6 Switch, right hand	48	___
01215	Custom Trax No. 6 Switch, left hand	48	___
01216	Custom Trax No. 8 Switch, right hand	50	___
01217	Custom Trax No. 8 Switch, left hand	50	___
01218	Flextrack, 36" roadbed	15	___
01219	HomaBed 48' Straight	69	___
01220	HomaBed 48' Curved	74	___
01221	HomaBed 48' Straight/Curved	81	___
01222	Monon Composite Side Hopper Car 3-pack	100	___
01223	Monon Composite Side Hopper Car	50	___
01224	LV Composite Side Hopper Car 3-pack Set B	100	___
01225	LV Composite Side Hopper Car #8	50	___
01226	PRR Composite Side Hopper Car 3-pack Set B	100	___
01227	PRR Composite Side Hopper Car #8	50	___
01228	36" Weathered Rail, Code 131, 33 pieces	70	___
01229	CB&Q SW1 Diesel #1	200	___
01230	CB&Q SW1 Diesel #2	200	___
01231	CNJ SW1 Diesel #1	200	___
01232	CNJ SW1 Diesel #2	200	___
01233	Erie-Lackawanna SW1 Diesel #1	200	___
01234	Erie-Lackawanna SW1 Diesel #2	200	___
01235	GN SW1 Diesel #1	200	___
01236	GN SW1 Diesel #2	200	___
01237	B&M SW8 Diesel #1	200	___
01238	B&M SW8 Diesel #2	200	___
01239	BN SW8 Diesel #1	200	___
01240	BN SW8 Diesel #2	200	___
01241	C&NW SW8 Diesel #1	200	___
01242	C&NW SW8 Diesel #2	200	___
01243	CRI&P SW8 Diesel #1	200	___
01244	CRI&P SW8 Diesel #2	200	___
01245	Conrail SW9 Diesel, scheme II #1	200	___
01246	Conrail SW9 Diesel, scheme II #2	200	___
01247	FEC SW9 Diesel #1	200	___
01248	FEC SW9 Diesel #2	200	___
01249	SLSF SW9 Diesel #1	200	___
01250	SLSF SW9 Diesel #2	200	___
01251	Lehigh Valley SW9 Diesel #1	200	___
01252	Lehigh Valley SW9 Diesel #2	200	___
01253	ATSF NW2 Diesel #1	200	___
01254	ATSF NW2 Diesel #2	200	___

S-HELPER SERVICE 1994-2012

____ **01255**	Chessie (C&O) NW2 Diesel #1	200
____ **01256**	Chessie (C&O) NW2 Diesel #2	200
____ **01259**	PRR NW2 Diesel, scheme I	200
____ **01260**	PRR NW2 Diesel, scheme II	200
____ **01261**	NW2 Diesel	200
____ **01262**	SLSF Extended Vision Caboose #1	70
____ **01263**	SLSF Extended Vision Caboose #2	70
____ **01264**	CB&Q Extended Vision Caboose, scheme II #1	70
____ **01265**	CB&Q Extended Vision Caboose, scheme II #2	70
____ **01266**	D&RGW Extended Vision Caboose #5	70
____ **01267**	D&RGW Extended Vision Caboose #6	70
____ **01268**	GN Extended Vision Caboose #3	70
____ **01269**	GN Extended Vision Caboose #4	70
____ **01270**	MEC Extended Vision Caboose, scheme III	78
____ **01271**	Silver Edge Beer Wooden Billboard Reefer	53
____ **01272**	Columbia Soups Wooden Billboard Reefer	53
____ **01273**	Niblets Corn Wooden Billboard Reefer	53
____ **01274**	Monarch Foods Wooden Billboard Reefer	53
____ **01275**	Wilson Milk Wooden Billboard Reefer #1 (Port Lines)	53
____ **01276**	Wilson Milk Wooden Billboard Reefer #2 (Port Lines)	53
____ **01277**	URTX MILW Wooden Billboard Reefer #1	53
____ **01278**	URTX MILW Wooden Billboard Reefer #2	53
____ **01279**	WFE GN Wooden Billboard Reefer #1	53
____ **01280**	WFE GN Wooden Billboard Reefer #2	53
____ **01281**	CNJ USRA Single-sheathed Boxcar #1	50
____ **01282**	CNJ USRA Single-sheathed Boxcar #2	50
____ **01283**	CMStP&P USRA Single-sheathed Boxcar #1	50
____ **01284**	CMStP&P USRA Single-sheathed Boxcar #2	50
____ **01285**	MKT USRA Single-sheathed Boxcar #1	50
____ **01286**	MKT USRA Single-sheathed Boxcar #2	50
____ **01287**	Wellsville, Addison & Galeton Single-sheathed Boxcar	50
____ **01288**	CB&Q F3 Diesel ABA Set, phase II, DC no sound	590
____ **01290**	BN Ore Car 5-pack	180
____ **01291**	BN Ore Car	40
____ **01292**	GN Ore Car 5-pack, scheme II	180
____ **01293**	GN Ore Car, scheme II	40
____ **01294**	DM&IR Ore Car 5-pack	180
____ **01295**	Coupler, Kadee style, 2 pair	6
____ **01296**	CNJ Composite Side Hopper 3-pack, scheme II (Hoquat)	100
____ **01297**	CNJ Composite Side Hopper, scheme II (Hoquat)	50
____ **01298**	DL&W Composite Side Hopper 3-pack, scheme II (Hoquat)	100
____ **01299**	DL&W Composite Side Hopper, scheme II (Hoquat)	50
____ **01300**	Public Service Composite Side Hopper 3-pack (Hoquat)	100
____ **01301**	Public Service Composite Side Hopper (Hoquat)	50
____ **01302**	AC/DC LocoMatic Sound Switcher Board	150

01303	Conrail SW9 Diesel Freight Set, 4 cars	300 ____
01304	C&NW F3 Diesel Freight Set, 4 cars	330 ____
01305	Chessie (C&O) NW2 Diesel Freight Set, 5 cars	370 ____
01306	D&RGW F7 Diesel Freight Set, 6 cars	430 ____
01307	CB&Q SW1 Diesel Freight Set, 6 cars	400 ____
01308	GN F7 Diesel Freight Set, 6 cars	430 ____
01310	Freight Coupler, short shank, AF compatible, pair	3 ____
01333	CMStP&P Wooden Billboard Reefer #1 (Badgerland)	53 ____
01363	CMStP&P Wooden Billboard Reefer #2 (Badgerland)	53 ____
01393	CMStP&P Wooden Billboard Reefer #3 (Badgerland)	53 ____
01402	DM&IR Ore Car 5-pack Set B	180 ____
01403	CMStP&P Wooden Billboard Reefer #4 (Badgerland)	53 ____
01413	CMStP&P Wooden Billboard Reefer #5 (Badgerland)	53 ____
01422	GN Ore Car 5-pack Set B, scheme I	180 ____
01423	Control Button, passing siding	8 ____
01432	CMStP&P Ore Car 5-pack Set B	180 ____
01433	Ore Car Sampler 10-pack	360 ____
01442	Flatcar with 4 Farmall tractors	60 ____
01443	D&RGW 40' Steel Rebuilt Boxcar (Boys RR Club)	50 ____
01452	D&RGW 40' Steel Rebuilt Boxcar (Boys RR Club)	50 ____
01453	Central of Georgia 40' Steel Boxcar (Boys RR Club)	50 ____
01501	MEC SW9 Diesel	200 ____
01502	MEC SW9 Diesel, holiday	200 ____
01503	MEC SW9 Diesel, AC/DC LocoMatic sound	290 ____
01504	MEC SW9 Diesel, holiday, AC/DC LocoMatic sound	290 ____
01505	MEC SW9 Diesel, DCC sound	290 ____
01506	MEC SW9 Diesel, holiday, DCC sound	290 ____
01507	MEC Locomotive and Caboose, holiday	270 ____
01508	MEC Locomotive and Caboose, holiday, AC/DC sound	360 ____
01509	MEC Locomotive and Caboose, holiday, DCC sound	360 ____
01510	Hood Milk Wooden Billboard Reefer #1 (Port Lines)	53 ____
01511	Hood Milk Wooden Billboard Reefer #2 (Port Lines)	53 ____
01512	Merchants Biscuit Wooden Billboard Reefer	53 ____
01513	E&A Opler Wooden Billboard Reefer	53 ____
01514	Carnation Milk Wooden Billboard Reefer	53 ____
01515	Great Falls Beer Wooden Billboard Reefer	53 ____
01516	Curve Beer Wooden Billboard Reefer #1 (NASG)	53 ____
01517	Curve Beer Wooden Billboard Reefer #2 (NASG)	53 ____
01518	B&M SW8 Diesel #1, AC/DC LocoMatic sound	290 ____
01519	B&M SW8 Diesel #2, AC/DC LocoMatic sound	290 ____
01520	BN SW8 Diesel #1, AC/DC LocoMatic sound	290 ____
01521	BN SW8 Diesel #2, AC/DC LocoMatic sound	290 ____
01522	C&NW SW8 Diesel #1, AC/DC LocoMatic sound	290 ____
01523	C&NW SW8 Diesel #2, AC/DC LocoMatic sound	290 ____
01524	CRI&P SW8 Diesel #1, AC/DC LocoMatic sound	290 ____

_____ 01525	CRI&P SW8 Diesel #2, AC/DC LocoMatic sound	290
_____ 01526	Conrail SW9 Diesel, scheme II #1, AC/DC LocoMatic sound	290
_____ 01527	FEC SW9 Diesel #1, AC/DC LocoMatic sound	290
_____ 01528	FEC SW9 Diesel #2, AC/DC LocoMatic sound	290
_____ 01529	SLSF SW9 Diesel #1, AC/DC LocoMatic sound	290
_____ 01530	SLSF SW9 Diesel #2, AC/DC LocoMatic sound	290
_____ 01531	Lehigh Valley SW9 Diesel #1, AC/DC LocoMatic sound	290
_____ 01532	Lehigh Valley SW9 Diesel #2, AC/DC LocoMatic sound	290
_____ 01535	Chessie (C&O) NW2 Diesel #1, AC/DC LocoMatic sound	290
_____ 01536	Chessie (C&O) NW2 Diesel #2, AC/DC LocoMatic sound	290
_____ 01539	PRR NW2 Diesel, scheme I, AC/DC LocoMatic sound	290
_____ 01540	PRR NW2 Diesel, scheme II, AC/DC LocoMatic sound	290
_____ 01541	NW2 Diesel, AC/DC LocoMatic sound	290
_____ 01550	Conrail Quality SW9 Diesel #1, DCC sound	290
_____ 01551	Florida East Coast SW9 Diesel #1, DCC sound	290
_____ 01552	Florida East Coast SW9 Diesel #2, DCC sound	290
_____ 01553	SLSF SW9 Diesel #1, DCC sound	290
_____ 01554	SLSF SW9 Diesel #2, DCC sound	290
_____ 01555	Lehigh Valley SW9 Diesel #1, DCC sound	290
_____ 01556	Lehigh Valley SW9 Diesel #2, DCC sound	290
_____ 01557	ATSF NW2 Diesel #1, DCC sound	290
_____ 01558	ATSF NW2 Diesel #2, DCC sound	290
_____ 01559	Chessie NW2 Diesel #1, DCC sound	290
_____ 01560	Chessie NW2 Diesel #2, DCC sound	290
_____ 01563	PRR NW2 Diesel, scheme I, DCC sound	290
_____ 01564	PRR NW2 Diesel, scheme II, DCC sound	290
_____ 01565	NW2 Diesel, DCC sound, DCC sound	290
_____ 01566	ATSF USRA Double-sheathed Boxcar, scheme I	50
_____ 01568	Duluth, South Shore & Atlantic Double-sheathed Boxcar	50
_____ 01569	Ivory USRA Double-sheathed Boxcar #1 (Miami Valley)	50
_____ 01570	Ivory USRA Double-sheathed Boxcar #2 (Miami Valley)	50
_____ 01571	NWP USRA Double-sheathed Boxcar #1	50
_____ 01572	D&RGW 40' Steel Rebuilt Boxcar #1 (Boys RR Club)	50
_____ 01573	D&RGW 40' Steel Rebuilt Boxcar #2 (Boys RR Club)	50
_____ 01574	D&RGW 40' Steel Rebuilt Boxcar #3 (Boys RR Club)	50
_____ 01575	Central of Georgia 40' Steel Boxcar #1 (Boys RR Club)	50
_____ 01576	Central of Georgia 40' Steel Boxcar #2 (Boys RR Club)	50
_____ 01577	Central of Georgia 40' Steel Boxcar #3 (Boys RR Club)	50
_____ 01578	Ann Arbor 40' Steel Rebuilt Boxcar	50
_____ 01579	Lancaster & Chester 40' Steel Rebuilt Boxcar #1	50
_____ 01580	Lancaster & Chester 40' Steel Rebuilt Boxcar #2	50
_____ 01581	Soo Line 40' Steel Rebuilt Boxcar #1	50
_____ 01582	Soo Line 40' Steel Rebuilt Boxcar #2	50
_____ 01583	B&O 2-8-0 Locomotive #3, hi-rail wheels, AC/DC sound	600
_____ 01584	B&O 2-8-0 Locomotive #3, hi-rail wheels, DCC sound	600

01585	B&O 2-8-0 Locomotive #3, hi-rail wheels	450 ____
01586	B&O 2-8-0 Locomotive #3, Code 110 wheels, AC/DC sound	600 ____
01587	B&O 2-8-0 Locomotive #3, Code 110 wheels, DCC sound	600 ____
01588	B&O 2-8-0 Locomotive #3, Code 110 wheels	450 ____
01589	Christmas Figure and Wreath Set	15 ____
01590	Santa and Mrs. Claus Figure Set	9 ____
01591	Matawan Junction Track Layout	430 ____
01592	Maybrook Bridge Line Track Layout	416 ____
01593	Tacoma Transfer Track Layout	410 ____
01594	Norwalk Crossing Track Layout	340 ____
01595	Macoon Yard Track Layout	630 ____
01596	Utica Terminal Track Layout	840 ____
01597	Decatur Exchange Track Layout	600 ____
01598	Gome & Dapgetid Track Layout	760 ____
01599	S-Helper Service Track Layout	620 ____
01601	B&M Double-sheathed Boxcar, scheme II #1 (Hoquat)	53 ____
01602	B&M Double-sheathed Boxcar, scheme II #2 (Hoquat)	53 ____
01603	DL&W Double-sheathed Boxcar, scheme II #1 (Hoquat)	53 ____
01604	DL&W Double-sheathed Boxcar, scheme II #2 (Hoquat)	53 ____
01605	Erie Wooden Billboard Reefer #1 (Hoquat)	53 ____
01606	Erie Wooden Billboard Reefer #2 (Hoquat)	53 ____
01607	NWX Wooden Billboard Reefer #6 (Hoquat)	53 ____
01608	NWX Wooden Billboard Reefer #7 (Hoquat)	53 ____
01609	PFE (WP) Wooden Billboard Reefer #1	53 ____
01610	PFE (WP) Wooden Billboard Reefer #2	53 ____
01611	SFRD "Super Chief" Wooden Billboard Reefer	53 ____
01612	Speaker/Switcher	40 ____
01613	NdeM 40' Steel Rebuilt Boxcar #1 (Mainstreeter)	50 ____
01614	NdeM 40' Steel Rebuilt Boxcar #2 (Mainstreeter)	50 ____
01615	Conrail SW9 Diesel Freight Set, 4 cars	300 ____
01616	SLSF SW9 Diesel Freight Set, 4 cars	300 ____
01617	Chessie (C&O) NW2 Diesel Freight Set, 5 cars	375 ____
01618	GN SW1 Diesel Freight Set, 5 cars	370 ____
01619	ATSF F7 Diesel Freight Set, 6 cars	430 ____
01620	Conrail SW9 Diesel Freight Set, 4 cars, sound	390 ____
01621	SLSF SW9 Diesel Freight Set, 4 cars, sound	390 ____
01622	Chessie (C&O) NW2 Diesel Freight Set, 5 cars, sound	460 ____
01623	NWP USRA Double-sheathed Boxcar, scheme I #2	50 ____
01624	Ann Arbor 40' Steel Rebuilt Boxcar #2	50 ____
01625	Domino Sugar PS-2 3-bay Covered Hopper	50 ____
01626	Jack Frost PS-2 3-bay Covered Hopper	50 ____
01627	B&O PS-2 3-bay Covered Hopper #1	50 ____
01628	B&O PS-2 3-bay Covered Hopper #2	50 ____

____	**01629**	C&NW PS-2 3-bay Covered Hopper, scheme II #1	50
____	**01630**	C&NW PS-2 3-bay Covered Hopper, scheme II #2	50
____	**01631**	SP PS-2 3-bay Covered Hopper #1	50
____	**01632**	SP PS-2 3-bay Covered Hopper #2	50
____	**01633**	AC/DC LocoMatic Sound Unit	180
____	**01634**	DCC Socket Set for Switchers #2	25
____	**01636**	MTC Brookside Wooden Billboard Reefer #3 (Port Lines)	53
____	**01637**	Sunrise Onions Wooden Billboard Reefer	53
____	**01638**	OTOE Food Products Wooden Billboard Reefer	53
____	**01639**	PFE Wooden Billboard Reefer, scheme III #1	53
____	**01640**	PFE Wooden Billboard Reefer, scheme III #2	53
____	**01641**	PFE Wooden Billboard Reefer, scheme III #3	53
____	**01642**	Heileman's Old Style Lager Wooden Billboard Reefer	53
____	**01643**	Domino Sugar Double-sheathed Boxcar #1 (Port Lines)	50
____	**01644**	Domino Sugar Double-sheathed Boxcar #2 (Port Lines)	50
____	**01645**	MEC Offset Hopper	50
____	**01646**	C&O USRA Rib Side Hopper #1	50
____	**01647**	C&O USRA Rib Side Hopper #2	50
____	**01648**	C&O USRA Rib Side Hopper #3	50
____	**01649**	C&O USRA Rib Side Hopper #4	50
____	**01650**	Waddell Coal USRA Rib Side Hopper #1	53
____	**01651**	Waddell Coal USRA Rib Side Hopper #2	53
____	**01652**	Waddell Coal USRA Rib Side Hopper #3	53
____	**01653**	Waddell Coal USRA Rib Side Hopper #4	53
____	**01654**	PRR Composite Side Hopper, scheme II #1	50
____	**01655**	PRR Composite Side Hopper, scheme II #2	50
____	**01656**	PRR Composite Side Hopper, scheme II #3	50
____	**01657**	PRR Composite Side Hopper, scheme II #4	50
____	**01658**	Spiral Hill USRA Rib Side Hopper #1 (Lehigh Valley)	50
____	**01659**	Spiral Hill USRA Rib Side Hopper #2 (Lehigh Valley)	50
____	**01660**	MKT 40' Steel Rebuilt Boxcar (TCA)	50
____	**01661**	Smoke Unit Funnels, 3 pieces	3
____	**01664**	Spiral Hill USRA Rib Side Hopper #3 (Lehigh Valley)	50
____	**01666**	Flatcar with 2 Humvees	60
____	**01667**	Flatcar with 2 Humvee ambulances	60
____	**01668**	ATSF F7 Diesel Freight Set, 6 cars, sound	490
____	**01669**	Locomotive Figure Set	6
____	**01670**	Tender Coupler, AF compatible, pair	3
____	**01671**	Speaker, 1-watt, 8-ohm	9
____	**01672**	Tender LED Light Set, golden white, pair	6
____	**01673**	Smoke Unit, pair	10
____	**01674**	Infrared Sensor, pair	10
____	**01675**	1.6mm Wrench	4
____	**01676**	Motor with flywheel, pair	15
____	**01677**	Flatcar with Bradley Fighting Vehicle	63

01678	Headlight LED Accessory, golden white, pair	10 ____
01679	Headlight Top LED Accessory, golden white, pair	10 ____
01680	Coal Load with snow	6 ____
01681	Mine Run Coal Load	6 ____
01682	Classification Lights, brass, pair	5 ____
01683	C&NW Stock Car #1 (Hoquat)	50 ____
01684	C&NW Stock Car #2 (Hoquat)	50 ____
01685	Grand Trunk Western Stock Car #1 (Hoquat)	50 ____
01686	Grand Trunk Western Stock Car #2 (Hoquat)	50 ____
01687	N&W Stock Car #1	50 ____
01688	N&W Stock Car #2	50 ____
01689	SLSF Stock Car #1	50 ____
01690	SLSF Stock Car #2	50 ____
01691	Santa Fe "Chief" Wooden Billboard Reefer (Hoquat)	53 ____
01692	Berkshire Wooden Billboard Reefer (Hoquat)	53 ____
01693	Peerless Beer Wooden Billboard Reefer	53 ____
01694	Skyland Eggs Wooden Billboard Reefer	53 ____
01695	Priebe Wooden Billboard Reefer	53 ____
01696	Central of Georgia 40' Steel Boxcar, red (Boys RR Club)	50 ____
01697	Central of Georgia 40' Steel Boxcar, black (Boys RR Club)	50 ____
01698	Central of Georgia 40' Steel Boxcar, maroon (Boys RR Club)	50 ____
01699	Central of Georgia 40' Steel Boxcar, blue (Boys RR Club)	50 ____
01700	MEC 2-8-0 Locomotive #1, Code 110 wheels	450 ____
01701	MEC 2-8-0 Locomotive #2, Code 110 wheels	450 ____
01702	NYC 2-8-0 Locomotive #1, Code 110 wheels	450 ____
01703	NYC 2-8-0 Locomotive #2, Code 110 wheels	450 ____
01704	Southern 2-8-0 Locomotive, Code 110 wheels	450 ____
01706	UP 2-8-0 Locomotive #1, Code 110 wheels	450 ____
01707	UP 2-8-0 Locomotive #2, Code 110 wheels	450 ____
01708	WM 2-8-0 Locomotive #1, Code 110 wheels	450 ____
01709	WM 2-8-0 Locomotive #2, Code 110 wheels	450 ____
01710	B&O 40' Steel Rebuilt Boxcar, blue roof (Boys RR Club)	50 ____
01711	B&O 40' Steel Rebuilt Boxcar, silver roof (Boys RR Club)	50 ____
01712	B&O 40' Steel Rebuilt Boxcar, blue roof (Boys RR Club)	50 ____
01713	B&O 40' Steel Rebuilt Boxcar, silver roof (Boys RR Club)	50 ____
01714	Great American Circus Steel Boxcar (Scenery Unlimited)	50 ____
01715	Great American Circus Steel Boxcar (Scenery Unlimited)	50 ____
01716	Great American Circus Steel Boxcar (Scenery Unlimited)	50 ____
01717	Great American Circus Stock Car (Scenery Unlimited)	50 ____
01718	Great American Circus Stock Car (Scenery Unlimited)	50 ____
01719	Great American Circus Stock Car (Scenery Unlimited)	50 ____
01720	MNS 40' Steel Rebuilt Boxcar #1 (Pines & Prairies)	50 ____
01721	MNS 40' Steel Rebuilt Boxcar #2 (Pines & Prairies)	50 ____
01722	Great American Circus Flatcar (Scenery Unlimited)	50 ____

_____	**01723** Great American Circus Flatcar (Scenery Unlimited)	50
_____	**01724** Great American Circus Flatcar (Scenery Unlimited)	50
_____	**01725** Great American Circus Flatcar (Scenery Unlimited)	50
_____	**01726** Great American Circus Flatcar (Scenery Unlimited)	50
_____	**01727** Great American Circus Flatcar (Scenery Unlimited)	50
_____	**01728** BN Christmas Bulkhead Flatcar #3 with presents	56
_____	**01729** GM&O Bulkhead Flatcar #1 with pipe load	56
_____	**01730** GM&O Bulkhead Flatcar #2 with pipe load	56
_____	**01731** BAAFC Wooden Billboard Reefer (NASG)	53
_____	**01732** BAAFC Wooden Billboard Reefer (NASG)	53
_____	**01734** 40" Unweathered Rail, Code 131, 33 pieces	70
_____	**01735** 33" Scale Wheel Set/Pickup, Code 110, 4-pack	5
_____	**01736** CB&Q (FWD) NW2 Diesel	200
_____	**01737** CB&Q NW2 Diesel	200
_____	**01738** CB&Q (FWD) NW2 Diesel, AC/DC LocoMatic sound	290
_____	**01739** CB&Q NW2 Diesel, AC/DC LocoMatic sound	290
_____	**01740** CB&Q (FWD) NW2 Diesel, DCC sound	290
_____	**01741** CB&Q NW2 Diesel, DCC sound	290
_____	**01742** ICG PS-2 2-bay Covered Hopper #1	50
_____	**01743** ICG PS-2 2-bay Covered Hopper #2	50
_____	**01744** SP PS-2 2-bay Covered Hopper, scheme III #1	50
_____	**01745** SP PS-2 2-bay Covered Hopper, scheme III #2	50
_____	**01746** Lancaster & Chester PS-2 2-bay Covered Hopper #1	50
_____	**01747** Lancaster & Chester PS-2 2-bay Covered Hopper #2	50
_____	**01748** Maryland Midland PS-2 2-bay Covered Hopper (NASG)	50
_____	**01749** Maryland Midland PS-2 2-bay Covered Hopper (NASG)	50
_____	**01750** Kerr-McGee PS-2 2-bay Covered Hopper	50
_____	**01751** 2-8-0 Locomotive, AC/DC LocoMatic sound	600
_____	**01752** B&O 2-8-0 Locomotive #1	600
_____	**01753** B&O 2-8-0 Locomotive #2	600
_____	**01754** ATSF 2-8-0 Locomotive #1	600
_____	**01755** ATSF 2-8-0 Locomotive #2	600
_____	**01756** C&NW 2-8-0 Locomotive #1	600
_____	**01757** C&NW 2-8-0 Locomotive #2	600
_____	**01758** Erie 2-8-0 Locomotive #1	600
_____	**01759** Erie 2-8-0 Locomotive #2	600
_____	**01760** MEC 2-8-0 Locomotive #1	600
_____	**01761** MEC 2-8-0 Locomotive #2	600
_____	**01762** NYC 2-8-0 Locomotive #1	600
_____	**01763** NYC 2-8-0 Locomotive #2	600
_____	**01764** Southern 2-8-0 Locomotive #1	600
_____	**01766** UP 2-8-0 Locomotive #1	600
_____	**01767** UP 2-8-0 Locomotive #2	600
_____	**01768** WM 2-8-0 Locomotive #1	600
_____	**01769** WM 2-8-0 Locomotive #2	600

01771	2-8-0 Locomotive, DCC sound	600 ____
01772	B&O 2-8-0 Locomotive #1	600 ____
01773	B&O 2-8-0 Locomotive #2	600 ____
01774	ATSF 2-8-0 Locomotive #1	600 ____
01775	ATSF 2-8-0 Locomotive #2	600 ____
01776	C&NW 2-8-0 Locomotive #1	600 ____
01777	C&NW 2-8-0 Locomotive #2	600 ____
01778	Erie 2-8-0 Locomotive #1	600 ____
01779	Erie 2-8-0 Locomotive #2	600 ____
01780	MEC 2-8-0 Locomotive #1	600 ____
01781	MEC 2-8-0 Locomotive #2	600 ____
01782	NYC 2-8-0 Locomotive #1	600 ____
01783	NYC 2-8-0 Locomotive #2	600 ____
01784	Southern 2-8-0 Locomotive #1	600 ____
01786	UP 2-8-0 Locomotive #1	600 ____
01787	UP 2-8-0 Locomotive #2	600 ____
01788	WM 2-8-0 Locomotive #1	600 ____
01789	WM 2-8-0 Locomotive #2	600 ____
01790	GTW USRA Rebuilt Covered Hopper #1	50 ____
01791	2-8-0 Locomotive, DC, no sound	450 ____
01792	B&O 2-8-0 Locomotive #1	450 ____
01793	B&O 2-8-0 Locomotive #2	450 ____
01794	ATSF 2-8-0 Locomotive #1	450 ____
01795	ATSF 2-8-0 Locomotive #2	450 ____
01796	C&NW 2-8-0 Locomotive #1	450 ____
01797	C&NW 2-8-0 Locomotive #2	450 ____
01798	Erie 2-8-0 Locomotive #1	450 ____
01799	Erie 2-8-0 Locomotive #2	450 ____
01800	Chicago Macaroni Wooden Billboard Reefer	53 ____
01801	Hamm Brewing Wooden Billboard Reefer	53 ____
01802	Westcott & Winks Wooden Billboard Reefer	53 ____
01803	Marhoefer Wooden Billboard Reefer #1	53 ____
01804	Flatcar with 2 Stuart tanks	60 ____
01807	Santa Fe Flatcar with trailer, scheme II #1	63 ____
01808	Santa Fe Flatcar with trailer, scheme II #2	63 ____
01809	Reading Flatcar #1 with trailer	63 ____
01810	Reading Flatcar #2 with trailer	63 ____
01811	Flatcar with REA trailer, 2007 Christmas Car	63 ____
01812	SP Flatcar #1 with trailer	63 ____
01813	SP Flatcar #2 with trailer	63 ____
01814	CGW Bulkhead Flatcar with pipes #1	56 ____
01815	CGW Bulkhead Flatcar with pipes #2	56 ____
01816	ACL Bulkhead Flatcar #1 with pipes	56 ____
01817	ACL Bulkhead Flatcar #2 with pulpwood	56 ____
01818	ATSF Standard Flatcar #2, red	50 ____

01819	ATSF Standard Flatcar #3, red	50
01820	Reading Standard Flatcar #1	50
01821	Reading Standard Flatcar #2	50
01822	ACL Standard Flatcar #1	50
01823	ACL Standard Flatcar #2	50
01824	PRR Standard Flatcar #4	50
01825	PRR Standard Flatcar #5	50
01826	SP Standard Flatcar, scheme II #1	50
01827	SP Standard Flatcar, scheme II #2	50
01828	Santa Fe Wooden Billboard Reefer #1	53
01829	Santa Fe Wooden Billboard Reefer #2	53
01830	Carling Black Label Billboard Reefer #3 (Port Lines)	53
01831	B&O USRA Single-sheathed Boxcar, scheme II #1	50
01832	B&O USRA Single-sheathed Boxcar, scheme II #2	50
01833	CNJ USRA Single-sheathed Boxcar #1	50
01834	CNJ USRA Single-sheathed Boxcar #2	50
01835	MEC USRA Single-sheathed Boxcar #1	50
01836	MEC USRA Single-sheathed Boxcar #2	50
01839	PRR USRA Single-sheathed Boxcar #3	50
01840	PRR USRA Single-sheathed Boxcar #4	50
01842	Canada Southern USRA Rebuilt Covered Hopper #1	50
01843	Canada Southern USRA Rebuilt Covered Hopper #2	50
01845	RFP Express USRA Double-sheathed Boxcar #1	50
01846	RFP Express USRA Double-sheathed Boxcar #2	50
01847	DCC Interface PCB for Switchers	25
01848	B&O USRA Rebuilt Covered Hopper #1	50
01849	B&O USRA Rebuilt Covered Hopper #2	50
01850	CNJ USRA Rebuilt Covered Hopper #1	50
01851	CNJ USRA Rebuilt Covered Hopper #2	50
01852	C&O USRA Rebuilt Covered Hopper #1	50
01853	C&O USRA Rebuilt Covered Hopper #2	50
01854	D&H USRA Rebuilt Covered Hopper #1	50
01855	D&H USRA Rebuilt Covered Hopper #2	50
01856	LNE USRA Rebuilt Covered Hopper #1	50
01857	LNE USRA Rebuilt Covered Hopper #2	50
01858	LV USRA Rebuilt Covered Hopper #1	50
01859	LV USRA Rebuilt Covered Hopper #2	50
01861	MEC USRA Rebuilt Covered Hopper #2	55
01862	NYC USRA Rebuilt Covered Hopper #1	50
01863	NYC USRA Rebuilt Covered Hopper #2	50
01864	NKP USRA Rebuilt Covered Hopper #1	50
01865	NKP USRA Rebuilt Covered Hopper #2	50
01866	Reading USRA Rebuilt Covered Hopper #1	50
01867	Reading USRA Rebuilt Covered Hopper #2	50
01868	Cambria & Indiana Offset Hopper #1	50

01869	Cambria & Indiana Offset Hopper #2	50 ____
01870	USRA Rebuilt Covered Hopper, gray	50 ____
01871	PRR Standard Flatcar #4	50 ____
01872	S-Helper Service 35' Trailer, horizontal corrugations	20 ____
01874	ATSF 35' Trailer, horizontal corrugations, scheme II	20 ____
01875	Reading 35' Trailer, vertical ribs	20 ____
01876	Moxie Wooden Billboard Reefer #1 (NASG)	53 ____
01877	Moxie Wooden Billboard Reefer #2 (NASG)	53 ____
01878	REA 35' Trailer, vertical ribs	20 ____
01879	SP 35' Trailer, horizontal corrugations	20 ____
01880	ATSF 35' Trailer, vertical ribs, scheme II	20 ____
01881	Weber Wooden Billboard Reefer #1 (Badgerland)	53 ____
01882	Weber Wooden Billboard Reefer #2 (Badgerland)	53 ____
01883	Weber Wooden Billboard Reefer #3 (Badgerland)	53 ____
01884	Sampson Canning Wooden Billboard Reefer	53 ____
01885	ATSF USRA Double-sheathed Boxcar #1	50 ____
01886	ATSF USRA Double-sheathed Boxcar #2	50 ____
01887	CB&Q USRA Double-sheathed Boxcar #1	50 ____
01888	CB&Q USRA Double-sheathed Boxcar #2	50 ____
01889	CH&D USRA Double-sheathed Boxcar #1	50 ____
01890	CH&D USRA Double-sheathed Boxcar #2 (Miami Valley)	50 ____
01891	NKP USRA Double-sheathed Boxcar #1 (Hoosier)	50 ____
01892	NKP USRA Double-sheathed Boxcar #2 (Hoosier)	50 ____
01893	NKP USRA Double-sheathed Boxcar #3	50 ____
01894	NKP USRA Double-sheathed Boxcar #4	50 ____
01895	NWP Double-sheathed Boxcar, scheme II #1 (O West)	50 ____
01896	NWP Double-sheathed Boxcar, scheme II #2 (O West)	50 ____
01897	NWP USRA Double-sheathed Boxcar, scheme II #3	50 ____
01898	NWP USRA Double-sheathed Boxcar, scheme II #4	50 ____
01899	Frank Fehr Brewery Wooden Billboard Reefer	53 ____
01900	Buffalo Creek & Gauley USRA Rib Side Hopper #1	50 ____
01901	Buffalo Creek & Gauley USRA Rib Side Hopper #2	50 ____
01902	Buffalo Creek & Gauley USRA Rib Side Hopper #3	50 ____
01903	Buffalo Creek & Gauley USRA Rib Side Hopper #4	50 ____
01904	C&O USRA Rib Side Hopper #5	50 ____
01905	C&O USRA Rib Side Hopper #6	50 ____
01906	PRR USRA Rib Side Hopper, scheme II #1	50 ____
01907	PRR USRA Rib Side Hopper, scheme II #2	50 ____
01908	GTW USRA Rebuilt Covered Hopper #2	50 ____
01909	CB&Q NW2 Diesel Freight Set, 5 cars	350 ____
01910	SLSF SW9 Diesel Freight Set, 5 cars	350 ____
01911	MP F7A Diesel Freight Set, 6 cars	430 ____
01912	GN SW1 Diesel Freight Set, 4 cars	315 ____
01913	CRI&P 40' Steel Rebuilt Boxcar #1 (State Line)	50 ____
01914	CRI&P 40' Steel Rebuilt Boxcar #2 (State Line)	50 ____

_____	**01915** CRI&P 40' Steel Rebuilt Boxcar #3 (State Line)	50
_____	**01916** ATSF "Chief" 40' Steel Rebuilt Boxcar #1	50
_____	**01917** ATSF "Chief" 40' Steel Rebuilt Boxcar #2	50
_____	**01918** C&O 40' Steel Rebuilt Boxcar #3	50
_____	**01919** C&O 40' Steel Rebuilt Boxcar #4	50
_____	**01920** P&LE (NYC) 40' Steel Rebuilt Boxcar #2	50
_____	**01921** P&LE (NYC) 40' Steel Rebuilt Boxcar #3	50
_____	**01922** MP "Eagle" 40' Steel Rebuilt Boxcar #3	50
_____	**01923** MP "Eagle" 40' Steel Rebuilt Boxcar #4	50
_____	**01941** CNJ USRA Rebuilt Covered Hopper #3	50
_____	**01942** CNJ USRA Rebuilt Covered Hopper #4	50
_____	**01943** Moxie Wooden Billboard Reefer #3	53
_____	**01944** Moxie Wooden Billboard Reefer #4	53
_____	**01946** Santa Fe Wooden Billboard Reefer #3	53
_____	**01947** Santa Fe Wooden Billboard Reefer #4	53
_____	**01951** PFE Wooden Billboard Reefer, scheme IV #1	53
_____	**01952** PFE Wooden Billboard Reefer, scheme IV #2	53
_____	**01957** PFE Wooden Billboard Reefer, scheme IV #3	53
_____	**01958** B&A 40' Steel Rebuilt Boxcar #1 (Daniel Lundy)	50
_____	**01959** B&A 40' Steel Rebuilt Boxcar #2 (Daniel Lundy)	50
_____	**01960** B&A 40' Steel Rebuilt Boxcar #3 (Daniel Lundy)	50
_____	**01961** B&A 40' Steel Rebuilt Boxcar #4 (Daniel Lundy)	50
_____	**01962** Sherman Williams PS-2 2-bay Hopper #1 (CVSG)	50
_____	**01963** Sherman Williams PS-2 2-bay Hopper #2 (CVSG)	50
_____	**01964** Sherman Williams PS-2 2-bay Hopper #3 (CVSG)	50
_____	**01965** Sherman Williams PS-2 2-bay Hopper #4 (CVSG)	50
_____	**01966** Sherman Williams PS-2 2-bay Hopper #5 (CVSG)	50
_____	**01967** Union Carbide "Bakelite" PS-2 3-bay Covered Hopper	50
_____	**01968** ATSF PS-2 3-bay Covered Hopper #1	50
_____	**01969** ATSF PS-2 3-bay Covered Hopper #2	50
_____	**01970** Erie PS-2 3-bay Covered Hopper #1	50
_____	**01971** Erie PS-2 3-bay Covered Hopper #2	50
_____	**01972** Erie PS-2 3-bay Covered Hopper #3	50
_____	**01973** CRI&P 40' Steel Boxcar, scheme II #2 (State Line)	50
_____	**01976** GN PS-2 3-bay Covered Hopper #3	50
_____	**01977** GN PS-2 3-bay Covered Hopper #4	50
_____	**01978** SW8/9 Diesel, DCC sound	290
_____	**01979** C&NW (CGW) PS-2 3-bay Covered Hopper #1	50
_____	**01980** C&NW (CGW) PS-2 3-bay Covered Hopper #2	50
_____	**01981** Marhoefer Wooden Billboard Reefer #2	50
_____	**01982** Marhoefer Wooden Billboard Reefer #3	50
_____	**01983** CP Stock Car #1	50
_____	**01984** CP Stock Car #2	50
_____	**01985** CB&Q Stock Car #3	50
_____	**01986** CB&Q Stock Car #4	50

01987	UP Stock Car #7	50 ____
01988	UP Stock Car #8	50 ____
01989	B&O Composite Side Hopper #5	53 ____
01990	B&O Composite Side Hopper #6	53 ____
01991	PRR Composite Side Hopper, scheme II #5	53 ____
01992	PRR Composite Side Hopper, scheme II #6	53 ____
01993	Black Fishbelly Hopper	53 ____
01994	Red Fishbelly Hopper	53 ____
01995	Akron, Canton & Youngstown Fishbelly Hopper #1	53 ____
01996	Akron, Canton & Youngstown Fishbelly Hopper #2	53 ____
01997	Akron, Canton & Youngstown Fishbelly Hopper #3	53 ____
01998	Akron, Canton & Youngstown Fishbelly Hopper #4	53 ____
01999	ACL Fishbelly Hopper #1	53 ____
02000	ACL Fishbelly Hopper #2	53 ____
02001	ACL Fishbelly Hopper #3	53 ____
02002	ACL Fishbelly Hopper #4	53 ____
02003	B&O Fishbelly Hopper #1	53 ____
02004	B&O Fishbelly Hopper #2	53 ____
02005	B&O Fishbelly Hopper #3	53 ____
02006	B&O Fishbelly Hopper #4	53 ____
02007	CNJ Fishbelly Hopper #1	53 ____
02008	CNJ Fishbelly Hopper #2	53 ____
02009	CNJ Fishbelly Hopper #3	53 ____
02010	CNJ Fishbelly Hopper #4	53 ____
02011	C&O Fishbelly Hopper #1	53 ____
02012	C&O Fishbelly Hopper #2	53 ____
02013	C&O Fishbelly Hopper #3	53 ____
02014	C&O Fishbelly Hopper #4	53 ____
02015	D&H Fishbelly Hopper #1	53 ____
02016	D&H Fishbelly Hopper #2	53 ____
02017	D&H Fishbelly Hopper #3	53 ____
02018	D&H Fishbelly Hopper #4	53 ____
02019	LV Fishbelly Hopper #1	53 ____
02020	LV Fishbelly Hopper #2	53 ____
02021	LV Fishbelly Hopper #3	53 ____
02022	LV Fishbelly Hopper #4	53 ____
02023	N&W Fishbelly Hopper #1	53 ____
02024	N&W Fishbelly Hopper #2	53 ____
02025	N&W Fishbelly Hopper #3	53 ____
02026	N&W Fishbelly Hopper #4	53 ____
02027	NS Fishbelly Hopper #1	53 ____
02028	NS Fishbelly Hopper #2	53 ____
02029	NS Fishbelly Hopper #3	53 ____
02030	NS Fishbelly Hopper #4	53 ____
02031	Reading Fishbelly Hopper #1	53 ____

Retail

____ **02032**	Reading Fishbelly Hopper #2	53
____ **02033**	Reading Fishbelly Hopper #3	53
____ **02034**	Reading Fishbelly Hopper #4	53
____ **02035**	WM Fishbelly Hopper #1	53
____ **02036**	WM Fishbelly Hopper #2	53
____ **02037**	WM Fishbelly Hopper #3	53
____ **02038**	WM Fishbelly Hopper #4	53
____ **02039**	Ballantine Beer Wooden Billboard Reefer #3 (Hoquat)	53
____ **02040**	Ballantine Beer Wooden Billboard Reefer #4 (Hoquat)	53
____ **02043**	DL&W Reefer #1	53
____ **02044**	DL&W Reefer #2	53
____ **02045**	Eatmor Cranberries Wooden Billboard Reefer	53
____ **02046**	Falstaff Wooden Billboard Reefer #1 (NASG)	53
____ **02047**	Falstaff Wooden Billboard Reefer #2 (NASG)	53
____ **02048**	Lemp Falstaff Wooden Billboard Reefer #1 (NASG)	53
____ **02049**	Lemp Falstaff Wooden Billboard Reefer #2 (NASG)	53
____ **02050**	Prima Special Wooden Billboard Reefer	53
____ **02051**	CB&Q NW2 Diesel Freight Set, 6 cars	390
____ **02052**	BN SW8 Diesel Freight Set, 4 cars	346
____ **02053**	CRI&P SW8 Diesel Freight Set, 5 cars	360
____ **02054**	GN 2009 Christmas Boxcar	63
____ **02055**	Toronto, Hamilton & Buffalo Double-sheathed Boxcar #2	50
____ **02056**	3M USRA Double-sheathed Boxcar #1	50
____ **02057**	3M USRA Double-sheathed Boxcar #2	50
____ **02058**	Flatcar with 4 wrapped steel coils	63
____ **02059**	Mine Run Coal Load	7
____ **02060**	Gluek Brewing Billboard Reefer, blue (Hoquat)	53
____ **02061**	Gluek Brewing Billboard Reefer, red (Hoquat)	53
____ **02065**	Gray Steel Coil Loads	63
____ **02066**	Metal Rail Joiners, unweathered, 36 pieces	7
____ **02070**	Laser Cut Reels with rack	75
____ **02071**	PRR 2D-F1 Archbar Truck, code 110, pair	25
____ **02072**	PRR 2D-F1 Archbar Truck, hi-rail, pair	25
____ **02073**	B&O USRA Rib Side Hopper, scheme II #1	53
____ **02074**	B&O USRA Rib Side Hopper, scheme II #2	53
____ **02075**	B&O USRA Rib Side Hopper, scheme II #3	53
____ **02076**	B&O USRA Rib Side Hopper, scheme II #4	53
____ **02077**	Reading USRA Rib Side Hopper #5	53
____ **02078**	Reading USRA Rib Side Hopper #6	53
____ **02079**	ATSF Composite Side Hopper #5	53
____ **02080**	ATSF Composite Side Hopper #6	53
____ **02081**	CB&Q Composite Side Hopper #5	53
____ **02082**	CB&Q Composite Side Hopper #6	53
____ **02083**	LV Composite Side Hopper #9	53
____ **02084**	LV Composite Side Hopper #10	53

02086	C&O Composite Side Hopper #5	53 _____
02087	C&O Composite Side Hopper #6	53 _____
02109	GN 40' Steel Rebuilt Boxcar, scheme III #3	53 _____
02110	GN 40' Steel Rebuilt Boxcar, scheme III #4	53 _____
02111	NKP Steel Rebuilt Boxcar #1	53 _____
02112	NKP Steel Rebuilt Boxcar #2	53 _____
02113	NKP Steel Rebuilt Boxcar #3	53 _____
02114	NKP Steel Rebuilt Boxcar #4	53 _____
02115	Seaboard "Orange Blossom Special" Rebuilt Boxcar #2	53 _____
02116	Seaboard "Orange Blossom Special" Rebuilt Boxcar #3	53 _____
02117	SP Steel Rebuilt Boxcar #1 (S Scale West)	53 _____
02118	SP Steel Rebuilt Boxcar #2 (S Scale West)	53 _____
02119	SP Steel Rebuilt Boxcar #3 (S Scale West)	53 _____
02120	SP Steel Rebuilt Boxcar #4 (S Scale West)	53 _____
02127	40" SW/NW Wheelset, Code 110	16 _____
02128	40" SW/NW Wheelset, AF compatible	16 _____
02129	40" F unit Wheelset, Code 110	16 _____
02130	40" F unit Wheelset, AF compatible	16 _____
02149	WM Fishbelly Hopper, scheme II #1	53 _____
02150	WM Fishbelly Hopper, scheme II #2	53 _____
ART-5400	DC Power Pack, 24VDC	50 _____
20064	Rock Island Boxcar, silver (State-Line S Gaugers)	45 _____
20070	Rock Island Boxcar, green (State-Line S Gaugers)	45 _____

Unnumbered Items

Train Pack Lube Set   15 _____

		Good (P-5)	Exc (P-7)
	1946		
___ **D1451**	Consumer Catalog	35	150
___	with red binder	75	450
___ **D1455**	Dealer Catalog	27	115
___ **D1457**	Gilbert Scientific Toys	10	21
___ **D1458**	Appointment Card	1	2
___ **M2499**	Instruction Sheet		1
___	Envelope for D1451	2	7
	1947		
___ **D1462**	Catalog Mailer	14	60
___ **D1472**	Catalog Mailer	14	50
___ **D1473**	Consumer Catalog	27	80
___ **D1482**	Dealer Catalog	20	75
___ **D1492**	Erector Fun and Action	4	13
___ **D1495**	What Retail Stores Should Know	4	13
___ **D1496**	Display Suggestions	45	270
___ **D1502**	Advance Catalog	13	41
___ **M2502**	Instruction Book	2	5
___	Envelope for D1473	2	4
	1948		
___ **D1505**	Advance Catalog	10	52
___ **D1507**	Consumer Catalog	15	49
___ **D1508**	Superman	17	100
___ **D1508**	Consumer Catalog	10	24
___	with prepaid postage	5	18
___ **D1517**	HO Catalog	9	23
	1949		
___ **D1524**	Gilbert Scientific Toys Catalog	5	9
___ **D1525**	Bang Bang Torpedo	45	115
___ **D1530**	Advance Catalog	18	50
___ **D1531**	Gilbert Scientific Toys Catalog	5	9
___ **D1536**	Consumer Catalog	9	30
___ **D1547**	Catalog Envelope	1	4
___ **D1552**	How to Sell American Flyer	5	18
M2690	Instruction Booklet		
___	(A) Yellow cover	1	5
___	(B) White cover	4	7
	1950		
___ **D1578**	Dealer Catalog	13	40
___ **D1579**	Gilbert Toys	5	16
___ **D1581/A**	Red/Blue Ad		180
___ **D1604**	Consumer Catalog	16	45

GILBERT PAPER 1946–1967		Good (P-5)	Exc (P-7)	
D1610	Catalog Envelope	1	4	____
D1629	Dealer Action Displays Sheet		NRS	____
D1631	Dealer TV Ad	9	18	____
	Ready Again Booklet		300	____

1951

D1637	Dealer Catalog	13	45	____
D1637A	Advance Catalog	8	34	____
D1640	Consumer Catalog	15	40	____
D1641	Erector and Gilbert Toys Catalog	2	5	____
D1652	Facts About AF Trains		60	____
D1656	AF and Toys	5	9	____
D1660	Gilbert Electric Eye	5	9	____

1952

D1667	Advance Catalog	10	40	____
D1667A	Advance Catalog	11	41	____
D1668A	Consumer Catalog		40	____
D1670	Single Sheet 200 Series Buildings	2	9	____
D1677	Consumer Catalog	8	30	____
D1678	Facts About AF Trains	7	11	____
M2978	AF Model Railroad Handbook	5	9	____
M2984	Instruction Book	1	3	____
	Advance Catalog		NRS	____
	Consumer Catalog, Spanish		NRS	____

1953

D1699	Consumer Catalog		50	____
D1703	Erector and Other Toys	3	7	____
D1704	Dealer Catalog	9	30	____
D1714	Dealer Catalog, East	8	30	____
D1715	Consumer Catalog, West	11	29	____
D1727	Tips on Selling AF Trains	5	9	____
D1728	Tips on Erector	2	8	____

1954

D1734	Catalog Envelope	1	4	____
D1740	Erector and Gilbert Toys	1	4	____
D1744	AF and Erector Ad Program	4	16	____
D1746	Dealer Catalog			
	(A) Pulp	8	30	____
	(B) Glossy	8	45	____
D1748	Catalog, East			
	(A) Consumer	3	15	____
	(B) Dealer	4	20	____
D1749	Dealer Catalog, West	11	29	____
D1750	Dealer Displays		NRS	____
D1751	Microscope Flysheet	1	2	____
D1760	Consumer Catalog, East	10	44	____
D1761	Consumer Catalog, West	12	37	____
D1762	Boys Railroad Club Letter	1	5	____

		Good (P-5)	Exc (P-7)
____ **D1769**	Read All About Ad Campaign		NRS
____ **D1774**	Erector and Other Gilbert Toys	2	5
____ **D1777**	Reply Postcard	1	2
____ **M3290**	Instruction Book	1	4

1955

____ **D1782**	Dealer Catalog	8	30
____ **D1783**	Certificate of Registry	5	9
____ **D1784**	Erector and Other Gilbert Toys		80
____ **D1801**	Consumer Catalog, East	7	20
____ **D1802**	Consumer Catalog, West	9	20
____ **D1814**	Choo Choo Sound Foldout	1	4
____ **D1816**	Dealer Catalog	9	29
____ **D1820**	HO Consumer Catalog	1	5
____ **D1835**	Tips for Selling Erector	1	2
____ **D1840**	Envelope	1	4
____ **M3450**	Instruction Book	1	5

1956

____ **D1866**	Consumer Catalog, East	7	15
____ **D1867**	Consumer Catalog, West	10	15
____ **D1874**	Dealer Catalog	14	39
____ **D1879**	Gilbert and Erector Toys	1	6
____ **D1882**	AF and Erector Displays	1	7
____ **D1892**	Store Banner (Dealer)		525
____ **D1893**	Store Banner		1250
____ **D1899**	Big Value AF Trestle System Special Set Brochure		100
____ **D1904**	Gilbert HO Catalog	2	6
____ **D1907**	Dealer Catalog	6	28
____ **D1920**	How to Build a Model Railroad	2	15
____ **D1922**	Miniature Catalog	6	25
____ **D1925**	Erector Folder	2	7
____ **D1926**	Envelope for D1922 Catalog	1	4

1957

____ **D1937**	Dealer Catalog	9	35
____ **D1966**	Consumer Catalog	2	10
____ **D1973**	Erector and Other Toys	1	2
____ **D1980**	Cardboard		35
____ **D1981**	Same as D1980		35
____ **D2006**	Consumer Catalog, East	5	15
____ **D2007**	Consumer Catalog, West	13	20
____ **D2008**	Erector and Toys	1	4
____ **D2022**	Dealer Flyer		55
____ **D2031**	Consumer Catalog		41
____ **D2037**	Erector and Gilbert Toys	1	5
____ **D2045**	Gilbert Promotion Kit		NRS
____ **M3817**	HO Instructions	2	7
____	Same as M3450 (1955) but without number		20

		Good (P-5)	Exc (P-7)	

1958

		Good (P-5)	Exc (P-7)	
D2047	Consumer Catalog	21	90	___
D2048	Catalog, West	25	75	___
D2058	Erector and Toys	1	5	___
D2060	Erector and Gilbert Toys	2	10	___
D2073	Advance Catalog	6	17	___
D2080	Smoking Caboose		125	___
D2086	Consumer Folder, East	2	10	___
D2087	Consumer Folder, West	1	10	___
D2088	Consumer Folder	2	11	___
D2101	Career Building Science Toys	1	2	___
D4106	HO Catalog	1	4	___
M4195	Accessory Folder	1	4	___
M4202	Color Billboards		10	___

1959

		Good (P-5)	Exc (P-7)	
D2115	Dealer Catalog	12	50	___
D2118	AF No. 20142, Willit		15	___
D2120	Career Building Science Toys	1	12	___
D2125	Overland Express Sheet	1	2	___
D2132	HO Catalog		34	___
D2146	Consumer Catalog	1	10	___
D2148	Consumer Catalog	1	7	___
D2171/-79	Dealer Promotional Set		NRS	___
D2179	Promotional Sheet, Franklin Set	1	5	___
D2180	Gilbert Science Toys	1	4	___
M4225	Train Assembly and Operating Instructions		NRS	___
M4326	Accessory Catalog	1	4	___
M4869	AF Maintenance Manual	1	2	___
	Canadian D2115 Catalog		NRS	___
	Catalog, Gilbert Toys		NRS	___

1960

		Good (P-5)	Exc (P-7)	
D2192	Catalog			
	(A) Dealer	5	28	___
	(B) Advance		33	___
D2193	Consumer Catalog	2	9	___
D2193REV	Revised Consumer Catalog	2	7	___
D2196	Dealer Catalog		120	___
D2197	Dealer Display Catalog		85	___
D2198	Action and Fun Catalog	2	6	___
D2205	Gilbert Toys	2	9	___
D2208	Dealer Advance Catalog		75	___
D2223	Gilbert Science Toys	1	4	___
D2224	Consumer Folder	1	5	___
D2225	Consumer Folder	3	6	___
D2226	Consumer Folder	1	4	___
D2230	Consumer Catalog	9	40	___
D2231	Consumer Catalog	2	7	___
	Truscott Set Promotional Sheet		50	___

		Good (P-5)	Exc (P-7)
1961			
D2238	Career Building Science Toys	2	25
D2239	Consumer Catalog	4	15
D2242REV	Auto Rama Catalog	1	2
D2255	1961–62 Retail Display	1	2
D2266	Gilbert Science Toys	1	5
D2267	Consumer Catalog	4	15
D2268	Auto Rama Folder	1	2
1962			
D2277REV	Career Building Science Toys	7	24
D2278	Dealer Catalog	2	19
D2278REV	Revised Dealer Catalog	2	10
D2282	Dealer Catalog		35
D2283	HO Trains and Accessories	2	8
D2307	Consumer Ad Mats		75
D2310	Consumer Catalog	4	17
D2329	HO Catalog		45
M6874	Instruction Booklet	1	4
	The Big Ones Come From Gilbert		35
1963			
D2321	Dealer Catalog	1	5
D2321REV	Revised Dealer Catalog	5	14
D2328	Consumer Catalog		16
X863-3	Consumer Catalog	4	31
1964			
X264-6	Consumer Catalog	3	21
564-11	Dealer Catalog	2	7
	Similar to X264-6, 8 pages		NRS
	Similar to X264-6, black binding		NRS
1965			
X165-12	Dealer Catalog	6	29
X165-12REV	Revised Dealer Catalog	6	13
X365-10	Consumer Folder	1	5
T465-5REV	Dealer Folder	1	2
1966			
T166-6	Dealer Catalog	4	21
T166-7	Gilbert Action Toys	6	32
X466-1	Consumer Catalog	3	14
T1065-11	Dealer Sales Folder		200
M6788	All Aboard Instructions	3	8
1967*			
	Four-page Folder	1	4

*Gilbert train production ended in 1966; however, an American Flyer Industries Folder was released for 1967.

ABBREVIATIONS

Descriptions

AF	American Flyer
AFL	American Flyer Lines
ART	American Refrigerator Transit Co.
BAAFC	Baltimore Area American Flyer Club
CC	Command Control
CD	Center discharge
CVSG	Cuyahoga Valley S Gauge Association
EMD	Electro-Motive Division
FGE	Fruit Growers Express
FM	Fairbanks-Morse
GP	Diesel locomotive
GM	General Motors
MDT	Merchants Despatch Transportation
MOW	Maintenance-of-way
NASG	National Association of S-Gaugers
NETCA	New England Division, TCA
NMRA	National Model Railroad Association
PA	Alco diesel with cab
PB	Alco diesel without cab
PFE	Pacific Fruit Express
PM	Pike Master
REA	Railway Express Agency
s-i-b	Smoke in boiler
s-i-t	Smoke in tender
TCA	Train Collectors Association
TTOS	Toy Train Operating Society
UFGE	United Fruit Growers Express
USRA	United States Railroad Administration
WFE	Western Fruit Express
1-D	One dome
3-D	Three dome

ABBREVIATIONS
Railroad names

ACL	Atlantic Coast Line
ATSF	Atchison, Topeka & Santa Fe
B&A	Boston & Albany
BAR	Bangor & Aroostook
B&LE	Bessemer & Lake Erie
B&M	Boston & Maine
BN	Burlington Northern
BNSF	Burlington Northern Santa Fe
B&O	Baltimore & Ohio
CB&Q	Chicago, Burlington & Quincy
CMStP&P	Chicago, Milwaukee, St. Paul & Pacific
CN	Canadian National
CGW	Chicago Great Western
CNJ	Central of New Jersey
C&NW	Chicago & North Western
C&O	Chesapeake & Ohio
CP	Canadian Pacific
CRI&P	Chicago, Rock Island & Pacific
C&S	Colorado Southern
CUVA	Cuyahoga Valley Railway
D&H	Delaware & Hudson
D&RGW	Denver & Rio Grande Western
DT&I	Detroit, Toledo & Ironton
DM&IR	Duluth, Missabe & Iron Range
Erie-Lack.	Erie-Lackawanna
FEC	Florida East Coast
FWD	Fort Worth & Denver
GM&O	Gulf, Mobile & Ohio
GN	Great Northern
GN&W	Genesee & Wyoming
GTW	Grand Trunk Western
IC	Illinois Central
ICG	Illinois Central Gulf
IGN	International-Great Northern
KCS	Kansas City Southern

L&N	Louisville & Nashville
LNE	Lehigh New England
LV	Lehigh Valley
MEC	Maine Central
MILW	Milwaukee Road
MKT	Missouri-Kansas-Texas
MNS	Minnesota, Northfield & Southern
MP	Missouri Pacific
M&StL	Minneapolis & St. Louis
NdeM	Nacionales de Mexico Railway
NH	New Haven
NKP	Nickel Plate Road
NOT&M	New Orleans, Texas & Mexico
NP	Northern Pacific
NS	Norfolk Southern
N&W	Norfolk & Western
NWP	Northwestern Pacific
NYC	New York Central
NYO&W	New York, Ontario & Western
NYNH&H	New York, New Haven & Hartford
OSL	Oregon Short Line
P&LE	Pittsburgh & Lake Erie
PC	Penn Central
PRR	Pennsylvania Railroad
PMKY	Pittsburgh, McKeesport & Youghiogheny
PTM	ST Rail System
RFP	Richmond, Fredericksburg & Potomac
SF	Santa Fe
SLSF	St. Louis-San Francisco
SP	Southern Pacific
SSW	St. Louis Southwestern
T&P	Texas & Pacific
TP&W	Toledo, Peoria & Western
UP	Union Pacific
WM	Western Maryland
WP	Western Pacific

Build your toy train library

101 Classic Toy Trains

Whether you're a collector or an operator, you'll find *101 Classic Toy Trains* a valuable reference guide to the finest toy trains produced in the classic post-World War II era. Get tips on the top toy train accessories, locomotives, and railcars and discover why each one is so collectible. Each item includes a colorful photo, fascinating history, fun facts, collectible information, and approximate value.

64100 • $24.95

Trackwork for Toy Trains

This essential guide addresses O gauge trackwork from nearly all of today's major manufacturers. Peter H. Riddle provides an overview of the various lines of sectional and flexible track, then demonstrates with step-by-step photography the basic techniques for cutting, bending, wiring, and layout installation. Also includes tips and tricks for working with special trackwork, such as switches, crossings, and accessory-activation sections.

10-8365 • $19.95

Marx Trains Pocket Price Guide Ninth Edition

This new edition features updated pricing and newly recorded variations of products for Marx trains and related toys. Conveniently sized for easy portability, be sure to take it with you to train shows and auctions so you can make informed buying and selling decisions.

10-8910 • $12.95